ARTS OF DARKNESS

ARTS OF DARKNESS

American Noir *and the*
Quest for Redemption

THOMAS S. HIBBS

SPENCE PUBLISHING COMPANY • DALLAS
2008

Published in the United States by
Spence Publishing Company
111 Cole Street
Dallas, Texas 75207

Library of Congress Control Number: 2007929180

ISBN 978-1-890626-71-6

Printed in the United States of America

For my parents,
Bill and Shirley Hibbs

Contents

List of Films Discussed

American Beauty (1999)
Angel (1999-2004)

Basic Instinct (1992)
Ben Hur: A Tale of the Christ (1955)
Blade Runner (1982)
Body Heat (1981)
Bound (1996)
Buffy the Vampire Slayer (1997-2003)

Cape Fear (1962, 1991)
Casablanca (1942)
The Children of Men (2006)
Chinatown (1974)

Dark City (1998)
Dawson's Creek (1998-2003)

Detour (1945)
Dogma (1999)
Donnie Darko (2001)
Double Indemnity (1944)

The End of the Affair (1955, 1999)
The Exorcist (1973)

Fight Club (1999)
The File on Thelma Jordon (1950)

The Getaway (1972)
The Gospel according to St. Matthew (1964)

Happiness (1998)
Harry Potter (2001-2005)
Hostel (2005)

Acknowledgments

SOME PORTIONS OF THE CURRENT BOOK were published in previous forms in other places. The section on *The Matrix* began as an essay ("Notes from the Underground: Nihilism and *The Matrix*") in *The Matrix and Philosophy*, edited by William Irwin (Open Court, 2002); the section on *Buffy the Vampire Slayer* was originally published as an essay ("Buffy the Vampire Slayer as Feminist *Noir*") in *Buffy the Vampire Slayer and Philosophy*, edited by James South and William Irwin (Open Court, 2003). Some of the writing on Pascal's thought that informs the book was first published as "Reasons of the Heart: Pascal and the Ethics of Thought," in *International Philosophical Quarterly* (Summer, 2005). Some reflections on John Lyden's book, *Film as Religion*, began as a review published in *Crisis* (January, 2004). Although not included in this book, an essay "The Human Comedy Perpetuates Itself: Nihilism and Comedy in Coen Neo-*Noir*," which appeared in *The Philosophy of Neo-Noir*, edited by Mark Conard (University Press of Kentucky, 2006) gave me an opportunity to think through issues related to the current book. A similar chance to explore noir themes was afforded me by *Books and Culture*, which published my review: "Seeking with Groans: The Moral Universe of Film *Noir*"

(March-April 2007). Much of writing on recent films included in this book began as short reviews for *National Review Online*, whose editor Kathryn Jean Lopez has proven remarkably accommodating of my passion for dark films.

Whatever clarity, vigor, and cogency there is in the prose of this book is at least partly due to the helpful, critical comments I have received over the years from a number of generous editors, including Jody Bottum at *The Weekly Standard* and *First Things*; Rod Dreher at *The Dallas Morning News*; Kathryn Jean Lopez at *National Review Online*; and John Wilson at *Books and Culture*.

The ideas for this book began germinating not long after I finished my first book on popular culture, *Shows about Nothing* (Spence, 2000). I was then teaching in the philosophy department at Boston College, where three colleagues in particular sparked engaging and entertaining conversation about film: Brian Braman, always eager to talk about the links between films and books, Jorge Garcia, who sees and remembers every film released every year, and Ron Tacelli, S.J., who loves film despite never having found any particular film satisfactory. I have been discussing film, culture and faith with my friend, Fr. Bill Parent, for more than twenty years and he can continues to prompt my thinking and writing about these important matters. I also had the opportunity to try out some of these ideas in a philosophy class with a particularly astute group of Boston College undergraduates. I would also like to thank audiences, especially students, at Covenant College, the University of Notre Dame, the University of San Francisco, and—on numerous occasions—at Baylor University.

At Baylor, where I remain on the academic dark side as a dean, none of what I get done would get done without the organizational skills and generous spirit of my administrative assistant, Paulette Edwards. To Paulette, many thanks. Also at Baylor, three graduate student assistants (Jay Bruce, Tony Bartl, and Julianne Romanello) read sections of the book in draft form and made helpful comments. I am particularly grateful to Julianne who proofread the entire manuscript and supplied the index. Stephen Swanson provided critical comments on a number of chapters.

I have had the good fortune of working again with Spence Publishing. Tom Spence, Mitch Muncy, and Linda Roney have been unflaggingly generous in their support of both projects and in their enthusiasm in promoting my work. Mitch in particular is largely to be blamed for my developing an avocation in commentary on film and popular culture. He was willing, with *Shows*, to take on what was initially a somewhat amorphous project. He helped not only to make it into a book but into an accessible read for those without training in philosophy.

My wife, Stacey, and children—Lauren, Daniel, and Sara—have done much more than be patient with my preoccupation with books, films, and my own writing. They have very often been active participants, discussing films and books and the relationships between the two. It is a great joy to watch my childrens' growing awareness of, and observations about, these and other things.

A debt of another sort is owed to my parents, Bill and Shirley Hibbs, who gave me life, love, and education and who, while not always concurring with my taste in film, continue to provide enthusiastic support for my reflections on film, philosophy, and culture. Particularly as I raise my own children, I look back both in gratitude and occasionally in amazement at their good work in attempting to form my less than compliant character.

To my parents I dedicate this book.

Preface

—

Seeking with Groans

ORMAC MCCARTHY'S LATEST NOVEL, *The Road*, is a post-apocalyptic tale of a quest for a new beginning amid the ruins of
the contemporary world.[1] In an America enduring a nuclear
winter, a father and son travel south in search of warmth, water, and
the remnants of human community. The minimalist style, which often
shifts without antecedent clues from present experiences to memories
of the past to dreams, consists mostly of concise description of the
daily tasks of finding food, keeping warm, and hiding from canni-
balistic hordes. The clipped dialogue between father and son reflects
the necessity and fear of speech, the uncertainty of what to say, how
to communicate what has been lost, where they now are, and what
they dare hope for in the future. The question of what, if anything,
we have to hand on to the next generation—the central question of
civilization—is particularly vexing in this world. The narrator worries
that he will not be able "to enkindle in the heart of the child what was
ashes in his own."

"Darkness implacable" is the way the narrator describes the obstacle to finding one's way at night, in a world where night and day
are barely distinguishable: "nights dark beyond darkness and the days

each more grey than the one before." McCarthy's book exemplifies arts of darkness, the attempt to depict accurately and name adequately the absences, the loss of distinctions that give life meaning and structure, the dissolution of every assumed framework, from the domestic to the cosmic. Even more difficult than naming the absences is the task of expressing the nearly indefatigable human longing for hope, where the great temptation is not simply to lose hope but to transfer one's hope from life to death. The inhabitants of post-apocalypse America grasp for analogies: "We're not survivors. We're the walking dead in a horror film." They craft similes: "Like pilgrims in a fable swallowed up and lost among the inward parts of some gigantic beast." Or again: "Then they set out upon the road again, slumped and cowled and shivering in their rags like mendicant friars sent forth to find their keep." Despite the theological imagery, the calling to mind of the pre-modern religious quest, this is a world in which God is present, if at all, through his striking absence. And yet, both because of what remains behind, held in the memory of the father, and what, in spite of all rational calculation, might lay ahead, the most painful mystery here is not evil or destruction, but the lingering prospect of beauty and love. "There were times when he sat watching the boy sleep that he would begin to sob uncontrollably but it wasn't about death. He wasn't sure what it was about but he thought it was about beauty or about goodness."

From its supposition of a contemporary wasteland through its sense of the way the past, in both its horror and its glory, weighs down upon the present and on to its nearly hopeless and implicitly theological quest to recover some semblance of an elusive order, McCarthy's book is one of the more impressive examples of a certain kind of contemporary narrative—the dark quest for redemption. From cult movie hits like *Fight Club* and *Donnie Darko*, to television shows like *24* and *Buffy the Vampire Slayer*; from the films of M. Night Shyamalan (*The Sixth Sense* and *Signs*) to the movies of Paul Thomas Anderson (*Magnolia* and *Punch-Drunk Love*); from the resurgent genre of comic book super-hero films such as *Spider-Man*, *X-Men*, and *Batman Begins*

to science fiction films such as *Blade Runner, Dark City, The Matrix,*
and *The Children of Men*—dark tales of the quest have proven to be
surprisingly popular, and, often enough, artistically complex and philosophically weighty.

Some of these films, dark tales of the quest, hearken back to the
classic period of film *noir*. Although the current book aims to study a
cultural phenomenon, in one respect, broader and, in another, more
narrow than that found in the genre of film *noir*, it does take its initial
bearings from the films in the early period of *noir* and considers a
number of later films often classified as neo-*noir*. Indeed, the argument
of the book could not have been developed except for what it owes to
the splendid and growing literature on noir, from authors such as R.
Barton Palmer, Nicholas Christopher, Foster Hirsch, James Naremore,
Alain Silver, Andrew Spicer, and J. P. Telotte. The focus of the book is
broader than film *noir* in that it takes under its purview films that are
not technically *noir* films; it is more narrow in that its interest in *noir*
films is primarily in those marginal *noir* films in which the religious
quest figures prominently.

If film critics have found it impossible to come up with a unifying
definition of *noir* as a genre, the films grouped under the *noir* label
still exhibit what philosophers call family resemblances, including recurring themes (criminality, infidelity, get rich quick schemes, and
seemingly doomed quests), dominant moods (anxiety, dread, and oppressive entrapment), typical settings (cities at night and in the rain),
and peculiar styles of filming (sharp contrasts between light and dark
and tight, off-center camera angles). *Noir* is certainly a counter to the
optimistic, progressive vision of post-war America. Subverting the
rationality of the pursuit of happiness, *noir* turns the American dream
into a nightmare. Noir also undercuts the enlightenment vision of the
city as the locus of human bliss, wherein human autonomy and rational
economics could combine to bring about the satisfaction of human
desire. Instead of enlightenment progress, with its lucid sense of where
we are and where we are going, noir gives us disconcerting shadows

and a present tense that is incapable of moving forward because it is overwhelmed by the past. In the noir universe, progress and autonomy are debilitating illusions.

In classic *noir*, the violation of limits is rarely, if ever, successful and whatever glimpse of redemption characters may have is always partial rather than revolutionary, and personal rather than political. The ending of many a *noir* and neo-*noir* film manages to combine physical brutality with enduring longing for communication, understanding, even at times, love. Some films suggest that, even in the midst of a corrupt world, a certain kind of integrity is still possible and that, in certain circumstances, defeat can be victory. *Noir* also exhibits an ethical thrust, what J.P. Telotte identifies as the desire to "speak the truth about the human condition," or at least to narrate the "difficulty" of speaking that truth.[2] Repudiating old-fashioned American optimism but never quite succumbing to despairing nihilism, *noir*'s most captivating characters are those who, in the words of Blaise Pascal, "seek with groans."[3]

As we shall see in the body of the book, Pascal, the seventeenth-century mathematician, philosopher, satirist, and Christian apologist, anticipates many a *noir* theme. One of the underlying arguments of the book is that Pascal is a neglected resource for contemporary cultural criticism, particularly for the strain of narrative that deals with dark quests. Writing at the very advent of modernity and in response to Descartes' announcement of one of the defining ambitions of modernity (to render us masters and possessors of nature through science and technology), Pascal might well be termed the first post-modern writer. He dissects the root motivations, the human, social, and theological consequences of radical modernity. His account of the paradoxes and seeming contradictions of the human condition regularly strikes a noir note. He writes, for instance, "When I see the blind and wretched state of man, when I survey the whole universe in its dumbness and man left to himself with no light, as though lost in this corner of the universe, without knowing who put him there, what he has come to do, what will become of him when he dies, incapable of knowing anything, I am moved to terror, like a man transported in his sleep to some terrifying desert island, who wakes up quite lost and with no means of escape."[4]

Pascal highlights the sense of entrapment and disorientation, the tragic tensions between human longing and human achievement. But Pascal thinks despair is a consolation in which we cannot afford to indulge. Here skepticism counters skepticism—we simply do not know enough to resign ourselves to defeat or to rest in uncertainty and despair. Between presumption and despair, translucent certitude and paralyzing doubt, human life takes on the shape of a tenuous quest. Pascal's vocabulary for describing the world of noir overlaps to some extent with Telotte's philosophically astute comments on noir. As Telotte puts it, noir gropes for understanding and communication amid "troubling shadows rather than a clear point of attack, more absence than presence." Without a present awareness of what is lacking or at least an awareness that something is lacking, we would have no notion of absence. In this paradoxical sense, redemption, too, can be present in noir, as a haunting absence.

Just as *noir* is suspicious of Enlightenment proclamations concerning progress and the intelligibility of nature and human life, so too Pascal is dubious about the way religious believers often naively affirm the obviousness of God's existence and the intelligibility of divine providence to the human intellect. In contrast to the comforting platitudes of conventional Christian practice, Pascal insists that Christianity does not teach that the existence of God is palpable to any observer; instead, it teaches, "God is a hidden God." But the hiddenness of God does not necessarily undermine the quest or even the possibility of redemption. Although neglected in the literature on *noir*, strategies of redemption are not entirely alien to classic noir dramas. In his recent essay, Barton Palmer argues that narratives of redemption have been unduly neglected in the critical reception of noir. Palmer is careful to note that, where redemption occurs in *noir* films, it is not by means of "cheap grace"; redemption is thoroughly penitential and its final outcome always tenuous and with an aching sense of loss and cost. There is no facile transcendence in dark tales of the quest.[5]

While paying some attention to what critics take to be the family resemblances of noir films, the present study is less an attempt to define *noir* than an investigation of a broader but in some ways easier to grasp phenomenon—the convergence of a dark depiction of the human condition with the religious quest. Thus, as our study progresses, the use of "*noir*" will become more fluid, even as the analysis remains focused on religious quest. Precisely this combination of an unsettling and shadowy vision of contemporary life with the theme of a quest for deeper understanding lies at the heart of our study.

Such a study should have at least three implications. First, it will help us to pay more attention to a neglected sub-genre within the field of noir and neo-*noir* films. The book aims to make a small contribution to the growing and increasingly sophisticated literature on film *noir*. Second, it will bring the thought of Pascal to bear on contemporary culture, the critique of modernity, and the revival of the quest. The hope is that Pascal will be taken more seriously as a thinker with a penetrating diagnosis of the human condition and a cogent prognosis involving the restoration of human life as a quest. Third, it will open up consideration of an often-ignored theological element in our popular culture. Christians and other believers regularly complain about the degradation of our popular culture and about Hollywood's bias against religious believers. And there is much to lament. But too often the supposition is that we need more pleasant, gently affirming films. Provided they avoid the sophomoric and the saccharine, such films would certainly be welcome. But the current book implicitly argues that the most powerful religious narratives in our culture may be those that do not so much circumvent tragedy and the unsavory features of the human condition, but rather pass through them.

PART I

THE ROOTS OF AMERICAN *NOIR*

Arts of Darkness

Unless we are willing to accept our artists as they are, the answer to who speaks for America today will have to be the advertising agencies. They show us our unparalleled prosperity and our almost classless society. They could never be accused of not being affirmative. Where the artist is still to be trusted, he will not be looked to for assurance. Those who believe art proceeds from a healthy and not a diseased faculty of mind will take what he shows them as a revelation, not of what we ought to be but of what we are at a given time and under given circumstances, that is, as a limited revelation but a revelation nonetheless.[1]

Flannery O'Connor

I N HER COMMENTS about the predicament of art in the modern age, Flannery O'Connor does not abandon the traditional vocation of the artist as one who reveals truth about the human condition. But she does resist the temptation to grasp for comprehensive, affirmative visions where only negations and partial insights are possible. O'Connor was motivated to clarify her vision of the vocation of the artist in part by criticisms of her own work as bleak and insufficiently affirmative, even nihilistic.[2]

As a writer whose vision was informed by a religious sensibility, O'Connor was particularly sensitive to the gap between contemporary religious platitudes and the deeper realities to which she wanted to point in her own fiction. The problem for a religious writer in our culture is that the basic vocabulary of religion, as of virtue and vice, has become trivialized and stripped of meaning. Walker Percy once noted how difficult it is to talk about baptism in a world where that sacrament had become a "minor tribal rite," equivalent to the Christmas ritual of taking the kids to visit "Santa at the department store." In a context where distortions seem natural to us, the artist must resort to freaks and monsters, to a Gothic sensibility that enables us to see anew what we thought we understood. When it appears in such fiction, grace will seem, not "warm and binding," but "dark and disruptive." A writer in the position of O'Connor or Percy must seek to effect a double dislocation of the reader. The fundamental goal is to induce in the reader a sense that something is deeply awry in the human condition. But to accomplish that in present circumstances the author must induce in the reader another sort of alienation, from optimistic assumptions of contemporary beliefs in progress, intelligibility, and the pursuit of happiness. The author must force the reader to take up an unwelcome quest.

Not particularly orthodox in its religious symbolism, the recent film *Donnie Darko*, a surprise cult hit featuring an alienated teen who has visions of a giant bunny predicting the apocalypse, is a "dark and disruptive" film of religious quest. First released in the fall of 2001, just after the attacks of 9/11, *Darko*'s plotline of a jet engine crashing through a suburban house was hardly the sort of tale for which Americans had any appetite. But DVD release gave the film new life, and it has become a much-discussed film among today's youth and a favorite among film critics. The eponymous main character is a strange sort of superhero willing to plumb the depths of our contemporary culture in the hope of discovering some clue to the purpose of life.

As with most teen movies, *Donnie Darko* is all about teen angst, here exaggerated for effect. Donnie (Jake Gyllenhaal) is on medication, has regular visits with a psychiatrist, sleepwalks, has dim memories of being involved in destructive acts, begins dating the new girl at school (Jena Malone as Gretchen Ross), and develops an interest in the physics and metaphysics of time travel. In the midst of all this, he enjoys regular visits from a giant, ominous looking bunny, who commands Donnie to perform destructive acts and repeatedly warns him about the end of the world.

Donnie's version of the quest is inextricably entangled with big questions. The most direct attempts by characters in the film to address Donnie's angst and confusion do not prove fruitful. A local self-help guru, Jim Cunningham (Patrick Swayze), encourages students to "face their ego reflection" and overcome fear with love. In an entertaining send-up of the self-esteem movement, Cunningham sees lack of self-love as the cause of every teen vice from drug use to premarital sex. Donnie's skepticism about the optimistic self-help movement is actually a sign of health and some degree of intellectual integrity.

And Donnie has lots of intellectual questions. He spends time with a teacher discussing time travel, a vehicle through which the film formulates questions of determinism, contingency, and human freedom. Donnie's official therapy meetings are more like philosophy or theology seminars, as the conversation turns repeatedly to the question of the existence of God. He states at one point, "There is no God if everyone dies alone." Donnie gradually learns to frame the question whether everyone dies alone in the form of another question, whether anyone can die for anyone else. Donnie is a teen dark knight of the soul on a quest for purposeful action. Through interpretations of bizarre visions and the physics of time travel, Donnie seeks for a lost code of redemption or sacrificial love in the confused maze of adolescent America.

Donnie Darko's title, gloomy vision of contemporary life, and theme of a quest through the ruins of conventional society are all symptomatic of contemporary American *noir*, an approach to American culture that has proven artistically fruitful and immensely popular.

The phrase "American *noir*" calls to mind the classic film *noir* of the 1940s and 1950s: films such as *Double Indemnity*, *The Maltese Falcon*, and *Touch of Evil*.[3] It was also during this period that at least marginally religious artists, such as Graham Greene and Alfred Hitchcock, wrote and produced stories with a religious sensibility remarkably akin to O'Connor's and Percy's.[4] One might argue for a natural affinity between a certain kind of religious sensibility, evident in films such as Greene's *The Third Man* or *The End of the Affair*, or Hitchcock's *I Confess*, and a certain strain of film *noir*. Although neglected in the literature on *noir*, strategies of redemption are not entirely alien to classic *noir* dramas. In a recent essay, Barton Palmer argues that narratives of redemption have been unduly neglected in the critical reception of *noir*. Palmer is careful to note that, where redemption occurs in *noir* films, it is not by means of "cheap grace"; redemption is thoroughly penitential and its final outcome always tenuous and with an aching sense of loss and cost. There is no facile transcendence in *noir*; instead, there is only what Palmer calls "difficult spiritual growth."[5]

In this book, I will examine a neglected convergence between the two genres of the *noir* film and the religious film—the *noir* narration of the quest for redemption. An equally neglected author will be a useful guide in this study: the great seventeenth-century mathematician, inventor, controversialist, and Christian apologist, Blaise Pascal. In his trenchant and aphoristic observations on the "monstrous" character of the human condition, Pascal anticipates many a *noir* theme. He writes, for instance, "When I see the blind and wretched state of man, when I survey the whole universe in its dumbness and man left to himself with no light, as though lost in this corner of the universe, without knowing who put him there, what he has come to do, what will become of him when he dies, incapable of knowing anything, I am moved to terror, like a man transported in his sleep to some terrifying desert island, who wakes up quite lost and with no means of escape."[6]

Pascal is acutely aware of the fragmentation of our knowledge and of the vulnerability of the self to forces, internal and external, beyond its control or even its conscious awareness. He underscores the way reason is often prey to the passions, the way it can be bent and twisted in virtually any direction by habit and trauma. Yet our ability to recognize that something is awry in the human condition and to acknowledge our enslavement to a variety of forces and habits are signs that reason is not utterly corrupt and that a residue of liberty remains to us. The combination of these two themes—encroaching forces beyond our control and the attempt to respond to these forces in a human way—is essential both to *noir* and to Pascal's account of the inherently paradoxical nature of the human condition.

Pascal's vocabulary for describing the world of *noir* overlaps to some extent with that of J. P. Telotte, the most philosophically astute commentator on *noir*. As Telotte puts it, *noir* gropes for understanding and communication amid "troubling shadows rather than a clear point of attack, more absence than presence."[7] Without a present awareness of what is lacking or at least an awareness that something is lacking, we would have no notion of absence. In this paradoxical sense, redemption can be present in *noir* as a haunting absence. As Mark Conard has recently proposed, the absence that haunts *noir* is what Nietzsche calls "the death of God": "Seeing *noir* as a response or reaction to the death of God helps explain the commonality of the elements that critics have noted in *noir* films. For example, it explains the inherent pessimism, alienation, and disorientation in *noir*. It affirms that *noir* is a sensibility or an outlook, as some hold. It explains the moral ambiguity in *noir* as well as the threat of nihilism and meaninglessness that some note."[8]

Nietzsche once quipped that Pascal's blood ran through his own veins. Of course, Pascal is not a nihilist and nowhere proclaims the death of God. But for Pascal, and in contrast to the comforting platitudes of conventional Christian practice, Christianity does not teach that the existence of God is obvious; instead, it teaches that "God is a hidden God." It does not teach that we can see that this is the best of all possible worlds. As O'Connor insisted, we cannot even begin to appreciate redemption until we experience how lost we are and how great is the "price of restoration." Aiming to capture human souls, Pascal's God is a God of ironic distance and violent, surprising intervention in the human world.[9]

In the face of the rationalism and scientific progressivism of the nascent Enlightenment, Pascal had a decidedly tragic view of the human condition (at least on this side of grace and redemption), a point eloquently stated in the Marxist Lucien Goldmann's famous book on Pascal, *The Hidden God: A Study of Tragic Vision*.[10] Goldmann focuses on Pascal's apprehension of the integral connection between part and whole: "How could it be possible for a part to know the whole? But he may perhaps aspire to a knowledge of at least those parts which are on the same scale as he himself. But the different parts of the world are all so closely linked and related together that I hold it to be impossible to know one without knowing the others and without knowing the whole."[11] Caught in the middle, between the twin infinities, the infinitely small and the infinitely large, human beings cannot link one extreme to the other, much less gain a comprehensive knowledge of parts and whole. For Pascal, this puts into question the entire modern rationalist project. Goldmann identifies the failure of the rationalists as a neglect of the "value of the tragic position."[12] The tragic position of Pascal emerges directly out of the most important scientific discovery of seventeenth-century rationalism, that of geometrically infinite space, about which Pascal observed: "The eternal silence of these infinite spaces casts me into dread." Pascal thus highlights the "gulf that lies between physical and cosmological reality, on the one hand, and human reality on the other."[13]

Goldmann calls Pascal the first modern man and the initiator of historical-dialectical thought, a line of thinking that culminates in Hegel and Marx. It certainly makes more sense to align Pascal with Hegel and Marx than with the rationalist tradition from Descartes through Kant. But it is not clear that Pascal can be described as an imperfect modern, since he would resist the temptation to which both Hegel and Marx succumb, namely, that of attempting to encompass the whole within a system. In this sense, Pascal might more accurately be described as the first post-modern, one who accentuates the continued dislocation of the human person from God, from society, indeed from himself.

The alienation resulting from the individual's sense that the universe does not directly answer to human desire underlies the tragic situation of many a *noir* protagonist. Goldmann reads Pascal through the interpretive lens of Georg Lukacs, who speaks of "tragic man" as awaiting an illuminating judgment from God.[14] But "the world around him still follows the same path, indifferent to both questions and answers. No word comes from either created or natural things." Again, the silence of God gives rise to an "unbearable world of error and illusion," an awareness of which creates an "unbridgeable gap separating certain men from the human and divine world."[15] Tragedy arises not just because it is "impossible to live a valid life in this world," but also because it is necessary to continue on a quest for such a valid life.[16]

Admittedly, *noir* does not fit the classical, Aristotelian definition of tragedy. The characters in *noir* are ordinary and democratic, often given to amorality, even perversion. They are not "tragic heroes," not the nobler-than-average characters that authors from Aristotle to Shakespeare have described as befitting tragic dramas. As Ian Jarvie has argued, settings for *noir* films are often so exotic and the characters so unprincipled that audiences have only a superficial engagement with them.[17] He concludes, on the basis of the "disconnection" between drama and audience, that *noir* cannot perform the cathartic function of purging pity and fear that Aristotle sees as central to tragedy. Lacking the grandeur of the older tragic heroes, contemporary *noir* protagonists always risk seeming simply pathetic or thoroughly corrupt. It is important in this context to stress the variability of *noir* plots and characters, some of which do indeed fit Jarvie's description, while others come a bit closer to fulfilling at least some of what Aristotle supposes is essential to tragedy. To what extent, in what ways, and at what points in the story do we sympathize with Sam Spade (*The Maltese Falcon*) or Thelma Jordon (*The File on Thelma Jordon*) or Scottie Ferguson (*Vertigo*)? Different answers would have to be given for each of these characters, since we sympathize to various degrees and at varying points with each of them. Moreover, the very use of the term "tragedy" shifts quite a bit from Aristotle and Shakespeare to Lukacs and Goldmann's Pascal. As the latter conceive it, tragedy does indeed seem to fit the *noir* film.

In his recent book on *noir*, John Irwin proposes that *noir* revises the traditional detective story, which is principally an intellectual puzzle to be solved by the cleverness of the detective. In the *noir* detective story, the solution is rarely so clear; indeed, it is often unclear what the clues are or even precisely what the mystery is to be resolved. To put it another way, we might say that the *noir* detective story makes the detective himself into a mystery. Or, as Irwin formulates it, the mystery is driven by character more than by plot.[18] Although classical tragedy is certainly driven by character as well as plot, something of a parallel to Irwin's contrast between classic and *noir* detective stories can be seen in the relationship of old to new tragedy, classical to modern, the latter of which puts into greater question the agent himself who is undertaking the quest and the standard assumptions about the intelligibility of the mystery. Similarly, Pascal's objection to the deism of modern natural theology, which focuses on pure data and deductive reasoning, is that it fails to allow for the confusion inherent in the evidence and to put into question the agent pursuing the investigation.

Tragedy, in Pascal's sense, is a direct response to the failure of a certain radical strain of the Enlightenment project. Modernity, to an early version of which Pascal was responding, is bent on refashioning nature to render it more accommodating to human needs and wishes. Its project of "mastery and possession of nature" aims to alleviate the inconveniences of the human condition. As Sara Melzer explains, Pascal seeks to demystify modern science which itself reposes upon a demystification of ordinary experience and received theology. She writes, "From Pascal's perspective, Descartes and the believers in the 'new science' sought to reverse the effects of the Fall and create a human-made paradise that would eliminate the notion of a lack and thus eliminate desire . . . The new science provided humans with the tools that would allow them to measure, to weigh, to explain, and ultimately to manipulate the world around them."[19]

Indeed, the twin goals of Descartes's method, "utility and certainty," may not be fully compatible with one another. Of these two goals, Stanley Rosen writes: "The first is to identify the structure of nature, and so all of rational order, with mathematical properties of extension; the second is to give man mastery over this order, thanks to the new technique of mathematics. If order is to provide man with certitude and security, it must be eternal, regular, and independent of, although accessible to, subjective mental activity. Unfortunately, if man is to be master of this order, it must be subject to his will."[20] Rosen underscores the way Descartes's project creates contradictions between knowledge and volition, between intelligibility of the real as independent of human volition and the construction by the human will of the conditions for knowing the real.

Melzer concurs with Goldmann that Pascal uses one of modern science's chief discoveries, namely, that of the infinite, against modern science. We cannot adequately grasp the infinite and hence our apprehension of whatever we know is but limited, partial, and haunted by uncertainty.[21] The infinite surfaces in another way in Pascal, in connection with desire. Modernity promises satisfaction of desire in a linear fashion, but this, Pascal insists, results not in satisfaction but rather in the indefinite postponement of satisfaction. Even as we expend enormous effort, time, and money in an attempt to control nature, to alleviate pain and suffering, and to postpone death, we realize at some level that we can never fully succeed in this project. "Being unable to cure death, wretchedness, and ignorance, men have decided, in order to be happy, not to think about such things."[22]

By making inordinate promises for the amelioration of the human condition, modernity exacerbates our sense of alienation, even as it deprives us of a vocabulary for expressing that sense of loss. The gap between promise and realization creates an unbearable tension. According to Pascal, at the root of our alienation, our flight from self-knowledge, is fear of death, a resistance to our own mortality: "It is easier to bear death when one is not thinking about it than the idea of death when there is not danger."[23] Modern society has thus of necessity become as effective at distracting us from our ills as it is at eliminating the ills. Yet for Pascal, there is a positive thrust underlying the obsession with self-deceiving illusion: "despite these afflictions man wants to be happy, only wants to be happy, and cannot help wanting to be happy."[24] Present unhappiness combined with the natural desire for happiness is at the root of our restlessness and our sense that the next pursuit, the next promotion, the next experience of love, will remedy our wretchedness and make us happy: "What causes inconstancy is the realization that present pleasures are false, together with the failure to realize that absent pleasures are vain."[25] This is the trap of many a *noir* character. This is Pascal's way of accounting for the phenomenon of repetition, the apparently senseless and self-lacerating habit of recurring, destructive behavior. As Lukacs puts it in a passage dear to Goldmann, "the present becomes secondary and unreal, the past threatening and full of danger, the future already known and long since unconsciously experienced."[26] In *noir*, as in Pascal, the quest, often deluded by self-interest and vanity, perdures even in the midst of the deepest uncertainty.[27]

Nicholas Christopher observes that the *noir* drama centers upon a "labyrinth," a "set of conditions producing amazement," symbolic of "meaning's multiplicity and elusiveness."[28] While the populist films of the 1940s offer affirmative visions of American life, *noir*-style films of the same period capture the sense that something is awry in contemporary life, that the sunny, public discourse of happiness and success conceals a dark underside of American life. Whatever might be the social and political sources of *noir*, it is never reducible to a simple negation. *Noir* is stylistically and dramatically complex. Its emphasis on darkness and shadows, absence over presence, and the duality of personal identity underscore the depth and mystery inherent in the most mundane of experiences. Into such a disorienting, threatening and inviting world, *noir* thrusts its protagonist, who sets out on a quest to solve a particular mystery. Of course, the quest is rarely rooted in pure motives and often enough its roots are self-interested curiosity. Typically, we find a mixture of impulses—from base desires to prey on others out of greed and lust to the awareness of, and desire for, something more, for intelligibility, communication, even love. The dialectic of force and freedom is, according to Pascal, one of the clues to the paradoxes of the human condition.

By calling our conventions into question, *noir* opens the possibility of a more fundamental inquiry into the human condition. Its accent on darkness and mystery, its skepticism about rational progress, and the calculation, regulation, and satisfaction of desire by scientific means—all this is an affront to Enlightenment confidence in transparent intelligibility and humane, technological progress. According to the most bold strain in the modern Enlightenment, we know where we are, where we want to go, and precisely how we are to get there. Film *noir* exhibits persistent skepticism about these claims; to varying degrees, it recovers a conception of human life as an always tenuous quest, whose success is dependent on veiled clues and the uncertain assistance of others. For all its emphasis on psychotic loners and individuals devoted to calculative self-interest, *noir* often highlights the inextricably social condition of human beings. Although fulfillment is never secure and is often foreclosed, the longing for communication, friendship, and love remains at the very center of the plot. Autonomy, the centerpiece of Enlightenment ethics and politics, can be a debilitating illusion; bold self-assertion, a self-destructive vice. Film *noir* engages, without necessarily succumbing to, nihilism.

According to J. P. Telotte, *noir* accentuates "our difficulty in ever seeing or speaking the truth of our human condition." Telotte offers an instructive comment on a crucial scene from the seminal classic film *noir, Double Indemnity*, in which Walter Neff confesses his murder plot to his colleague, Barton Keyes: "I just wanted to set you right about something you couldn't see because it was right smack up against your nose." Telotte commends *noir* for helping us "to recognize what we 'couldn't see' normally" and for shifting focus "to what which is, disconcertingly, too close to be seen, too much a part of our personal and cultural lives for us to see and assess clearly." The deeper point here is that we are so constituted as to resist actively, if not consciously, the knowledge of what is most obvious. As Pascal puts it, "We run heedlessly into the abyss after putting something in front of us to stop us seeing it."[29] Here we come up against the greatest of obstacles, our own multiple aversions to truth, especially to the truth about ourselves: "we hide and disguise ourselves from ourselves."[30]

Despite the readiness with which film critics deploy the phrase "film *noir*," no one yet has come up with a persuasive definition of film *noir*; indeed, some critics have cautioned against the very project and urged that the best we can hope for is to identify a loose set of characteristics, concerning style, mood, character types, and plot themes.[31] If the determination of the core features and boundaries of classic film *noir* is elusive, achieving such clarity regarding so-called neo-*noir*, which runs from the late 1960s to our own time, is impossible. Typically encompassed by the neo-*noir* label are films such as *Chinatown*, *Body Heat*, *The Usual Suspects*, *Memento*, and *Minority Report*. But the phenomena of interest in this book are much broader than what fall under the title of *noir*, narrowly construed. Sometimes these dark stories of the quest share stylistic or plot themes with *noir*, but more important for us is the way they share *noir*'s suspicion of Enlightenment progress, rationality, individualism, and optimism. Instead of light and straightforward resolution of problems, there is darkness and the enduring sense of vulnerability to catastrophe. Instead of the pursuit of happiness and an optimistic embrace of the future, there is a sense of entrapment in a past that can never quite be overcome. Instead of peremptory restoration, there is at best a penitential path tentatively groping for redemption.

If we move beyond the issue of criteria for inclusion in the *noir* or neo-*noir* canon, we can see that dark tales are everywhere nowadays, as they have always been in American film. From cult movie hits like *Fight Club* and *Donnie Darko*, to television shows like *24* and *Buffy the Vampire Slayer*; from the films of M. Night Shyamalan (*The Sixth Sense* and *Signs*) to the movies of Paul Thomas Anderson (*Magnolia* and *Punch-Drunk Love*); from the resurgent genre of comic book super-hero films such as *Spider-Man*, *X-Men*, and *Batman Begins* to mainstream Oscar winners such as *American Beauty*. What is significant about these films is not just that they present a dark and dismal world but that they display their main characters as on a quest for love, truth, justice, and even redemption. While paying some attention to what critics take to be the family resemblances of *noir* films, this book is less an attempt to define *noir* than an investigation of a broader but in some ways easier to grasp phenomenon—the convergence of *noir* with the religious quest. Thus, as our discussion progresses, the use of "*noir*" will become more fluid, even as the analysis remains focused on religious quest.

Precisely the combination of an unsettling and shadowy vision of contemporary life with the theme of a quest for deeper understanding lies at the heart of the three biggest stories, in the worlds of film and books, over the past few years. In the spring of 2004, two narratives dominated the movie and book industries in America: Mel Gibson's *The Passion of the Christ* and Dan Brown's *The Da Vinci Code*. An R-rated film, in Aramaic and Latin, focusing exclusively on the last hours of the life of Christ, and featuring gruesomely explicit violence, *The Passion* became the highest grossing R-rated film in movie industry history. In dramatic contrast to *The Passion*, *The Da Vinci Code* unravels the entire orthodox Christian theological tradition and puts in its place a sort of new-age gnosticism. Meanwhile, J. K. Rowling's *Harry Potter* series about a boy wizard caught up in a cosmic battle of good and evil continues to dominate the book world and to have a huge impact on film. All three of these stories offer stark visions of the human condition, accentuate the gap between appearance and reality, and feature characters on a quest or mission to reveal or uncover a deeper order of truth about human life.

Whatever *The Passion*'s ethical, theological, or dramatic flaws, its success indicates that many Americans hunger for something more than the vapid spirituality of a happy-go-lucky Jesus (humorously sent-up in the film *Dogma*, in which a statue of the "Buddy Jesus" winks and gives the thumbs-up sign to parishioners at a Catholic Church, as part of a new promotional strategy, called "Catholicism Wow!").[32] It is of course dangerous to generalize about any cultural phenomenon. In the same culture and at the same time period that *The Passion* was setting box office records, a very different sort of religious story, also about the quest for the truth concerning the man called Christ, was all the rage at local bookstores and has since become a hugely popular film. Dan Brown's *The Da Vinci Code* is a very contemporary quest story about the battle to unlock the code, important portions of which are allegedly woven into Leonardo's famous paintings, concerning the Holy Grail.[33] In *The Da Vinci Code*, the greatest story ever told is a hoax, perpetrated in the name of political power and the oppression of women. If one story forces viewers to confront the radical truth-claim at the heart of the Gospel, the other deconstructs the Christ-story and puts in its place a sort of post-modern gnosticism that conveniently accommodates contemporary sexual mores.

As debates over *The Passion* and *The Da Vinci Code* occupied the cultural headlines, J. K. Rowling's *Harry Potter* series continued its market ascendancy, a dominance that would have been more prominently noted had it not been for a rather arbitrary decision to reclassify the books as children's literature.[34] The story of the wizard "boy who lived," *Harry Potter* narrates the life of an orphan, the only survivor of an attack on his family by the diabolical wizard, Lord Voldemort. At Hogwarts School, Harry receives training in defense against the dark arts, arts he may have to deploy in his quest to fend off attacks from others bent on power and destruction. In the darkest moments in the novels, Harry himself comes under suspicion, in part because his powers so closely mimic those of Voldemort. Harry finds himself frequently trapped in a labyrinth, a maze, through which he must travel in his attempt to defend the innocent. The maze here, as in *noir*, is symbolic of the many layers of meaning and intelligibility, of the way appearances can deceive, and of the complexity of levels in Harry's own character and quest.[35]

The Passion, *The Da Vinci Code*, and *Harry Potter* are all quest stories involving the solution of codes, the navigation of a variety of mazes or traps, both physical and psychological, and the facing of conspiracy plots of various sorts. All three depict their characters as trapped and isolated from others in their immediate surroundings precisely because they bear secret truths or are engaged in a task inexplicable to others. Each demands a radical reappraisal of conventional assumptions. All involve the articulation and interpretation of a complex literary and religious iconography. What is striking about all three of these cultural phenomena is the way they combine a rather dark vision of the human condition with a quest to recover a lost code of virtue and vice, failure and success, loss and redemption. If American *noir*, at least taken in the wider sense in which I use it here, often involves a starkly negative vision of contemporary society, it need not end in despair.

NOIR AND THE RELIGIOUS QUEST

As we shall see in the rest of this book, there has been from the beginning a rich interplay between, on the one hand, the stylistic devices, themes, and plot structure of American *noir* and, on the other, the quasi-religious quest for a lost code of redemption. By way of illustration of the flexibility of *noir* narration and the fertile ways in which it can be connected to the religious quest, I would like to offer some brief, introductory remarks on two films not often juxtaposed. It might seem perverse to compare Frank Capra's Christmas tale of redemption, *It's a Wonderful Life,* with Quentin Tarantino's ironic and brutally violent neo-*noir Pulp Fiction*, but a comparison reveals a certain unnoticed alliance between *noir* and the religious quest.

Capra's films are much darker than has traditionally been acknowledged. Everyone remembers the happy ending of *Wonderful Life*, as George Bailey (Jimmy Stewart) is reunited with his family and friends, who gather round the Christmas tree to sing joyous songs. The happy ending makes us apt to forget that, to reach this point, George Bailey had to travel through a living hell, the result of his suicidal impulse for non-being. Facing bankruptcy, public humiliation, and perhaps time in jail because of the apparent loss of a large sum of money from his business, George is more than half in love with easy death. An angel of mercy, the avuncular Clarence, rescues George from his attempted suicide by drowning. When George demands an outlet from his current predicament, Clarence gives him what he wants, non-being in the midst of his town of Bedford Falls. George is now forced to continue his life in a town where no one knows him, where he exists in permanent isolation, and where those formerly closest to him now fiercely repudiate his memories and his sense of identity. Controlled by a ruthless capitalist, Bailey's small town of Bedford Falls becomes Pottersville, an American nightmare of frustrated aspiration and lost horizons. George Bailey thus enters the nightmare world of classic *noir*, a world of dislocation, without prospect of clear direction or the assistance of others.

What seems to George to be a curse is in fact the pedagogical working out of divine providence, offering George a second chance to be grateful for his life, family and friends. Of course, gratitude by itself will not make things right. Things are so bad in this world that only divine intervention can save George Bailey and his ordinary, representative town of Bedford Falls.

The suggestion that escape from the *noir* labyrinth is impossible apart from some sort of divine intervention is made with profound, comic power in Tarantino's *Pulp Fiction*. The very title of the film calls to mind the origins of classic American *noir* in the pulp fiction crime magazines and novels of the 1930s. Like many a classic *noir*, *Pulp Fiction* fashions a world without normal families, a world saturated with crime, drugs, and sexuality, a world void of law enforcement. Whatever order exists results from the raw will to power of the strongest, in this case the drug lord, Marsellus Wallace (Ving Rhames). Tarantino's slicing and restructuring of the temporal narrative of the action are also reminiscent of *noir*, as is the sense of characters trapped in a world to which they can imagine no real alternative. No quest seems possible or desirable; the characters have settled into the *noir* universe, a world no longer disturbing but normal. They have made a home in the *noir* world. Tarantino, a master of self-conscious irony, is toying with many *noir* conventions; his inverting or satirizing of *noir* motifs is palpable in his placing many of the most important events in the film in broad daylight, not in the dark, shadowy universe of classic *noir*. In this respect, *Pulp Fiction* follows the manipulation of *noir* themes prominent in Tarantino's *Reservoir Dogs*, a film whose famous torture scene occurs in broad daylight to the musical accompaniment of the 1970s upbeat pop hit from Steeler's Wheel, "Stuck in the Middle With You."

Tarantino's irony is most evident in the humor of these films, based largely on witty dialogue between hit men. The humor is laced with references to popular culture itself. Tarantino uses internal references to other works of popular culture to communicate directly with viewers, the most clever of whom share the knowing feeling that they are in on the joke. Of course, it is a self-canceling insight, one that exhausts itself within the framework of popular culture, a self-referential culture, ultimately about nothing but its own internal referents. As the *Pulp Fiction* character Butch (Bruce Willis) explains in response to an inquiry about the meaning of his name, "This is America, lady. Our names don't mean shit."

Just as in *Wonderful Life*, here chance plays an important role, indeed a much more prominent role. Tarantino's repudiation of linear narration suits a world out of joint where character development and unified storytelling are impossible. The sequence of events in the film pivots around a remarkable chance event, the interpretation of which determines the destiny of the two central characters, Jules (Samuel Jackson) and Vincent (John Travolta). As they interrogate and then assassinate some college kids who had tried to cheat Marcellus Wallace of his fair share in a drug deal, Jules and Vincent are confidently in control of the situation. Unknown to them, however, another boy, armed and nervous, remains hiding in an adjacent room. Just as they finish killing the other boys, the hidden boy emerges through a door and fires multiple rounds directly at Jules and Vincent. Stunned at the surprise attack but even more surprised that none of the bullets hits them, Jules and Vincent pause in wonder before blowing the kid away. After the fact, Jules cannot let go of the sense that something astonishing just happened, something inexplicable by any rational means, something he feels compelled to describe as a miracle. By contrast, Vincent sees nothing worthy of wonder: "this shit happens." Jules, however, cannot go on as before. He tells Vincent that he is renouncing violence, a commitment he exhibits in the final scene of the film, in which Jules defuses a potentially violent hold-up in a coffee shop.

A violence saturated neo-*noir*, *Pulp Fiction* gives the lie to the claim that in the world of *noir* "otherworldly answers are ruled out."[36] Or rather, Tarantino's film reveals the flaw in the easy contrast between this-worldly and other-worldly, since it is not clear that the answer Jules seeks is "otherworldly." As Jules describes the miracle, "God got involved"—here and now, in this world. Capra's film goes much further in the direction of delivering redemption, both for George and for his community, as it reaffirms the goodness of small-town American life. By contrast, Jules's conversion never suggests any possible transformation of America. Instead, Jules's quest, his interpretation of the chance event as a miracle, isolates him from everyone else in the film.

As different as they are in plot and setting, *Wonderful Life* and *Pulp Fiction* provide evidence of the flexibility of *noir* narration and of a potential link between *noir* and the religious quest. In most *noir* films, God is absent, if not dead. As we have noted, Mark Conard contends that *noir* is best understood as embodying the problems of human life in a world where the existence of God is no longer a viable assumption. After an examination of the various attempts by film critics to define *noir* or to argue that definition is not possible, Conard concludes that the task of defining *noir* in any strict sense is doomed to failure. There are, nonetheless, certain standard features in *noir*: inherent pessimism, a sense of alienation and disorientation, and a pervasive preoccupation with the problem of seeing and speaking the truth. Borrowing heavily from Nietzsche, Conard suggests that the pre-eminent source of these various common elements in *noir* is the death of God. The *noir* universe is characterized by the absence of any overarching framework, of any clearly identifiable meaning or purpose—all of which Nietzsche saw as the result of the death of God and the devaluation of the highest values. As Raymond Borde and Etienne Chaumeton put it in "Toward a Definition of Film *Noir*," the intended effect of *noir* is to "create a specific alienation," resulting from "the state of tension instilled in the spectator when the psychological reference points are removed."[37]

If the link between *noir* and penitential redemption opens up an underdeveloped theme in the literature on film *noir*, it also exposes an underappreciated approach to religion in popular film and television. The literary scholar and cultural critic Mark Edmundson argues that our culture is trapped in a dialectic between facile transcendence, evident in films such as *Forrest Gump*, which offer happy endings achieved by the avoidance of difficulty and complexity, and debased Gothic, a pervasive, unrelenting, and unredeemable sense of evil evident in the popular genre of contemporary horror.[38] We are forced to choose between tales of ineradicable evil and stories of cheap grace, where the difficulties of our world are quickly overcome by good intentions and a benevolent providence. We lack, Edmundson declares, stories of redemption that encompass, rather than simply avoid, the darkness, suffering and deprivations of our world. The mixing of *noir* and redemption promises a way of overcoming that division; it suggests the possibility of stories of renewal or redemption that, instead of ignoring or glossing over the darkness, embrace, transform, and redeem it.

THE LOST CODE OF REDEMPTION

Noir never delivers final redemption for its characters, but it does present characters in a quest for a lost code of redemption. Such quests are present from the beginning in *noir*, if not universally. Although I will not limit myself to films firmly entrenched in the *noir* canon, I will begin with the classic period of film *noir* in the 1940s and 1950s. In *noir* classics such as *Double Indemnity*, *The Maltese Falcon*, *Detour*, and *The File on Thelma Jordon*, I will look carefully at the tension between the fatalism of classic film *noir* and themes of the quest and redemption.[39] Fatalism of mood and narrative structure are embodied in the most famous *noir* device of the confessional flashback, in which the viewer knows the ending because the future is prefigured in the past.

But the degrees and sources of fatalism in *noir* films vary a great deal from one film to another. The flashback voiceover, furthermore, can be construed not just as underscoring determinism but also as working against it. As J. P. Telotte cogently argues, the voiceover embodies a second-order quest for communication, for truth, and sometimes even for reconciliation or redemption that cuts against, and in some measure transcends, the fatalism of the first order of events. Framing our study of classic *noir* and redemptive strategies will be the religiously tinged *noir* stories from Graham Greene's fiction (*The Third Man* and *End of the Affair*) and Hitchcock's films (*Vertigo*, *The Wrong Man*, and *I Confess*).

After an examination of classic *noir*, I will turn to neo-*noir*, an even more elusive category than that of classic *noir*. The accent in classic *noir* is on the universality of the human condition, its inherent limitations and the inevitable and usually destructive consequences that attend certain desires or types of action. By contrast, an influential strain of neo-*noir* film features characters impervious to the laws of the human condition; these characters "get away" with lives of criminality. This shift constitutes a movement in the direction of nihilism and a recoiling from the fundamentally democratic world of classic *noir*, in favor of a form of aristocratic nihilism. The most resourceful of these characters, for example in *The Usual Suspects*, are in control of the *noir* plot, using their cunning and artistry to ensnare others. The aristocratic nihilism so prominent in a certain strain of neo-*noir* involves a strange form of transcendence, an odd conflation of the facile transcendence Edmundson decries and the debased Gothic plot starring amoral super-heroes. Here redemption is impossible for the many and unnecessary for the few.[40] The quest becomes pointless.

Another sort of transcendent control is operative in modern science's obsession with technology, a theme prevalent in science fiction neo-*noir*. The modern, technological aspiration for knowledge and control generates ignorance and enslavement. The materialism of modern science creates other conundra for mankind. The very notion of a soul—as indicative of a source of animation, of what lives and dies, rather than simply functioning and then ceasing to function—becomes problematic. The quest in sci-fi *noir* aims not simply at the solution of a particular crime or at the discovery of a set of individual identities, but at what, if anything, distinguishes human from machine. This is the key question for P. K. Dick, the famous sci-fi author and favorite author of neo-*noir* directors. These themes are prominent from *Terminator* and *Blade Runner* to *Dark City* and *The Matrix*, the latter pair of which features a quasi-religious quest to overcome human alienation, even as they fall prey to the Gnostic temptation to equate salvation with an escape from the bodily conditions of human life.[41]

The temptations to aristocratic nihilism and to Gnosticism exhibit something of the instability of *noir* narration, which, at its best, embodies a tension between the dramatic sense of the entrapment of the protagonist and the nobility of his or her quest. In the nihilistic films, the quest is simply undone, a pointless distraction from the tasks of self-creation and the manipulation of others. But certain features of *noir* narration, particularly of the wrong man caught in a trap, can also give rise to depictions of strikingly noble characters. Some of these narratives are quite distant from classic *noir*, although they retain the themes of quest in the midst of an alien and hostile universe. Both tendencies—toward aristocratic nihilism and toward the nobility of the quest—can be found in contemporary feminist neo-*noir*.

Neo-*noir* films are often seen as liberating characters from constricting conventional moral codes or oppressive political systems. Too often, they are infantile exercises in amoral wish fulfillment, adolescent fantasies of sexual freedom and domination of others. They achieve nothing more than a hollow and self-canceling transcendence of convention. The theme of sadomasochism, the bold exercise of power over the bodies of others, insinuates itself into a number of neo-*noir* films, including feminist films, from *Body Heat* to *Basic Instinct*. The latter unleashes the Sadean impulses of violent sexuality that have always had a place in *noir*. The difference here is that these impulses are sources of liberation instead of self-destruction.[42]

But *Basic Instinct* is not the last word on feminist neo-*noir*. A cult television hit, about the sort of teen world operative in *Donnie Darko*, *Buffy the Vampire Slayer* (*BtVS*) is a kind of feminist neo-*noir*, which hearkens back to many of the themes of classic *noir*, especially the emphatic sense of the inherent limitations of the human condition. The series, as creator Joss Whedon insists, is all about "girl power," but it is not in the grip of illusory feminist theories of autonomous freedom or unbridled self-creation. Like many classic *noir* films, *BtVS* portrays human life as a quest, whose success depends largely on our ability to decipher uncertain clues and on the help of others. It thus counters Enlightenment themes of transparent certitude with shadowy mystery and of independent autonomy with inescapable dependency. *BtVS* presents human life itself as part of a cosmic labyrinth, a universal battle between forces of good and evil, whose outcome for individuals and for humanity is perpetually in doubt.

In many ways, *BtVS* is emblematic of the popularity of the contemporary dark tale of spiritual quest, whose features are even less amenable to generic determination than are those of film *noir*. In its focus on an adolescent quest for identity in the midst of a cosmic battle between good and evil, *BtVS* at once embraces and transcends the dominant trends in the teen genres of the 1990s, which range from television series such as *Dawson's Creek* to popular horror films such as *Not Another Teen Movie* and the *Scream* trilogy. *BtVS*'s implicitly raises the question of who or what, if anyone or anything, ultimately is in control of the cosmic battle between good and evil, the question of providence, which surfaces in other contemporary dark tales of the quest, the chief example of which is the Oscar-winning *American Beauty*. Beyond its dramatically compelling illustrations of the twin nihilisms of suburban, consumerist paradise and of endless youth—themes prominent in *BtVS*—*American Beauty* contains a sustained, if finally incoherent, reflection on the resources for redemption and transcendence. Others dark films of quest that raise the issue of providence would include Paul Thomas Anderson's films, *Magnolia* and *Punch-Drunk Love*, and the neglected, *Thirteen Conversations About One Thing*, of which one commentator has written, "The fundamental yearning for human happiness, the film suggests, drives us to recognize that this most basic need cannot be satisfied within the confines of immanent reality, but demands reference to a transcendent source of meaning."[43]

Reference to a transcendent source of meaning and to the possibility that what appears to be mere chance is in fact a providential orchestration of events are pervasive themes in M. Night Shyamalan's dark tales of spiritual quest. From his best known films, such as *The Sixth Sense* and *Signs,* to less well known films such as *Wide Awake* and *Unbreakable*, Shyamalan depicts unhappy, haunted, guilt-laden characters on spiritual quests, quests they pursue sometimes consciously (*Wide Awake* and *Unbreakable*), sometimes unconsciously (*The Sixth Sense*), and sometimes positively resist (*Signs*). Shyamalan has a penchant for creatively reworking existing sub-genres, in the horror film and of the comic book superhero. Among the standard *noir* films, there has often been an overlap with horror, as for example, in the vintage *noir* film, *Night of the Hunter*. Contemporary films such as *Donnie Darko* and television series such as *BtVS* exploit the possible points of convergence between *noir* styles and themes and standard motifs in the genres of horror and of the superhero.

Many contemporary dark films of the quest borrow symbols and themes rather freely from diverse sources: Christian, pagan, and eastern religions. That would be true of *Harry Potter, BtVS, American Beauty,* and the films of Shyamalan. By contrast, Mel Gibson's *The Passion of the Christ* is a sustained reflection on the central and exclusive claims and symbols of the Christian faith.[44] Like most of the contemporary films we examine in the latter part of the book, *The Passion* falls outside the bounds of film *noir*. It is, nonetheless, by far the darkest of any of the American film treatments of the life of Christ, a depiction of the last hours of Christ's life that hearkens back to an older tradition of meditation on the passion. It also builds, as do many *noir* tales of spiritual quest, upon the conventions of the contemporary horror genre. To put it that way, however, may be to get the causal connection backwards, at least in one important respect. An anonymous review on the horror film website, ESPLATTER, describes *The Passion* as providing an articulation of the "iconography" of the horror genre. In whatever ways the film might be ethically, theologically, or artistically flawed, it remains one of the most significant examples of American *noir* and the quest for a lost code of redemption.[45]

For Gibson as for Pascal, the life of Christ sheds light on the otherwise unintelligible and intractable paradoxes of the human condition. As we noted above, Goldmann offers a truncated account of Pascal, which never moves beyond Pascal's observations about the tragedy of our alienated condition. But Pascal sees in the image of a humiliated and crucified God a counter to the endemic vices of the human condition. Christ meets pride and despair with humility and hope. Yet redemption here does not overcome the tenuous, penitential path and the lingering possibility of going astray. Even in the incarnation, God remains hidden. Pascal comments: "He has qualified our knowledge of Him by giving signs which can be seen by those who seek Him and not by those who do not." Obscurity, combined with a complex ethical pedagogy, ill suits the deist conception of the deity, but it befits the Christian account, according to which nature is infected and in need of healing.[46] If there were a Pascalian objection to *The Passion*, it may be that it at times forgets the lessons of the hiddenness of God. Thus, an examination of this film will provide occasion for drawing out what otherwise might be missed in Pascal—his account of the cure for the *noir* condition of humanity.[47]

The Dangerous Edge of Things

FLANNERY O'CONNOR'S SUGGESTION that, unlike the advertising industry, American art should "not be looked to for assurance" provides an apt interpretive starting point for classic film *noir*. There is an instructive point of convergence here between O'Connor's Gothic sensibility and certain strains of film *noir*, an overlap that is particularly evident in the writings of Graham Greene. Known for his many novels, Greene's most lasting fame may be in film rather than literature. A film critic early in his career and the author of a number of scripts for the cinema, Greene wrote the script for and was involved in the production of the *noir* classic, *The Third Man*. In 1999, on the fiftieth anniversary of its release, the British Film Institute selected *The Third Man* as the greatest British film ever; in the same year, it was released on a Criterion Collection DVD. The film ranks alongside *The Maltese Falcon*, *Double Indemnity*, and *Sunset Boulevard* as an exemplary film *noir*. In his fine book on film *noir*, *More Than Night*, James Naremore describes *The Third Man* as "one of the best and more representative films of a period when a certain kind of high art had fully entered public consciousness and when European sobriety and American entertainment sometimes worked in tandem."[1]

Greene's interest in film antedates his great collaboration with director Carol Reed on *The Third Man* and *The Fallen Idol*. In fact, the interest runs to the very beginning of his career, to his time as a film critic.[2] A writer by instinct and habit, Greene nonetheless sought to appreciate film on its own terms, as a distinct medium. He had a preference for the early silent films and argued that film depends primarily on "picture and movement," perhaps with musical commentary, and only secondarily on dialogue. He also thought it was a mistake to denigrate film because of the democratic tastes it sought to meet. "Cinema," he wrote, "has to appeal to millions." Its "popularity is a virtue not to be rejected as vile."[3] For all his emphasis on the peculiar artistic traits of film, he admitted that his own writing was deeply influenced by film. He once stated, "When I describe a scene, I capture it with the moving eye of a camera."[4]

On both text and screen, Greene's dramas conjure up a seedy world of infidelity, greed, and betrayal, a world that critics have labeled "Greeneland." Greene bristled at that nomenclature, for he thought it suggested the construction of a deranged fantasyland detached from real life. He in turn accused the critics of not looking carefully enough at everyday life and the evils that pervade modern society. This is not to say that Greene's work is unadorned or free from artistic complexity; on the contrary, as James Naremore observes, the settings of Greene's novels are "thoroughly urban, rendered through a vivid, imagistic prose; his narration made use of internal monologues and complex shifts in point of view; and his endings were darkly ironic, pervaded by a sense of Kafkaesque guilt."[5] For all the modernist elements in Greene's fiction and films, he held to a very traditional description of the goal of film. It has a poetic role, to depict "life as it is and as it should be."[6] Greene thought very highly of some of Capra's films, such as *Mr. Deeds Goes to Town*, a film that captures a "sense of the common life."[7] He was not always so kind to American films of this sort; he castigated Capra's *You Can't Take it With You* for its "easy Benthamite morality" that honesty is the best policy.[8]

Greene intends for his own work to have an unsettling effect on audiences. He regularly uses the verb "excite" to describe the first and indispensable task of the filmmaker. Excitement is achieved through some sort of gripping dramatic situation; in Greene's case, the preference is for "blood melodrama," the sort of writing that in America and Britain contributed to the development of film *noir*. After exciting the audience, Greene thought, the filmmaker could then display "horror, suffering, and truth."[9] He loved the quotation from Robert Browning about the "dangerous edge of things." He commented that the "dangerous edge of things remains what it always has been—the narrow boundary between loyalty and disloyalty, between fidelity and infidelity, the mind's contradictions, the paradox one carries within oneself. This is what men are made of." These are precisely the paradoxical boundaries or tensions that provide creative sustenance to film *noir*.

The sense of the "mind's contradiction" and the tension between virtue and vice suggest an approach to the dramatic resources of *noir* that is an alternative to the more theoretically charged attempt to align *noir* with, say, existentialism, according to which the *noir* protagonist transcends meaninglessness through the creation of value. As we have already noted, this interpretation of *noir* faces a huge obstacle, the fatalism inherent in many *noir* dramas. Where the fatalism is overcome, it is not through the autonomous creation of value but through a tenuous quest for intelligibility, communication, and love.

Because many of those involved in the writing and production of *noir* narratives were leftists and because *noir* contains often relentless criticisms of America—its alleged benevolence and freedom, its system of justice, its belief in equality, dignity, and the pursuit of happiness—*noir* is often envisioned as part of a leftist, even communist, movement in Hollywood.[10] Capitalist greed might well be said to be the chief passion in *noir*, since even lust typically ends up subordinate to, or just another manifestation of, greed. It is not unreasonable to offer a Marxist interpretation of the fake bird, around which the entire action of *The Maltese Falcon* pivots, as a commodity fetish. But *noir* has proven equally congenial to conservatives and for good reason. For all its radical stylistic experimentation and its fascination with the ordinary citizen turned criminal, *noir* (from *Double Indemnity* to *A Simple Plan*) expresses deeply conservative instincts about limits, about the natural and social constraints on human passion and ambition.

Running from films of the early 1940s such as *The Maltese Falcon* and *Double Indemnity* up to 1959s Orson Welles's classic, *A Touch of Evil*, film *noir* is a counter to American optimism. Instead of the narrative moving toward an affirmation of the American dream, of the efficacy of democratic virtues and the resiliency of the communal foundations of American life in the family, the dream becomes a nightmare, and the vices of greed, envy, and lust predominate. Faith in progress is seen as naïve, replaced by a haunting sense that misdeeds of the past cannot be overcome or rectified. *Noir* characters are highly susceptible to irrational passion; in their dependence on circumstances beyond their control, they exhibit a potentially fatal vulnerability. Characters find themselves trapped in a sort of labyrinth, in the midst of which they embark upon a quest to solve a set of mysteries, usually involving both a crime and a woman. But the quest is often enough equally a search for self-knowledge, for love, and for friendship; it involves a desperate desire to communicate one's predicament, to make clear, if not the answer, at least the precise shape and source of the dilemma. One might be tempted to call film *noir* the anti-Capra genre, since his films exhibit the buoyancy of American democracy and end with affirmations of family, community, and America. But, as we have already urged, Capra often manages, nowhere more so than in *It's a Wonderful Life*, to inscribe *noir* within a happy ending. Jimmy Stewart's George Bailey becomes a classic *noir* protagonist when he is given the dubious gift of non-existence. The ensuing transformation of his small town of Bedford Falls, locus of the American dream, into Pottersville, an American nightmare of merciless capitalism, is archetypal *noir*. That Capra's classic piece of Americana can contain an extended *noir* narrative illustrates the breadth of the influence of *noir* in American film.

Because *noir* does not offer a happy resolution or any clear way out, it has with some regularity been decried as nihilistic, a degenerate art form. Such pejorative evaluations can be traced as far back as the mid-1940s when the French invented the phrase "film *noir*." In his seminal essay on *noir*, Jean-Pierre Chartier expressed distaste for the new wave of dark, American films because of their "pessimism and disgust for humanity." American *noir* contains no "fleeting image of love that gives hope for a better world"; its characters are "monsters," who fail to "rouse our pity or sympathy."[11] Many other critics have followed Chartier's lead, even if they appear to applaud what Chartier repudiates. Some critics see *noir* as reaching its pinnacle in the shattering of narrative and identity and in despair over the possibility of the fulfillment of human aspiration.[12]

Film *noir* embodies a dialectic of enlightenment, wherein the pursuit of light darkens the mind. The motto of the Enlightenment is Kant's hortatory "dare to know." Enlightenment theorists advocate the unlimited pursuit of truth, which is thought ultimately to be transparent to human intelligence and the self-conscious, scientific reorganization of human life and society in light of truth. By contrast, *noir* persistently reminds us that certain kinds of knowledge are forbidden, that knowing as seeing, experiencing, or enjoying can be destructive, even deadly. The human condition is not malleable to human wishes in the way certain optimistic modern thinkers have believed.

Enlightenment theorists promise liberation from various types of external authority: familial, religious, and political. But an unintended consequence of the implementation of Enlightenment theories is the elimination of freedom. Shigalyov, the theorist from Dostoevsky's *Demons*, states the problem succinctly: "I got entangled in my own data, and my conclusion directly contradicts the original idea I start from. Starting from unlimited freedom, I conclude with unlimited despotism."[13] In its initial years, *noir* often embodied its anti-Enlightenment themes in a specific post-war milieu: the dislocation of men returning from battle to domestic life, the tension created by the freedom women experienced during the war, the haunting sense that something has been lost that cannot be recovered, and a pervasive sense of rot and corruption.

In all these ways, *The Third Man* is vintage film *noir*. Set in post-war Vienna, in a city divided into four zones (Russian, American, British, and French), *The Third Man* is the story of an attempted reunion, between Holly Martins (Joseph Cotten), an American author of popular westerns, and Harry Lime (Orson Welles), currently residing in Vienna. Just as Martins arrives in Vienna, he is told that Lime is dead and that his funeral is currently underway. Arriving at the end of the ceremony, Martins encounters a number of acquaintances of Lime, including his lover and a British major named Calloway (Trevor Howard), who in a series of increasingly explicit conversations reveals information about the unsavory life and illegal practices of Lime. Perplexed by conflicting accounts of the circumstances surrounding Lime's death in an alleged car accident, Martins suspects foul play and begins to conduct his own investigation, a task made particularly difficult by the city itself, a linguistic and legal labyrinth, where, in passing from one street to another, any sense of confidence about one's environment can vanish rapidly.

The style of the film is paradigmatic *noir*. Camera angles are skewed in nearly every scene, as the images of the characters are multiplied, reflected and refracted in glass and water, even in glasses of beer. The sense of spatial disorientation is pronounced from the very beginning, when Holly visits the building where Lime had been living. He stands on a lower level of a spiral staircase and looks up at a porter who is framed off center. The camera alternates between high and low shots as the porter in German explains matter-of-factly that Lime is dead, "already," he adds, "in hell or heaven." As he says hell, he points upward and, as he says heaven, he points downward. The manner of framing the scene and the gestures of the actor unsettle our expectations about the ultimate frame of reference for human justice and orientation. But the film never quite abandons these frames of reference; indeed, its lingering sense of justice links the horrifying violation of natural justice to a loss of an ultimate standard of judgment, to the death of faith in a God who protects the innocent. In this way, Greene's script depicts not the positive influence of the supernatural or the escape from the *noir* labyrinth through faith, but the entrapment and haunting sense of loss that result from its abandonment.

The Third Man's penchant for tight shots and for decentralized framing of characters and objects underscores the limited vision, the disorientation, of the characters in the story. The sharp and often rapid contrast between dark and light as well as the ample use of shadows reinforce the sense of mystery and danger. Through such devices, *noir* films place the viewers in the same situation as that of the protagonist, thus allowing for maximum identification with his dilemma, his sense of being trapped in a labyrinth.

Greene senses the comic resources of the *noir* predicament. If the sense of alienation becomes too great, the drama can degenerate into absurdity and turn comic, as the quest for a way out of the labyrinth becomes pointless. So, in the scene where the porter, with whom Holly had previously met, is murdered, Holly is identified as a suspect and quickly bundled up and forced into a car that rapidly leaves the scene. Both Holly and the audience fear the worst, that he will be the next murder victim. But he is quietly delivered to the British Cultural Centre for a planned lecture on the modern novel. There, his own rather mundane and illiterate training is mocked and dismissed by the serious European audience members, many of whom leave after issuing derisive remarks.

Greene is also having some fun with the divide between popular entertainment and serious fiction, even as he engages in a subtle critique of the dangers of American innocence, a topic that would become the central theme of his later novel, *The Quiet American*. Holly writes westerns, which here are seen to embody a simplistic division of good and evil and to result in unambiguously happy endings for the just. Indeed, the plot of the *The Third Man*—which reveals not only that

Harry has faked his own death, but also that he has been involved in a money-making scheme to water down doses of penicillin with the result that children end up permanently maimed—will lay bare just how naïve Martins is. To convince Martins of Harry's malice, Calloway has to take him to the hospital ward where the deformed children are under permanent care.

Martins's obliviousness is also evident during the question period after his lecture on modern literature. He appears never to have heard of stream of consciousness and, when asked about his chief literary influences, responds by citing Zane Grey. When he receives the initial invitation to speak, he is told he should address the modern novel and the crisis of faith. When he responds, "What's that?", he is told, "I thought you'd know. You're a writer."

Of course, the film does have something to say about the crisis of faith, even if its religious themes are more muted than in some of Greene's other works. Perhaps the most famous lines in the film, lines Orson Welles contributed during filming, occur in a late exchange between Holly and Harry. In an historical and philosophical self-justification, Lime asserts, "In Italy for thirty years under the Borgias, they had warfare, terror, murder, and bloodshed, but produced Michelangelo, Leonardo da Vinci, and the Renaissance. In Switzerland, they had brotherly love. They had five hundred years of democracy and peace, and what did that produce? The cuckoo clock." The Borgias, by Lime's account, embody a Nietzschean spirit of transcending good and evil through aesthetic self-fashioning.

As justifiably famous as this insouciant defense of aesthetic nihilism is, it is not Lime's most telling speech. Immediately preceding the discussion of the Borgias, there is a conversation, taken directly from Greene's book, that cuts to the heart of the threats of modern politics. When Holly inquires about the accusations concerning the doses of penicillin, Lime urges him to "leave it alone" but then adds a sort of justification. Gesturing to the streets far below, which are populated with unrecognizable individual human beings, he states, "Look down.

See all those dots. Victims? Would you really feel any pity if one of those dots stopped moving—forever. . . . In these days, old man, nobody thinks in terms of human beings. Governments don't. So why should we?" Lime's thesis is that care for individual lives runs against the utilitarian logic and instrumental rationality of modern politics, in both its socialist and capitalist guises. The potential for nihilism lurks just beneath the surface of the benevolent progressivism of modern utilitarianism, whose goal is the maximization of the good conceived in terms of pleasure, the greatest good for the greatest number.

In this brief statement, Greene encapsulates a line of reasoning about modernity prominent in both Nietzsche and Dostoevsky. The Godlessness of the theory is the first thing that pops into the mind of Martins, who challenges Lime, "You used to believe in God." Lime responds sardonically, "I still do . . . I'm not hurting anybody's soul by what I do . . . the dead are happier dead." Here Lime resorts to what Walker Percy described as the great heresy of the modern age, angelism, the denial that human beings are bodily by nature. It is remarkable how deftly and how succinctly Greene sums up in these brief exchanges the doctrinaire modern myths of dualism, progressivism, and utilitarianism.

For all his superficial allure, Lime is himself among the already dead, the living dead. The first we learn of him, he is being buried, placed beneath the earth, on the way to becoming lime, as his name not so subtly indicates. His apparent resurrection is the greatest wonder in the film. But what sort of life does he have? While he celebrates the great artistic creations of the renaissance, the period of rebirth, he has created little except vile destruction. He has no great hopes or aspirations. He escapes underground into the slimy sewer, which has become his natural habitat.

Lime is a character peculiar to modernity, the wasteland that was post-war European culture. T.S. Eliot's famous poem has proved to be an enduring influence on film *noir*. The great *noir* novelist, Dashiell Hammett, was fascinated with *The Waste Land*. As we shall see in greater detail later, Paul Schrader, the author of the script for the neo-*noir* film, *Taxi Driver*, described the spiritual and psychological crisis he endured while writing the script as akin to the crisis portrayed in *The Waste Land*.[14] Eliot's poem contains many *noir* themes, with its cities cut off from nature, facing an inexplicable apocalypse, its sterile and mechanical sexuality, its spiritually aimless protagonist and narrator, haunted by the past yet unable to piece the fragments of memory together, whose quest seems doomed, but who is under some sort of compulsion to continue, to tell the tale of contemporary dislocation and alienation, to pursue the veiled clues buried amid the ruins of western civilization. As Nancy Gish observes in her perceptive study of the poem, "All of the characters live in a world without love, relationships, action, or religion, where nothing fulfills and desire fails. But it is not their plight alone that moves us. Despite the many voices and shifting scenes, we sense a central consciousness whose perspective colors all we perceive and whose longing and despair most deeply affect us."[15]

Noir films may not always feature a central consciousness, but the mixing of the failure of desire with an inexorable longing overlaps nicely with *noir*. In his fine study of film *noir*, *Voices in the Dark*, J. P. Telotte describes the dramatic narrative of *noir* in terms of a "pattern of desire," desire "for a kind of communication-or to be more accurate, for a way of formulating our place in the cultural landscape and articulating that formulation for others."[16] In the modernist tradition of Eliot, to which certain *noir* films bear a striking resemblance, the desire for articulation of the landscape takes the form of a religious quest.

Like Eliot, Greene gives us characters whose dislocation and temptation to despair are fundamentally defects of spirit or, to put it more bluntly, sins against God, even if they struggle to identify their failure as sin. One feature of their alienation is precisely the inability to articulate what has been lost. Of course, the residue of faith in the lives of many of Greene's characters functions less as a consolation than as a source of the labyrinth into which the characters plunge. In one of his most famous novels, *The Heart of the Matter*, one of the main characters, Scobie, goes to confession fully aware that he is not capable of giving up the adulterous sin that he plans to confess. He hopes for a "miracle," that the priest will "find the word, the right word." No such miracle is forthcoming and he frankly admits to the priest that he cannot promise to commit this sin no more, "It would be no good my promising that, Father." On his way to suicide, Scobie succumbs to despair and damnation: "I am damned already—I may as well go the whole length of my chain."[17] Much of Greene's fiction is an attempt to articulate the lost code of redemption; it longs to speak the truth about our condition in such a way that truthful telling, confession of past sins, might be opportunities for grace. Of course, his characters often bespeak damnation rather than redemption; or rather, his characters exist on the dangerous edge of things, where the language of redemption and damnation borders on the unintelligible. Even where absent or dissipating, that code of redemption haunts the characters and the drama. By marking its absence, Greene renders it present.

Some critics have seen these spiritual trials as spurious dilemmas, invented for drama's sake. Orwell accused Greene of developing the "cult of the sanctified sinner" and of feigning belief in hell.[18] But this is too harsh. Greene's dilemmas work precisely because his characters retain, at a minimum, a residual sense of the divine, of God's haunting absence, if not His glorious presence. This is the strategy of his most explicitly religious novel, *The Power and the Glory*. This is the story of the whiskey priest, who in the midst of the Mexican persecution of the Church and burdened by his own sins, is never quite able to shake off his sense of his own vocation. Burdened with a daughter for whom he cannot care, the result of a sin of passion, he knows that his continued functioning as a priest is apt to cause scandal or worse. Government authorities are pursuing him for performing the now forbidden sacramental rites of the church; anyone associating with or assisting him could be subject to punishment. And yet,

If he left them, they would be safe, and they would be free from his example. He was the only priest the children could remember; it was from him they would take their ideas of the faith. But it was from him too they took God—in their mouths. When he was gone it would be as if God in all this space between the sea and the mountains ceased to exist. Wasn't it his duty to stay, even if they despised him, even if they were murdered for his sake? Even if they were corrupted by his example? He was shaken with the enormity of the problem. He lay with his hands over his eyes; nowhere, in all the wide flat marshy land, was there a single person he could consult. He raised the brandy to his mouth.[19]

The pervasive and deeply paradoxical sense of the continued, commanding presence of an absent God enables Greene's *noir* dramas to avoid succumbing to absurdity, despair, and nihilism. If *noir* wallows in confusion, disorder, and disproportion, it risks losing its sense of the purpose of any quest. Without the possibility of God or goodness, evil itself loses its gravity. Greene knew this perhaps better than any other twentieth century author. In response to the sort of objections voiced by Orwell, Greene offered a rejoinder worthy of Flannery O'Connor, who was herself accused of being a "hillbilly nihilist." He said that he "often tried to show the mercy of God. You cannot show it by portraying only virtuous people." By taking this indirect and negative path to God, Greene offers us precisely what O'Connor describes as a "limited revelation, but a revelation nonetheless." At least in these quasi-religious *noir* dramas, Greene implicitly advances a revised version of Conard's thesis concerning *noir* and the death of God: the most dramatic form of the *noir* labyrinth is one that results, not from the death of God, but rather from a painful sense of the presence of God in his very absence. As Lukacs puts it in a passage central to Goldmann's interpretation of Pascal in *The Tragic Vision*, "The tragic man hopes that a judgment by God will illuminate the different struggles he sees in the world before him, and will reveal the ultimate truth. But the world around him still

follows the same path, indifferent to both questions and answers. . . .
Man must live alone and by himself. The voice of the Judge has fallen
silent for ever, and this is why man will always be vanquished, doomed
to destruction in victory even more than in defeat."[20]

Of course, for Pascal, Lukacs' conclusion that God has not and
cannot speak is too hasty; it reposes upon a misplaced confidence in
human reason's ability to reach a peremptory decision regarding the
divine. As we shall see later in this chapter, Greene's quasi-religious *noir*
dramas anticipate in striking ways the religious themes in the *noir* films
of Alfred Hitchcock, for example, *The Wrong Man* and *I Confess*. Yet,
for all of his influence on *noir*, Greene's narratives of failed redemption
or of the dark, penitential path toward redemption are clearly not the
norm in film *noir* history. In fact, the death of God, if it does supply
the background assumption for the *noir* universe, as Conard suggests,
has already in most *noir* films receded far into the background and
is no longer a conscious preoccupation of the protagonists. To gain
a sense of the *noir* universe in these standard *noir* films and before
turning to Hitchcock's own version of Greeneland, we will look at a
set of influential early *noir* films.

THE CONFESSIONAL QUEST

A sophisticated and influential early *noir* film, *The Maltese Falcon*, is
closely based on a book by the definitive American *noir* author, Dashiell
Hammett.[21] There is a decidedly romantic element to the classic *noir*
detective, who is, at least in this early period, a knight in a "realm
where knights have no meaning," as Raymond Chandler describes
the detective in *The Big Sleep*. As Telotte insists, the "moral stance" of
the detective, whatever degree of incoherence it might contain, is essential. If his conception of justice is flawed, it is nonetheless real. In
The Simple Art of Murder, Chandler, creator of the famous detective
Philip Marlow, captures the detective's character and code in a witty
and terse description:

Down these mean streets a man must go who is not mean himself, who is neither tarnished nor afraid. . . . He is the hero, he is everything. He must be a complete man and a common man and yet an unusual man. He must be, to use a rather weathered phrase, a man of honor . . . He must be the best man in his world and a good enough man for any world . . . He is a relatively poor man, or he would not be a detective at all. He is a common man, or he could not go among common people. He has a sense of character, or he would not know his job. He will take no man's money dishonestly and no man's insolence without a due and dispassionate revenge. He is a lonely man and his pride is that you will treat him as a proud man or be very sorry you ever saw him. He talks as the man of his age talks, that is, with rude wit, a lively sense of the grotesque, a disgust for sham, and a contempt for pettiness. The story is his adventure in search of a hidden truth, and it would be no adventure if it did not happen to a man fit for adventure. He has a range of awareness that startles you, but it belongs to him by right, because it belongs to the world he lives in. If there were enough like him, I think the world would be a very safe place to live in, and yet not too dull to be worth living in.[22]

Here the quest of the detective is not so much to discover a lost code of redemption, as it is to embody a new code, a code of action, work, and professional expertise. As Irwin notes in his interpretation of the writings of Chandler, that code is the best that can be found in a world without God.[23] The nobility of this early example of the *noir* detective is palpable; he stands out as the one to whom women gravitate and whom other men admire and fear. Given his precarious situation in a world saturated with betrayal and crime, he cannot afford to let his chivalry be seen as a weakness. Even when he acts nobly, he is likely to attribute his acts to self-interest. He is thus a singular example of the principle Tocqueville observed in nearly all Americans, who are so proudly devoted to the principle of rational self-interest that they claim it as their motive even for the most selfless acts.

What strikes the viewer at the outset of *The Maltese Falcon* is the apparent detachment of Sam Spade. In an early scene, a phone rings in the middle of the night in a dark room into which a bit of light and a soft breeze enter through an open window. The camera remains focused on a small table on which rest the phone and other objects—a book, a newspaper, and a clock. A hand reaches out and calmly grasps the receiver of the phone and answers it. The voice is identifiably that of the private detective, Sam Spade (Humphrey Bogart), who learns that his partner, Miles Archer, has been murdered. He registers this news calmly, dispassionately and agrees to come to the murder scene. Before leaving, he calls his secretary, Effie, and asks her to call Archer's wife and to keep the wife away from him.

Spade is the first and most memorable of all the *noir* detectives. He is a fusion of seeming contradictions: calm yet never relaxed, cool and calculative yet not without charm and a sense of his own limits, not prone to fighting yet prepared for conflict if necessary, far from pure in his motives or actions yet with a deep sense of honor and fair play. The death of his partner affects him in the way any other business loss would. He quickly orders that Miles's name be removed from the office door. Later, he will comment that, when your partner is murdered, you have to do something about it. Why? "It's bad for business." Of course, the gains from the business hardly equal the risks involved; thus does the principle of rational self-interest mask other, unspoken motives.

Spade sets out to solve the murder of Miles, who had been working for Miss Wonderly (Mary Astor), who had come to the detectives' office earlier in the day with a story about her sister running off from New York to San Francisco with a dangerous man named Thursby. Returning home after inspecting the crime scene, Spade has visitors, two cops, who inform him that Thursby was shot not long after Archer's murder. After some tough talk with the cops, who intimate that Spade might have been involved, he asks, "How did I kill him? I forget."

Preserving the code of the detective and hoping to stay ahead of the cops, Spade refuses to divulge the name of his client. He meets Wonderly and demands to know the truth. She confesses that her real identity is Brigid O'Shaugnessy and that she is searching, not for her sister, but for a rare and very expensive antiquity, the Maltese falcon. Spade now enters the quest for the black bird, the chief contestant for which is a man named Gutman (Sydney Greenstreet), the "fat man," to whom Spade soon pays a visit. Gutman expresses disdain and mistrust of altruists whose policies are "contrary to the laws of nature." He commends Spade for admitting that he is "looking out for himself." Gutman boasts that he alone knows about the history and worth of the falcon. When he is not as forthcoming as Spade would like, Spade flies into a rage, threatens Gutman, smashes a glass, and storms out of the apartment. Once outside, he smiles, pleased with his performance.

Spade's toughness with Gutman and others tells us much about the world he inhabits. Aggression may be, as Freud thought, the chief threat to civilization; yet, so long as civilization cannot alter human nature, it is wise to be prepared to exercise violence whenever, and in the precise measure, necessary. The laws of nature, of which Gutman speaks, are precisely the laws of the human condition Hobbes sought to articulate. The state of nature is a state of war of all against all; the natural condition of man is one of "restless desire for power after power that ceases only in death."[24] In this situation, it is perfectly rational for each individual to use whatever means he deems necessary to secure his safety and increase his power, which will help insure his future safety. As Hobbes puts it, in the state of nature, "every one is governed by his own reason; and there is nothing he can make use of that may not be a help unto him, in preserving his life against his enemies; it follows, that in such a condition, every man has a right to everything, even to one another's body."[25]

The state of nature is a state of war, in which even the strongest will live in a constant fear of violent death. For Hobbes, this means that all human beings are equal in the most telling respect: anyone can kill anyone else. As a remedy for this condition, Hobbes argues that "every man ought to endeavor peace, as far as he has hope of obtaining it." But he is careful to add a condition: "when he cannot obtain it, he may seek and use all helps and advantages of war."[26] Hobbes proceeds to argue that men should be willing, for the sake of peace, to lay down their natural rights so long as others are too. Despite the echoes of Hobbes, *The Maltese Falcon* is less concerned with political order and peace than it is with a code of honor and of personal prudence. If law enforcement has eliminated civil war, deadly battles continue on the "mean streets" of America's cities. And Spade is not the reformist type; he is indifferent to politics.

The falcon eventually falls into Spade's hands. After he stores the bird in a safe place, the whole gang comes together to decide on a strategy. In the midst of these deliberations, Spade and Gutman investigate a Hobbesian question: whether the imminent threat of murder is the only sure means of ensuring the compliance of others. Spade scoffs at Gutman's assertion that there are "other means of persuasion" besides a gun. Spade insists, "none are worth anything unless they are backed by the threat of death." Gutman does not disagree but counsels prudence: "As you know, in the heat of the action, men are likely to forget where their best interests lie and let their emotion carry them away." Spade responds: "And the trick from my angle is to make my play strong enough to tie you up, but not make you mad enough to bump me off against your better judgment." Gutman smiles: "You are a character." After they have agreed on a story and on terms of payment, Spade has Effie deliver the bundle. As everyone else eagerly hovers over the bird, Spade stands at a distance, attentive but unmoved. Gutman tries to scrape off the paint but becomes frantic when he realizes it is a fake. Gutman quickly recovers, laughs off their failure, and announces that he is ready to go to Istanbul to spend another year in his quest for the Falcon. He invites Spade, whom he admires as a man of "nice judgment and many resources," to come along, but Spade refuses. Gutman offers the *rara avis* to Brigid O'Shaughnessy as a memento and departs with Wilmer and Cairo. Spade calls the police on the lot of them.

Now alone with Brigid, he accuses her of shooting Miles. As she begs for mercy and proclaims her love for him, he states, "If they hang you, I'll always remember you." She tries to persuade him that they could run off together, but he sees it as a dead end. He refuses to "play the sap" for her. He could never trust her because they have so much dirt on each other. He would always have to worry that one day she would put a bullet in his back. Besides, "it's bad business, bad for your organization," to have your partner murdered without doing something about it. After citing all the reasons not to help her and putting them on one side, he admits that, on the other side, "maybe I love you and maybe you love me." But, he concludes, "I won't because all of me wants to regardless of consequences and because you've counted on that with me from the start." She asks how he can do this and he responds, "I'll have some rotten nights . . . but that will pass." She grabs him, says "if you loved me," and kisses him passionately just as the police arrive. He tells them, "She killed Miles." When the cops ask about the bird, he says, "it's the stuff that dreams are made of," pauses to look at Brigid as the police escort her into the elevator, then turns and walks slowly down the steps toward the exit of the building.

Spade's ability to sidestep the traps into which every other character falls has much to do with his ability to resist "dreams," destabilizing desires for money, power, or love.[27] Unlike leading male characters in most subsequent *noir*s, Spade does not succumb to the *femme fatale*, the alluring, mysterious, and potentially deadly female, who is often the provocation for the destructive plotline in *noir*. He manages to keep rational control over his passions. But this does not mean that reason eliminates passion; in fact, Spade is the most fiercely passionate character in the film. His remarkable attunement to others and to his environment is partly rooted in his greater capacity for feeling and

passion. Were this not the case, the conflict between reason and passion or between different passions would be spurious; but it is real and
ineliminable. Spade is not utterly invulnerable; his situation contains a
dose of tragedy, of real loss. There is no reason to doubt Spade's words
to Brigid here at the end. In this final conversation with her, Hammett
repeatedly describes Spade as "tender." Like many a *noir* character after
him, Spade seems bent, in spite of the apparent futility of speech, to
communicate the truth about his situation.

For all of his appreciation of the ruthlessness of the world, Spade
is not reducible to a character in a drama written by Thomas Hobbes.
His codes of action and speech embody a kind of poetry, precisely the
discipline most scorned by Hobbes. They also embody a tacit morality.
"Don't be too sure I'm as crooked as I'm supposed to be," is Spade's
ironic way of making this point. As one commentator has urged, the
lengthy deliberation, exemplified in the final conversation with Brigid,
over whether he should save her or allow her to receive justice indicates that Spade is the type of detective who inevitably becomes
personally involved in his cases to the point of risking his life to solve
the case and his freedom through love. As John Cawelti puts it, the
hard-boiled detective, in contrast to the detached classical detective
such as Sherlock Holmes, must adopt a "moral stance" toward those
around him, especially toward the criminal he encounters.[28] That is
what makes the final scene an appropriate dramatic culmination to
the entire story. The case is not solved for Spade until he has made a
moral appraisal of those implicated.

Hobbes is of course not the only philosopher whom interpreters
have invoked in their analysis of *The Maltese Falcon*. Many film critics have seen the end of the film, with its revelation that the bird is a
fake, as a symbolic critique of capitalism, a powerful illustration of
what Marxists call "commodity fetish," the irrational and essentially
unfulfilling desire for commodities.[29] Gutman's equanimity in the face
of the realization that the bird is fake and his continued pursuit of the
real bird provide a nice illustration of Pascal's observation that what

most human beings really want is, not the cessation of desire, but endless means of diversion. This sort of quest is, as Pascal saw long before Marx, inevitably empty: "What causes inconstancy is the realization that present pleasures are false, together with the failure to realize that absent pleasures are vain."[30]

Spade is the film's moral center and he exhibits no reformist tendencies; he seems an utterly apolitical character, an inappropriate vehicle for the communication of a revolutionary political ideology such as communism. Indeed, one of the chief lessons of the film is that any sort of idealism, political or otherwise, is a costly diversion in a *noir* world deeply unreceptive to dreams.

In Gutman and his lackeys, the film does indeed spoof a certain version of the quest. When he relates the history of the falcon to Spade, Gutman relishes every scholarly detail. He quotes liberally from ancient tomes to document the "astounding" history of the falcon, which dates back to the Crusades, to Malta, and then (after being taken from the east during the holy wars) to Spain, Sicily, Paris, and eventually San Francisco. Gutman seems as attracted to the fabulous history of the bird as he is to the extravagant claims about its monetary value. In the end, however, the real value of the bird—and, by implication of all the great quests since the Middle Ages—is its cash value. Beneath his refined manners and his romantic quest, Gutman harbors a ruthless, calculating spirit. As he says later about the rightful ownership of the bird, "there is no clear title except by right of possession."

But Spade embodies a different sort of quest, "the adventure in search of a hidden truth," as Chandler puts it. Sometimes the detective's clinging to a code in the midst of a hostile and seemingly meaningless universe is described as a kind of existentialism. In a famous article, "No Way Out: Existential Motifs in the Film *Noir*," Robert Porfirio rightly notes the overlap between existential and *noir* themes of isolation, alienation, and potential nihilism. According to Porfirio, what halts the "slide of existentialism toward nihilism" is "its heavy emphasis on man's freedom." As in existentialism, so too in *noir*, characters must choose between authentic and inauthentic ways of life, "since man is his own arbiter, he literally creates good and evil."[31]

Porfirio's article is entirely impressionistic, buttressed only by a few, quick quotations from existentialism and a few confirming references to characters in *noir* films. Film *noir*'s combined and paradoxical accentuation of absurdity and nobility is suggestive of existentialism. But there are problems with pushing this interpretation too far. First, there is the contradiction involved in advocating, as a remedy for nihilism, the arbitrary creation of values, a philosophical counsel that would seem to exacerbate, rather than alleviate, the crisis of meaning. Indeed, nihilism is incompatible with confidence in human freedom, since meaninglessness undermines every shred of human dignity. Second, Porfirio misses the significance of *noir*'s clear sense of limits, costs, and consequences. Unlike existentialism's proclamation of a heroic transcendence through freedom, an exulting embrace of pointless struggle, the *noir* universe does not offer such naïve consolations. In his famous essay, "The Myth of Sisyphus," Albert Camus goes so far as to speak of Sisyphus's "silent joy" in embracing the "series of unrelated actions which become his fate, created by him."[32] Neither joy nor the proclamation of self-creation suits the world of *noir*.

To clarify further the peculiar features of Hammett's *noir* world, we need only compare Bogart's role as Spade in *The Maltese Falcon* with his character in *Casablanca*, a film that shares much with *Falcon*, including actors such as Peter Lorrie and Sidney Greenstreet. Despite "containing practically everything we associate with the form," *Casablanca* has been regularly excluded from the *noir* canon, an exclusion that dates back to Borde and Chaumeton's influential *Panorama du film noir americain*. Those authors excluded it on the grounds that it is a "wartime propaganda film with a romantic ending"; yet, as Naremore notes, they include films that fit precisely that description.[33] The *noir* elements in *Casablanca* provide ample indications of the flexibility of *noir*, of the way it can be put at the service of very different types of narrative, even narratives with redemptive endings.

In *Casablanca*, Bogart plays Richard Blaine, a World War ii saloon keeper in Casablanca, a city of passage from occupied Europe to free America. Bogart plays the same sort of tough, frank speaking, detached character he played in *The Maltese Falcon*. Early in the film, the sycophantic Ugarte (Lorrie) enters Rick's office and fails in his attempts to ingratiate himself through flattery. He asks, "You despise me don't you, Rick?" Without pausing to look up from his table, Rick responds, "Well, if I gave you any thought, I probably would." A few scenes later, German curiae arrive to arrest Ugarte for the murder of German guards and the theft of letters of transit, which Ugarte has secretly entrusted to Rick. Ugarte panics, runs to Rick shouting, "Help me, Rick! Rick! Do something!" Rick remains unmoved and Ugarte is killed. When one of his associates tells Rick that he hopes he will be more helpful when the Germans come for him, Rick responds, "I stick my neck out for nobody." Toward the end of the film, Rick's penchant for action based on calculative, self-interest enables him to convince Captain Renault that he is absconding with Ilsa, the wife of Victor Laszlo, the leader of the French Resistance.

The final, noble sacrifice of Ilsa for Laszlow and his patriotic work would come as quite a surprise were it not for previous hints that Rick is more complex than he seems. In an early scene, another local entrepreneur, Ferrari (Greenstreet), shows up at Rick's Place and offers to pay Rick in exchange for Sam, Rick's longtime assistant and piano player at his saloon. "I don't buy and sell human beings," is Rick's curt reply. When a very young, newlywed begins bargaining with Captain Renault to gain exit visas for her and her husband, she asks Rick whether she should trust Renault. At first, Rick's answers are smug and ironic. To the question about what sort of man the Captain is, he responds, "Oh, like most men, only more so." But as he senses the girl's innocence and contemplates the sexual services Renault will demand in exchange for the visas, his tone alters. He finds the husband gambling and fixes the game so that the husband wins sufficient funds to pay for their exit visas.

Our picture of Rick deepens considerably with the arrival of Ilsa (Ingrid Bergman), whom he had met and fallen in love with in Paris. Just as the Germans invaded, the two agree to leave on the train together, but Ilsa fails to show. The night after her visit to Rick's place with her husband, Victor Laszlo, Rick remains at the bar well after closing, drinking and cursing his fate, the fate of an incurable romantic: "Of all the gin joints in all the towns in all the world, she walks into mine." The scene of a drunken, angry, and desperate Rick in the dark, except for the oddly angled slants of light piercing through the windows of his bar, has the feel of vintage *noir*, as does Rick's manner, dress, and mode of speech throughout the film. What frees Rick from the *noir* trap is the renewal of his love with Ilsa, who makes two private visits to him, and his realization that there is some larger, more significant cause in light of which he ought to understand his own desires. This is the insight of the ordinary citizen in the face of threats to order and peace, particularly in the face of the evils of the Nazi regime: "I'm no good at being noble . . . but it doesn't take much to see that the problems of three little people don't amount to a hill of beans in this world." Standard *noir* characters may grope for such an orientation or sense of purpose, but they rarely find it. The ending is a stirring call to arms, as Laszlo welcomes Rick back to the fight and promises confidently, "This time I know our side will win." Both Spade and Blaine have a code, an uneasy mix of Hobbesian self-interest and the medieval knight. The difference is that Blaine finds a confirmation, direction, and expansion of his code in the wider community. More than Blaine, Spade embodies the conflict between the mind and the world, "straining against each other without being able to embrace each other."[34] Yet Spade manages to negotiate his way in the world, to fend off its most serious threats; indeed, fortuitous circumstances allow him to dispense justice without being destroyed by it.

Although Spade may enjoy money or women, he strives to retain a sense of detachment, to be alert to the shifting of fortune and prepared to adapt to ensure his survival. He also lives by a code of honor; he is, as Chandler's description indicates, a sort of democratic hero. As already noted, he adopts a moral stance toward those with whom he interacts. But none of this makes him an existential hero, someone who creates his own conception of good and evil and, embracing the burden of his freedom, re-creates himself at each moment. Spade certainly improvises, but his freedom consists in a kind of adaptation to necessity, to what each situation requires of him. Moreover, while the existential hero is abstracted from the contingencies of time and place, Spade is very much wedded to a particular time and place. As he says of San Francisco, this is "my town, my game." He is less interested in transcendent moments of self-appropriation than in the prudential assessment of the present in light of the past. If the *noir* world of *The Maltese Falcon* shares with existentialism a sense of the conflict between the human agent and the world, it differs significantly over the resolution or negotiation of that conflict.

In this respect, Spade is a thoroughly democratic figure. He may be superior to the other characters in *The Maltese Falcon*, but his superiority consists precisely in his acknowledgment of the limits placed upon all human beings. The romantic and greedy aspirations of the other characters delude them into thinking that they can transcend these limits. Classic *noir* highlights the fundamental equality of human nature, the way all are subject to the human condition. Very few films contain characters who approximate Spade's ability to anticipate, and adapt to, the randomness of events. In fact, most *noir* characters find themselves tragically ensnared.

THE NON-CONFESSION CONFESSION

Ensnared is precisely the word to describe the character Walter Neff (Fred MacMurray), in another influential early *noir*, *Double Indemnity*.[35] In the dramatic opening of that film, a car rushes recklessly through city streets at night, runs a red light, and comes to a screeching halt at the offices of the Pacific All-Risk Insurance Company. Walter

Neff, an insurance agent, enters the office, sits at a desk lit by a single light, takes his boss's case recorder in hand, and begins to tape an office memorandum to his boss, Barton Keyes (Edward G. Robinson).

In precise terms and detached tone, Neff gives the date as July 16, 1938, and states that he wants to set him straight about a case, the Dietrichson case. "You'll probably call this a confession, but I don't like the word confession." Yet it is a confession, an attempt to make amends and set things right, to speak truthfully about past misdeeds in the hope of reconciliation. Neff wants the forgiveness, or at least the approval, of his friend and boss, whose heart is "as big as a house." Andrew Spicer goes so far as to say that Neff's goal is to "renew a bond of loyalty with Keyes which offers some form of redemption."[36]

"Redemption" is too strong a word in this context, but Spicer is on to something in seeing the voiceover recording as introducing a split into the narrative between the first order retelling of events (a tale of mechanical damnation and the inextricable bond between lust, greed, and death) and the second order commentary on those events, less a traditional commentary than a new quest for understanding and communication, a confession in a world without God or prospect of efficacious forgiveness.[37] It thus mimics the religious confession that recounts past events and acts, especially sins, in the present, in the hope of forgiveness and reconciliation. As John Irwin observes, Neff is driven by a perverseness "fueled . . . by boredom with his work, . . . by the moral indifference that work engenders," and by "a sort of intellectual pride, a professional's sense of superiority."[38] Neff seeks to understand his own perverseness, but an explanation eludes him. Although he knows where his pursuit will end, he never consciously grasps the intimate connection between such self-destructive perversity and death. He inhabits a kind of hell of perverse desire, not just without prospect of a purgatory or paradise, but without any ability to name where he is and how he got there.

An extended flashback begins with Neff making a routine visit to a California bungalow to persuade the owner to renew his auto insurance. The husband is out, but the wife, Phyllis, in a memorable scene, stands in a towel at the top of the stairs while Neff looks up from the doorway. She dresses, comes down the stairs, and they discuss insurance, especially, at her prompting, accident insurance for her husband. As Neff drives away, his voiceover states, "How could I have known that murder could sometimes smell like honeysuckle? Maybe you would have known, Keyes, as soon as she mentioned accident insurance, but I didn't. I felt like a million."

At a subsequent appointment, when Phyllis presses the issue of accident insurance, Neff leaps to the implication of a murder plot and demands that she forget about it. In a voiceover, Neff admits he was the one who could not stop thinking about it. He states that his job, trying to catch those who want to beat the system, made him vulnerable to Phyllis' suggestion: "You know how it is, Keyes. You can't sleep but think about all the tricks. Then you start thinking about how you could beat it." Neff's job has little to do with justice; it is about profit and loss, about management skills and calculative expertise. Neff begins to believe that his skill in catching others could be transferred to success in beating the system: "You're like the guy behind the roulette wheel, watching the customers to make sure they don't crook the house. And then one night you get to thinking how you could crook the house yourself and do it smart, because you've got the wheel right smack under your hands."

Neff cannot resist. He tells Phyllis, "I'm going to help you, but it's got to be perfect . . . straight down the line." She repeats weakly, "Straight down the line." As he watches her drive off, Neff says, "That was it, Keyes. The machinery had started to move and there was nothing we could do to stop it."

Neff is fond of these machine metaphors, images that call to mind the mechanistic materialism of Hobbes, who described life itself as "but a motion of limbs" and treated human choice as but the last desire prior to action, desire provoked and determined by a mechanistic interaction between the human body and its environment. There is a close connection in *noir* between money-thinking and rational thinking. As Hobbes bluntly and reductively puts it, reason is operative exclusively in matters that lend themselves to analysis through addition, subtraction, multiplication, and division.[39] Money certainly lends itself to calculative reasoning. In *noir* films, ordinary citizens turned criminals rarely talk about what they will do with money. Once considered to have merely an instrumental status in human life, money becomes an end in itself, toward which all our striving is ordered and in light of which all else is understood and appraised. Sex becomes another commodity. When Neff leaves Phyllis after their first meeting, he says he "felt like a million." Neff is interested not just in profit but in maximizing profit, as is indicated in the title of the film, *Double Indemnity*. He suggests to Phyllis that they make her husband's death look like a freak accident because such claims trigger a double indemnity clause: "It has to be the train, just as we discussed."

Neff returns home, makes some calls to establish an alibi, puts on a suit identical to the one Dietrichson will be wearing, and heads over the Dietrichson residence, where he sneaks into the car and lays down on the back floor. Phyllis drives her husband toward the train station but turns off onto an empty, dark road. At her signal, Neff kills him. The murder is not shown; we hear the victim's muffled cries as the camera remains fixed on Phyllis' unflinching facial expression. Combined with Neff's wearing of a dead man's suit, the tight shots in the car reinforce the sense of claustrophobia and entrapment of the murderous couple. The sense of inevitability highlights the futility and weakness of knowledge, once greedy, murderous desire has taken hold. Pretending to be Dietrichson, Neff enters the train and then hops off at a pre-arranged location along the track, where he meets Phyllis and they dump the dead man's body. In his voiceover, Neff says that, although everything went smoothly, he suddenly knew that "everything would go wrong. I couldn't hear my own footsteps. It was the walk of a dead man. . . . I tried to hold myself together, but my nerves were tearing me to pieces."

At first, Keyes is not suspicious. Just as Neff begins to feel comfortable and arranges for Phyllis to come to his apartment, Keyes shows up and admits his little man has been troubling him. It wasn't an accident and it wasn't suicide either. He suspects murder because of the astronomical odds against a man dying accidentally so soon after he took out accident insurance. Phyllis nearly knocks on the door, but hears voices and waits outside. As Keyes leaves, he stops to talk in the hallway and she stands behind the open door. In this masterfully orchestrated scene, the accent is on the helplessness and entrapment of Neff and Phyllis, whom the camera invites us to view almost as victims.

Phyllis tells Neff she's afraid, "not of Keyes, but of us. We did this to be together but it's pulling us apart." Of course, this is pure fiction. Although at least one scene strongly suggests sexual intimacy, the two have never been "together" and have never expressed genuine human emotion or passion. They embody the isolated nearness of city life, "human solitude in a world of steel," a world symbolized in the impersonal office space where Neff labors, in the redundant Spanish style house where Phyllis lives, and in the generic store in which the murderous lovers meet.[40] Even their sexual attraction is more artificial than romantic.

Double Indemnity captures, better than any other *noir*, the "gnawing loneliness within the supreme individualism of American life, the disillusionment that surfaces whenever the American dream of material success evaporates leaving nothing behind."[41] This is one source of the fatalism that Steven Sanders takes to be the defining feature of *noir*. But these interpretations work on only one level of the film, the first-order level of immediate action. Even here, the situation is more complicated. Neff is aware, in the very midst of carrying out the murder plot, of his guilt and condemnation. He is never reducible to the mere mechanics of desire; a residual sense of conscience is operative in him throughout, even if his conscience is unable to orchestrate a change of action. In an odd way, Neff illustrates the medieval conception of perplexity, the moral confusion and paralysis resulting from initial violations of conscience that renders one increasingly incapable of altering one's path, but never quite eclipses the awareness of one's own vice.

As their situation becomes more desperate, Neff calls Phyllis to arrange for a late-night meeting at her house. He tells Keyes in the voiceover that he now planned to be "free of the whole mess and of Phyllis too." As he makes his way to her house, we see Phyllis hide a gun under a cushion on her couch. Neff tells Phyllis, "I'm getting off the trolley car . . . another guy will finish my ride." As they argue, Phyllis shoots him; a wounded Neff comes close to her and invites her to "shoot again." Phyllis relents saying, "I'm rotten to the core. I used you just the way you said. I never loved you until a minute ago. I couldn't fire a second shot." Neff says, "I'm not buying, baby" and shoots her.

Many critics have been skeptical of Phyllis' belated repentance, a result, they suppose, of the filmmakers' desire to conform to production codes. However dubious might be Phyllis' conversion, Neff's remorseful "confession" seems genuine. As Neff finishes his recording, he realizes that Keyes has been watching and listening to him for some time. Keyes offers to call for a doctor, to which Neff responds, "What for? So they can patch me up? So I can walk into the gas chamber in San Quentin on my own power?" Claiming he needs just four hours to make it to the border, he heads for the exit but collapses in the doorway, as Keyes calls for an ambulance and the police. As Keyes kneels beside him, Neff says, "The guy you were looking for was too close, right across the desk from you." Keyes responds: "Closer than that, Walter." Neff says, "I love you, too."

Although Billy Wilder said that the ending made explicit that the story was ultimately a "love story between men," some critics have been preoccupied with the homoerotic subtext of the final frames, with the men's dialogue and posture and the sexual suggestiveness of Keyes' lighting a match for Neff's cigarette. The more important point is that Neff's "confession" and attempt at reconciliation lend a certain gravity and dignity to the tale of Neff's life. Telotte sees the lit match as symbolic of the "flickering light of truth that marks all discourse."[42]

The extended voiceover narrative frames the desire for money and sex within a more expansive quest for understanding, reconciliation, and friendship. It suggests that mechanical materialism and the determinism of self-destructive desire do not ultimately provide an adequate philosophical foundation for comprehending these characters. We do not merely react to external stimuli but we are aware of our world and ourselves. We can adopt a stance of critical self-awareness of our courses of actions and ways of living, and respond to circumstances in a variety of ways, some predictable, some not. We retain, except in the most extreme cases, a residual degree of self-determination and freedom and can achieve a limited degree of transcendence of our immediate situation. This is an impure or mixed freedom, not the absolutism of the existentialists. Pascal captures the duality when he urges readers to be aware that concupiscence automatically makes our decisions for us and then urges us to order our lives so that we are not dominated by passion. Of course, he does not believe there is much hope for success in the latter project by the power of natural reason alone. And he is acutely aware that human willing and thinking are never free from the influence of passion and imagination. But the mere fact that he thinks we can be made aware of that which dominates us and can marshal some effort in an opposite direction indicates that we are not utterly, and in a completely mechanical way, under the determining sway of the passions.

Of all the films that have given rise to the *noir* label among French critics, *Double Indemnity* is the one that seems most to warrant the pejorative appraisal of Jean-Pierre Chartier, who was repulsed by *noir*'s "pessimism and disgust for humanity" and its reduction of sex to an "obsessive criminal fatality." He argues that American film *noir* contains no "fleeting image of a love that gives hope for a better world" and no characters who "arouse our pity or sympathy." The characters are "monsters, criminals whose evils nothing can excuse, whose actions imply that the only source for the fatality of evil is in themselves."[43] This would be an apt judgment of *Double Indemnity* were it not for the quest embodied in narrative of the flashback voiceover. Constructed as a non-confession confession, the discourse of *Double Indemnity* hovers between an older code of confessional speech and a new code of psychological reductionism that is always tempted to view the discourse of repetition as merely an anxiety reflex. In his commentary on *Double Indemnity*'s voiceover technique, Telotte nicely points out that speech itself, the effort at self-understanding and self-communication through the confessional retelling of events, is a "human force that qualifies" and counters the "fatalism" of the film. An appropriate philosophical anthropology for *noir* would have to capture both the way in which we are prey to the machine-like workings of the passions and the way in which we retain a residual freedom and distance from those very passions. It needs a dialectical philosophy, as Goldmann describes Pascal's thought, a philosophy that embraces both sides of the paradox and resists anxious attempts at reductionism.

THE FILE ON THELMA JORDON

Truthfulness in the face of death and in light of one's own vices and infidelities is a staple of *noir*. Nowhere is the possibility of redemption, however partial and momentary, through truthful speech more evident than in the classic *noir* gem, *The File on Thelma Jordon*, a film in which the ennui of an ordinary middle class American husband provides the occasion for his entrapment by what appears to be a typical *noir* femme fatale. Yet this film neatly defies common expectations, as it shifts our attention decisively away from the male character and his fate and toward the surprising complexities of the character of Thelma. The story's beginning is commonplace *noir*, in scenes that call to mind a passage from Pascal: "How tiresome it is to give up pursuits to which we have become accustomed. A man enjoying a happy home-life has only to see a woman who attracts him, or spend five or six pleasant days gambling, and he will be very sorry to go back to what he was doing before. It happens everyday."[44]

This aphorism from Pascal underscores the way vagrant appetites render human beings subject to innumerable chance events. In most *noir* films, men have an even greater incentive to seek happiness outside the domestic realm, since they do not enjoy a "happy home-life." In the opening scene of *The File on Thelma Jordon*, a drunken assistant district attorney, Cleve (Wendell Corey), sits in his office and complains to Miles, his colleague, that his father-in-law dominates his life. After Miles leaves, a woman named Thelma Jordon (Barbara Stanwyck) arrives and says that she is looking for District Attorney Scott to discuss an attempted burglary at the estate of her elderly and sickly aunt. Cleve now shares his miseries with Thelma and they spend the evening together. Cleve arrives home and falls on his bed in a stupor as his wife asks, "Where were you on the night of May 25?" He falls asleep and she weeps.

After a morning fight, Cleve's wife proclaims her love for him and reminds him that she's headed to the beach house with the kids for the summer. When he asks her not to go, she tells him to think of the children: "We can't be selfish." She leaves and Thelma calls. She and Cleve begin a series of clandestine meetings in the hilly, wooded area near her aunt's estate. Thelma is secretive about her past. She admits to regrets and then to having been married to a man named Tony, from whom she claims to have separated. But an unknown male, later identified as Tony, lurks about in the woods, monitoring their meetings.

Then one evening, Aunt Vera is startled from sleep by a sound. There is a flash and Aunt Vera collapses in a heap. Meanwhile, Cleve unable to reach Thelma by phone, decides to go to the house. A shaken Thelma tells Cleve, "something's happened." She tells him that she suspects Tony and admits that, in a panic, she wiped the prints clean on the open window and the safe. Cleve tells her to rearrange everything as it was and put her prints back where they were. As the butler arrives at the main house, Cleve scurries out the open window leaving his footprints in the dirt, evidence for the police of the presence of a mysterious Mr. X.

At the beach house with his family, Cleve receives a call asking him to return to work on the case of Thelma Jordon, who has been accused of the murder of her aunt. Before Cleve returns, he admits to his wife that there is someone else. But his passion for Thelma leads not to love or freedom but to further confusion, exacerbated by police reports that she has never been married and photographs of her in a gambling raid. By this time, Cleve has so compromised his career that he cannot back out. He has plotted behind the scenes to take over the case of prosecuting Thelma. In a meeting with her attorney, she listens to him explain that there are "two kinds of criminals, the conscious and the unconscious." The latter are "split personalities," who do not let their "right hand know what their left hand is doing."

The discussion of dual personality is archetypal *noir*; Cleve's name—akin to the word "cleave" meaning a split or a severing—gives additional prominence to this theme. (His name also points to his cleaving to others, his pathetic dependence on women.) But the duality about which we wonder concerns Thelma. She certainly fits the part of the classic *femme fatale*, who seems, if only to her weak male victim, to be trustworthy. In Thelma's case, mounting evidence of a dark past contributes further to the motif of deceptive duality. Miles urges Cleve to ask Thelma in court about the pictures from the gambling raid: "let her try and explain away her past." An angry Cleve confronts Thelma in her prison cell: "Is that you as a blonde?" She responds haltingly, "No. It was me as I was once, but not now."

Thelma's defense attorney gives an inspired closing, arguing that the evidence for the presence of a mysterious Mr. X at the crime scene raises reasonable doubt about Thelma's guilt. She is acquitted. At this point, the official file on Thelma Jordon is closed, whatever one thinks about the outcome of the trial. But Cleve and the audience have lingering questions and suspicions. We are even less inclined than he to trust her assertions of change. What happens immediately after the trial seems to confirm our doubts.

Thelma returns to her aunt's home to find Tony already there. "Why did you have to come here?" she asks. They bicker. Thelma agrees to give Tony part of her aunt's annuity but adds a peremptory condition: "We're finished." When Cleve calls, Tony interrupts their conversation and hangs up the phone. Upon his arrival at the estate, Cleve finds Tony, and Thelma tells him that she loves Tony. She coldly admits that she killed her aunt: "You must have known but did not want to know." After she tells him, "You were the fall guy," Tony beats him and leaves with Thelma. More pathetic and needy than ever, Cleve illustrates a cycle in human behavior: "dependence, desire for independence, needs."[45]

In a surprising twist, Thelma herself ends up confirming this cycle but in a noble, rather than pathetic, way. As she drives off in the car with Tony, he tries to assuage her irritation by reminding her, now that the case is over, "you can get yourself back . . . fix your hair, get that sexy look." Tony here offers his own variation on Thelma's previous claim that she is not what she once was. However much she may have started out in agreement with Tony's plan, she is now incapable of continuing this way of life. An irate Thelma stuffs the car's cigarette lighter into Tony's face. He loses control of the car, which crashes and burns.

When we see Thelma again, she is on a stretcher in the hospital and has just finished giving the police a double confession for the murders of her aunt and Tony. Cleve arrives and his partner tells him that she has confessed to everything accept who Mr. X is. When Cleve asks why she won't tell, she says, "Because I love him, that's why." She explains, "I couldn't go on with him [Tony]. You did that for me, Cleve. I'm glad it's over . . . all my life struggling. Willis said that I was two people. He was right. You don't suppose they could just let half of me die." The film captures a more complete picture of Thelma's life and character than either the official police file or the unofficial rumors swirling about her past.

Internal division in *noir* is often conceived as concealing a dark side; *The File on Thelma Jordon* encompasses and transcends this standard, expected plot twist. The film depicts even the most weary and haunted of criminals as unpredictable, with a destiny partially contingent on free choice. The element of contingency is incompatible with depictions of humans as thoroughly necessitated. Pascal captures the complexity of the human being: "We think playing upon a man is like playing upon an ordinary organ. It is indeed an organ but strange, shifting, and changeable. Those who only know how to play an ordinary organ would never be in tune on this one."[46] Of course, Thelma's freedom is quite limited, constrained by the human condition and her past actions. She cannot remake the past or free herself from its burdens and punishments. Her ability to speak truthfully and to love nobly comes at a great cost, the extinction not just of the old, criminal self but of her entire life.

The File on Thelma Jordon presents a highly complex female character. Contemporary feminist interpretations of *noir* often criticize the *femme fatale* role as yet another stereotype of women, who seem to fall neatly into either of two categories, the dutiful wife and mother or the sexually alluring and morally compromised temptress. Moreover, the *femme fatale* ends up being punished for her deeds, often with the loss of her life. So the apparent liberation of the roles of women can actually be seen as a warning, a way of reinforcing traditional domestic function of women. Outside of this context, women are nothing more than symptoms of male anxiety or symbols of the capitalist reduction of all things, including persons, to commodities.

But there are serious weaknesses to this interpretation. First, it is not just women who pay for their violation of conventional mores. Men are subject to the same laws; no one wins in classic *noir*. Of course, the women often seem to pay more than the men, as is the case, for example, in *The File on Thelma Jordon*. Thelma's murderous and adulterous activities end with her death, while her partner, the married assistant district attorney, walks away with his life. But to look simply at external consequences is misleading. Thelma treats her death as a relief; it enables her to come clean about her nefarious activities and about her love for Cleve. Meanwhile, with his marriage shattered and his public image tarnished by scandal, Cleve faces an onerous future. Second, if *noir* provides moral lessons reinforcing conventional mores, it does so in a less than complete way. In vintage *noir*, there are few healthy, happy families to provide a counterexample to the conniving, lustful activities of the *femme fatale*. But this is to offer too generalized a picture of the *femme fatale*. Lizabeth Scott, who starred in many a *noir* film, argues that quite often the *femme fatale* is admirably complex; she "loves truthfully" and has the "greatest understanding."[47] These claims would seem to be borne out in the final words of Thelma Jordon.

If *noir* films tend toward skepticism of happy, normal, well-adjusted citizens and families, they also repudiate the criminal success story. In its assumption that a double, a dark self, lurks just beneath the surface of the most ordinary individuals, *noir* punctures naïve, conventional assumptions about human behavior. But the dark side is hardly liberating. Having crossed a line, *noir* characters face insuperable obstacles. Thus, *noir* seems to be at once radical and conservative. Moreover, characters are not reducible to the appetites that have led them astray. Their desires are often more complex than their tough, calculative modes of thinking and behaving would lead one to believe. Even where desire appears to operate in accord with laws of mechanical necessity, the characters evince an awareness of their situation that bespeaks a transcendence of it.

Now, the very notion of transcendence, let alone redemption, makes certain scholars of *noir* uneasy. But this, as I have already urged, entails too narrow a conception of *noir*, especially given that no one has yet come up with a persuasive definition of the genre. It also may entail too narrow a conception of redemption. Were it to exclude every glimmer of hope for transcendence or regeneration, *noir* drama would be indistinguishable from nihilism. To put the point more precisely, if negatively, nihilism has arrived, not when we cease to have happy or obviously just endings, but when the human longing for happiness, communication, love and justice is mocked as unintelligible, pointless, and absurd. However much *noir* may flirt with or engage the possibility of nihilism, it typically resists succumbing to it. *Noir* persists in depicting the human longing for love, for truth, and for communication as noble and admirable, as constitutive of what it means to be human. What *noir* precludes is a happy ending that restores all that has been lost. It denies that the slate can be wiped clean, that costs and consequences can be averted. Raymond Durgnant asserts that the only possible "happy ending in a true film *noir*" is quite limited: the "worst of danger is avoided with little amelioration or congratulation."[48] What Durgnant's claim misses is the trajectory of desire and speech in *noir*, a trajectory that Telotte traces in magnificent detail.

HITCHCOCK'S GREENELAND

The devastation that can be wrought by our inability to look away, our curious and self-destructive desire to know is nowhere more powerfully on display that in Alfred Hitchcock's famed *Vertigo*, a film steeped in tragic *noir*. Donald Spoto describes *Vertigo* as the "most tragic of Hitchcock's films."[49] In *Vertigo*, Hitchcock clearly wants viewers to sympathize with, if also to be appalled at, the dramatic quest and ethical dilemmas of John "Scottie" Ferguson (James Stewart). Only recently has Alfred Hitchcock begun to receive due recognition as a *noir* director; Foster Hirsch issues the revisionist judgment that "no director is more deeply *noir*" than Hitchcock.[50] We have already seen hints of the tragic temperament in *Double Indemnity* and *The File on Thelma Jordon*. By comparison with *Vertigo*, these films seem almost hopeful. Both Walter Neff and Thelma Jordon experience some measure of reconciliation. Significantly, they are still speaking as they die, still striving to communicate with someone they admire and love. By contrast, the main character in *Vertigo* is reduced to a motionless, psychologically crippling silence. Ferguson is one of many examples of the Oedipus theme in *noir*, perhaps the premier example from the classic period. Oedipus's unrestrained desire to know and his will to overcome all obstacles athwart his path lead to the discovery of a forbidden knowledge, a self-knowledge that marks at once the fulfillment of the quest and self-inflicted destruction.

The opening images of *Vertigo* stress the theme of seeing and knowing. It begins with tight shots of a pair of eyes glancing nervously back and forth, circular images of a spinning vortex, then a tight shot of a single unmoving eye. The opening gives way to a conventional cops and robbers chase scene across the rooftops of San Francisco buildings, a scene that ends in a very unconventional way. John Ferguson, a detective pursuing a fleeing suspect, slips as he makes the leap from one building to another; clinging desperately to a loose gutter, he glances down to the street many floors below and experiences vertigo. When one of the regular cops assisting him in the pursuit returns to help him, the cop himself slides off the roof to his death. The opening drama anticipates the plot of the entire film, with Ferguson playing the role of the desperate detective, failing at his task because of an enfeebling affliction and wreaking unintentional destruction on others.

Retired from the force, Ferguson, now in recuperation, spends time with his former girl friend, Midge. His physical recuperation reflects the deeper need for psychological recovery. He feels weak, ashamed, and guilty. As if to underscore his lack of control, Midge tells him the cop's death was not his fault, just before he proclaims he can "lick" his vertigo and faints trying. In a film that makes repeated reference to a masculine world of "freedom and power," a world now fading from San Francisco, Scottie is enfeebled and emasculated; he even wears a "corset."

In an effort to find something to do with himself, Scottie takes an assignment as a private detective on a very odd case. Gavin Elster, an old acquaintance, hires him to investigate his wife. Gavin asks Scottie: "Do you believe that someone out of the past, someone from the dead, can take possession of a living being?" He explains that his wife, Madeline (Kim Novak), regularly drifts into a kind of reverie and suddenly becomes "someone else, someone I don't know." She wanders the city preoccupied with a long dead woman named Carlotta Valdes. Elster himself admits to nostalgia for old San Francisco, to a time when men experienced "power and freedom," words that echo through the film.

San Francisco is in many ways the definitive *noir* city, the city that gives birth to *noir* in the fiction of Hammett and which provides the setting for both *The Maltese Falcon* and *Vertigo*. But, unlike any other *noir* film set in San Francisco, *Vertigo* presents the city in an unusually rich way. The difference in the presentation of the city, its history, its stylistic fusion of Spanish and European architecture, its mission churches, its lush foliage, and its location amidst ocean and bay, could not be more striking. None of this is on display in *The Maltese Falcon*; by contrast, *Vertigo* treats the city almost as if it were the main character in the film. Intertwining the geography and architecture of the city into the very fabric of the drama allows Hitchcock to offer a more lavish visual embodiment of the drama of the main characters than anything found in other *noir* films.

Indeed, the theme of the city as labyrinth, redolent of the quest motifs from classical myth, takes on enormous significance in *Vertigo*. Scottie's quest takes him into the heart of San Francisco and its architectural history. Superficially skeptical of Elster's story but secretly intrigued and needing the work, Scottie follows Madeline, to the old Mission church, where she visits the grave of Carlotta Valdes; then, to the Museum at the Palace of the Legion of Honor, where she sits transfixed before the portrait of Carlotta; and, finally, to a hotel formerly occupied by Carlotta. Scottie enlists one of Midge's academic friends to fill in the details on the history and legend surrounding Carlotta, a woman whom a wealthy man took in and cared for, and then abandoned after she gave birth to their child. "Men," Midge's friend comments, "could do that in those days because they had freedom and power."

Reporting back to Elster about what he's learned, Scottie adds sympathetically, "anyone could become obsessed with a history like that." Elster then informs Scottie that his wife's grandmother went insane and took her own life: "Her blood is in Madeline." With the introduction of these themes, Hitchcock takes a standard *noir* motif of the way the past bears down on the present, deepens it, and, as we shall see, develops it in novel ways. An obsession with the past, an inordinate desire to keep alive what is dead, can so mesmerize an individual that he or she has no present; in fact, Elster's comments present the past as an active and hostile agent, invading, possessing, and living parasitically off the present. The alluring but futile quest into the past calls to mind lines from T. S. Eliot's *Gerontion*:

> After such knowledge, what forgiveness? Think now
> History has many cunning passages, contrived corridors
> And issues, deceives with whispering ambitions,
> Guides us by vanities. Think now
> She gives when our attention is distracted
> And what she gives, gives with such supple confusions
> That the giving famishes the craving. Gives too late
> What's not believed in, or if still believed,
> In memory only, reconsidered passion. Gives too soon
> Into weak hands, what's thought can be dispensed with
> Till the refusal propagates a fear. Think
> Neither fear nor courage saves us.

With its elegant, old world architecture and its mission churches that predate the arrival of Enlightenment philosophy and the American founding, San Francisco, the locale for many *noirs*, is the ideal setting for this film. Scottie follows Madeline to San Francisco Bay, to the base of the Golden Gate Bridge; apparently in a sort of trance, she falls in and Scottie rescues her. He pulls her out, holds her close and anxiously and lovingly calls her name. The next scene indicates that a strange and premature intimacy has developed between the two of them. Madeline awakes in his bed, apparently naked and oblivious to what has transpired. When Scottie tells her about her fall into the bay, she says that she must have had a "dizzy spell and fainted." He meets her the next day and persuades her to join him on a trip outside the city. They drive to the sequoia forest to see the giant redwood trees, whose Latin root, Scottie explains, means "always green, ever living." The giant trees dwarf them. The span of their lives, as Madeline points out by gesturing to a cut section with concentric circles marking the age of the tree, is as nothing in comparison with the life of the tree. "Here I was born and there I died . . . only a moment for you—you took no notice." The scene is chilling in its expression of the brevity and insignificance of human life; in comparison to nature, each individual human life is as naught.

Aroused by her plight, Scottie desperately wants to take "notice." As they embrace by the crashing waves of the sea, she reveals images from a dream: a grave, a tower, and a bell. An excited Scottie figures out that she is talking, not about a building existing at another time and place, but about one of the California mission churches, San Juan Battista, south of San Francisco, "preserved exactly as it was 100 years ago, as a museum." He is nearly jubilant: "Don't you see? Now you've given me something to work on. We'll go there. You'll see it and remember and it will finish your dream, destroy your dream." Here Scottie expresses a naïve faith in psychoanalytic repetition, which promises liberation from past trauma through conscious confrontation with it. This is the optimistic Enlightenment side of Freud, who also sees in the re-experiencing of trauma the possibility of an exacerbation of trauma, the result of which could be the dissolution of the self. When they reach the mission, Madeline is more troubled than ever. They exchange vows of love, but Madeline adds mysteriously: "It's too late. There's something I must do." Scottie responds: "It's not too late. No one possesses you. You're safe with me." Madeline insists: "It's too late. It wasn't supposed to happen this way," to which Scottie responds, "it had to happen" because "we're in love." She then runs to the tower of the church; as Scottie pursues her, he experiences vertigo and, before he can make it to the top, watches in horror as she plunges to her death.

At the inquest, Madeline's death is declared a suicide, but not until after the chief examiner excoriates Ferguson for doing "nothing." Since the law has little to say about "things left undone," he leaves the matter to Ferguson and his conscience. Plagued by guilt and by the memory of Madeline, he visits her grave before lapsing into a catatonic state and being institutionalized. Finally well enough to rejoin society, Ferguson remains haunted by images of Madeline. He returns to the restaurant where he first saw her and mistakes a woman for her. Then as he stands on a street in the city, he sees a woman who resembles Madeline and follows her home, asks to speak with her, and badgers her with questions about her past. At first unnerved but then pitying, the woman, named Judy, states, "You really have got it bad, haven't you? Do I really look like her? She's dead, isn't she?"

After agreeing to meet him later for dinner, she pulls out her suitcase to pack and sits down to compose a letter to Ferguson, in which she confesses the entire plan. She was an instrument and the the victim of Elster's plan to murder his wife, for it was the wife who was tossed from the tower. Scottie was chosen to provide reliable corroborating evidence of her madness and suicidal tendencies and because his vertigo would preclude his making it to the top of the tower to discover the truth. She adds that she made a mistake, which was to fall in love with him: "I'll go now and you can give up your search." But just as she is about to finish the letter, she states: "If I had the nerve, I'd stay and lie." She pauses, tears up the note, and does just that. In its original release, critics objected to this sequence in the film, arguing that it reveals everything and renders the remainder of the film anticlimactic. But it serves at least two purposes: it makes her a more sympathetic character and it heightens audience expectation concerning whether and how Scottie will figure things out and how he will react. The confession reveals Madeline's Carlotta to be a "false enigma," replaced by a very real enigma of Judy, the woman who played Madeline.

Scottie remains preoccupied with Madeline. Before he discovers the truth, he engages in a sustained project of remaking Judy, an attempt at "possession" of her body, a project that Hitchcock bluntly described as necrophilia. Succumbing to his maniacal need to transform her into Madeline, she dresses like Madeline and has her hair done like Madeline. Just as the physical transformation into Madeline seems complete, she emerges from the bedroom shrouded in an almost supernatural light that gives her a ghostly appearance. As she stands in front of the mirror and asks Scottie to help her with a necklace, Scottie looks up and sees the necklace reflected in the mirror, the same necklace Madeline wore, an image of the one Carlotta wears in her portrait at the museum. He now knows the truth and his mood changes abruptly. He becomes physically forceful and demands that she accompany him, "for the last time," to the mission church. "I need you to be Madeline one more time and, when it's done, we'll both be free." When they arrive at the church, he forces her toward and up the tower, telling her that she is his "second chance." Informing her that the necklace gave her away, he pieces together the entire plot. "You were a counterfeit. He [Elster] made you over just like I did." Awareness that he is zeroing in on the truth increases his strength and apparently heals his vertigo. Before he realizes it, he's at the top of the tower, looks around and states confidently, "I made it."

Here Scottie engages in a doomed repetition of a repetition with predictably cataclysmic results. His attempt to wield freedom and power, to control the past in the present, to overcome seemingly irrational fears through knowledge and will, induces a psychic paralysis from which he is unlikely ever to recover. In its final scenes, *Vertigo* portrays an extreme version of what Sara Melzer calls the Pascalian "aporia of desire," based on the fact that the "true object of desire is always elsewhere." As Melzer explains, "the individual is torn apart by competing desires, none of which can ever be satisfied, all human existence is condemned to the misery of unfulfilled desire and of a perpetually deferred insight into reality."[51] Scottie's pivotal moment of insight concerns the recognition of the necklace, an apprehension of an image of an image of an image.

Fearfully, Judy says, "I loved you. I let you change me and keep me safe." Scottie responds angrily, "It's too late. There's no bringing her back." But she embraces and kisses him. Then a dark figure emerges from the shadowy stairway of the tower and Judy screams in horror and falls to her death. The figure is a nun who heard voices. "God have mercy," she says as she begins to ring the tower bells. Scottie is left standing, arms helplessly outstretched, staring vacantly at Judy's dead body below. The mysterious churches of Dolorosa and San Jaun Bautista, redolent of tradition and the rituals of judgment and atonement, are the occasion not so much of hopeful liberation but of entrapment in stultifying fear. The bells toll out death in life, damnation on the very grounds that should suggest salvation. The nun, a ghostlike appearance from the shadows, suggests a final, authoritative judgment rather than any prospect of mercy.

The ending is a severe tragedy indeed. In the moment of realization, fulfillment and cancellation are bound ineluctably together. Judy is in fact the woman, Madeline, he wanted to resurrect; yet, Madeline herself was not who she claimed to be. The original is a false copy. The ending appears to affirm nihilism by what it negates: love, communication, fulfillment of intelligibility and desire. Unlike other *noir* characters who, in spite of their blatant failures, continue to talk, to try to understand their own story and to communicate with others, Scottie is reduced to paralyzed silence. Yet, the longing for wholeness, for communication, for love remains present in its absence. Indeed, these longings perdure in the midst of Scottie's most twisted desires, his own peculiar form of necrophilia. Were the ending thoroughly nihilistic, we would not appropriately feel sorrow, pity, or horror at Scottie's destiny. Indifference or cynical, detached mockery would be more appropriate. If Scottie's trauma has once again removed him from the human community, the community of viewers still shares an appreciation of, and commiserates over, his destruction.

In his overwhelming desire to know, control, and gain freedom through an act of repetition, Scottie mimics the most tragic of Greek characters. Unlike *Oedipus*, *Vertigo* offers no sequel, no subsequent act whereby the main character might achieve a kind of vindication. Modern rationalism appears incapable of being brought into harmony with tragic wisdom. It leads inevitably and violently to unspeakable self-destruction. The early part of the film leads Scottie from his illusions of independence and his modern faith in rational self-control into an antique world of myth and superstition. In the film's most dramatically gripping paradox, Scottie's project of controlling and manipulating another woman, his attempt to reclaim the old male world of freedom and power, is itself an irrational obsession. Instead of exhibiting his independence, it reveals his pathetic dependence. Then, in a devastating repetition, just when Scottie through an act of will conquers his fear of heights, by traversing a spiral staircase, he confronts a paralyzing horror.

Now celebrated as a superbly crafted *noir*, *Vertigo* helped to solidify Hitchcock's reputation among critics. Still, among the harshest judges of Hitchcock's work is Graham Greene, who never reversed his early disdain for Hitchcock's *Secret Agent*. Hitchcock, Greene wrote, is a "specialist in sensation," treats his scripts "carelessly," and has a penchant for the "ingenious melodramatic situation."[52] He accused Hitchcock of being "tricky" and lacking imagination. Does Greene protest too much?

Greene's dismissal of Hitchcock may have less to do with their having diametrically opposed visions than with Greene's acute sense of how close they actually were. The director Neil Jordan describes Greene and Hitchcock as "two poets of English criminality and bad conscience."[53] Hitchcock may have had a better sense of the affinities, or at least less fear of collaboration, since he approached Greene about writing the script for *I Confess* and later tried to acquire the rights to Greene's novel *Our Man in Havana*. Greene refused on both occasions. In remaking for film Greene's *The End of the Affair* in 1999, Jordan was struck by the similarities between Greene's novel and Hitchcock's *Ver-*

tigo. In both stories, a husband approaches a friend about the strange behavior of his wife and asks for help in ascertaining the truth about her condition. In both cases, the friend becomes obsessed with the wife, so much so that it is difficult to distinguish love from hatred; try as he might to free himself from the past, he cannot do so. In both stories, one of the lovers seems to die but then reappears.

The most notable difference between *Vertigo* and *End of the Affair* is that God, or at least the possibility of God, plays a more explicit and more sustained role in Greene's story. As Francois Truffaut and others have noted, religious elements are not entirely absent from *Vertigo*, in the locations of crucial scenes and in the film's climax in the tower at the old church. Mercy in *Vertigo* appears in the form of harsh justice, as it often does in Greene. As we have already noticed, Greene goes about as far as any popular twentieth-century author toward making God an actual character in his stories. Replacing the *femme fatale*, God in *The End of the Affair* is the jealous and deadly lover who tempts, possesses, and will not let go of individual human beings. As the private investigator in the first film version of Greene's book puts it, "jealousy is the mark of true love," which is itself "man's noblest frailty."

The dramatic core of the story is contained in a scene that follows a bombing raid on London during the Blitz. Immediately after Sarah Miles and Maurice Bendrix have completed their afternoon of adulterous lovemaking, the bombs strike his residence. Sarah recovers quickly and discovers an apparently dead Bendrix buried underneath rubble. She returns to the bedroom, kneels and prays that he will be brought back to life; for that result, she promises never to be with him again. Suddenly, he is there, behind her, calling her name. With a look of alarm on her face, she utters, "You! Oh, God! Maurice you're alive." Increasing the mystery over whether he was in fact dead, he talks about what a strange sense of space and time he just experienced. She leaves abruptly and avoids his every attempt to contact her. His love turns to anger, resentment, and hatred, predicated on the assumption that she never really loved him. Her surprise at finding him alive, he conjectures, was because she had wanted him dead. That would have provided the easiest avenue of exit from the affair.

Only later, after her husband Henry (Peter Cushing) unwittingly asks for Bendrix's advice about whether Sarah could be having an affair, does Bendrix discover the truth of the matter. Against Henry's wishes, Bendrix hires a private investigator, who manages to gain hold of Sarah's diary in which she explains her prayer, her promise to God, and her struggle to remain distant from Bendrix, the only man she has ever truly loved. There are a series of mistaken identities here, akin to the wrong-man scenarios of classic *noir*. Henry mistakenly assumes that Bendrix is not Sarah's lover and that he is loyal enough to help investigate his wife in a dispassionate way. When the private investigator discovers a portion of one of Sarah's love letters, addressed to an unknown man, Bendrix angrily presents the evidence to Henry and suggests that he confront her: "Let Sarah clear herself, if she can." The lover is of course Bendrix. Perplexed at her clandestine wanderings around the city, Bendrix continues to think that another man has stolen her affections. But her secret love is not another man: it is God. From the diary, Bendrix learns of her conversations with a priest, to whom she complains that she made a God "out of her own imagination." "If there is a God," she nearly curses with anger, "then I hate him for it."

Once he learns the truth, Bendrix confronts Sarah and tries to use her own doubts and anger against her. Urging her to abandon her superstition, he decries God's "cruel and possessive love," which has given her only "suffering, loneliness, and despair." Now quite ill, she is resigned to continuing on the path of belief. She admits that she has "fought belief" longer than she has "fought love." After she dies, Bendrix discovers a letter from her dated just before her death, in which she announces that she cannot see him again but that she can love him without seeing him, a strange type of love to which she had alluded earlier in the story. There is of course an obvious parallel here between love of another, absent human being and love of God. As if to undercut our assumption that she has utterly left behind the sort of bodily love to which she was so devoted earlier, she urges, "You must pray the way you make love, with everything you've got."

Remaking the film in 1999, Jordan described it as a ghost story in which someone assumed dead returns to life and where the past haunts the main characters. This is an important clue about the latent resemblances Jordan detects between *Vertigo* and *End of the Affair*. Partly because he was working with better actors and a tighter script than in the first film version, Jordan executes the pivotal scene of the bombing more effectively than in the original. Pondering her promise to a God in whom she did not yet believe, she describes God's "knowledge" of her predicament as "cruel": "It knew what I would say before I said it." The impersonal pronoun "It" is striking. Yet she cannot sustain that sense of a distant, impersonal God. Later, she remarks that God "knows" her like Bendrix's "hands know" her "body." Following Greene, the filmmaker plays off the multiple connotations of the word "knowledge," at least one, scriptural meaning of which is explicitly sexual. The analogies between human and divine love, and the multiple ways in which they can compete with one another, suggest strongly that God is in fact an agent in the drama, a real character in the film. In this way, Greene provides an interesting response to Sanders's thesis that *noir* repudiates all "otherworldly" answers. *The End of the Affair* dares us to pose the questions, "what if someone from the other world were to become actively involved in this one? What would you do then?" In this case, the hypothetical character is not merely a ghost, but a living and very jealous God.

In the remake, there is a stirring ending with Bendrix at his typewriter directly addressing a God in whose existence he claims still not to believe. "I hate you as though you existed . . . I have only one prayer left. Forget about me. Leave me alone forever." Bendrix's destiny is uncertain; the final scene forces upon us certain tantalizing questions.

Does this constitute liberation? Or some form of knowing self-damnation? Or does it simply mimic the early, angry stages of Sarah's path to faith, her insistence that you cannot hate what does not exist?

The dramatic similarities between Hitchcock and Greene are multiple. In fact, some of Hitchcock's films embody precisely the sort of ambiguous religious sensibility found in Greene's novels. In the key scene in Hitchcock's *The Wrong Man*, for example, the wrongly accused Manny Balestrero (Henry Fonda) prays for God's help; as he kneels in prayer, Hitchcock superimposes the image of the real criminal on Manny's face, just as the criminal is about to commit a crime that will vindicate Manny. Of that scene, Truffaut commented, "It seems unlikely to me that anyone but a Catholic would have handled Henry Fonda's prayer scene as you did."[54] The film features an ordinary working man, a musician in New York City with a wife and two young children. During a discussion with his wife about how they will afford her dental work, she laments, "every time we're up, we get knocked back down." Her husband responds, "We're pretty lucky people." The next day, when he visits his bank to request a loan, Manny's luck takes a horrifying turn. A bank clerk identifies him as the man who recently robbed the bank. When the police find him, they lead Manny from one store to another, where workers repeatedly identify him as a thief. His handwriting is similar to that of the thief and none of his alibis work out. Trapped in a maze of incriminating circumstances beyond his control, he tells his lawyer, "The cards are stacked against us." His wife, Rose (Vera Miles), becomes increasingly despondent, reclusive, and afflicted with irrational guilt. She tells a psychiatrist that her own guilt, not that of her husband, is at the root of their bad luck: "They wanted to get me. It's useless trying."

After his first trial is declared a mistrial, he is at home with his mother who begs him to pray. He reacts with indifference; then, as he dresses in the bedroom he gazes up at a framed picture of Jesus and begins to pray. As he does, another image appears superimposed on Manny's, the image of the real criminal, whose face slowly blends with and then replaces Manny's. This is precisely the point at which the criminal attempts to rob another store but is caught and arrested. Spoto astutely observes that, when he is arrested, the new suspect re-iterates Manny's initial statement to police: "I haven't done anything. I have a wife and kids waiting for me at home." Spoto argues that the statement indicates a possible repetition of the injustice inflicted upon Manny and thus fosters complete skepticism about the public system of justice. But Spoto is making too much of this, since we have direct evidence that the man arrested at the end has committed at least one crime. Manny is thus cleared of all charges, but his redemption is not without continued cost. His wife remains diffident and with-drawn, although the final frames of the film offer an explanation that she emerged from the sanitarium two years later and returned to her family. Interestingly, this was an addition to which Hitchcock himself vigorously objected, in part because it was not factually correct in the actual events upon which the film was based. In those events, the wife remained in a psychotic state. Whatever redemption there is does not come in the form of cheap grace or a happy ending that heals all scars or eliminates haunting memories.[55] It comes, if at all, mysteriously in and through the *noir* labyrinth.

A similar, if less ambiguous, pattern, of redemptive suffering can be seen in the most artful religious film in the *noir* canon, Hitchcock's *I Confess*, another "wrong man" film, this one about a priest accused of a murder, the true perpetrator of which he can identify only by breaking the sacred seal of the confessional. Hitchcock thought the film's relative unpopularity was due to "the many critics who appar-ently felt that for a priest to guard a secret at the risk of his own life was absurd."[56] There is an instructive irony here, since the reception of the film mirrors the predicament of the main character whose se-cretiveness is inexplicable to those around him.

The film begins with a series of quick shots of towering church spires, from odd camera angles, and of a traffic sign, an arrow with the word "Direction" on it. The camera finally settles upon that sign and follows its lead through an open window to the scene of a dead body. Next we see a man in a priest's cassock walking the streets at night and then taking off the cassock. The subsequent scene is inside a Catholic Church where a distraught worker, Keller, at the church asks Fr. Logan (Montgomery Clift) to hear his confession. As the two take their positions in the confessional, the slats of the confessional window create the standard *noir* effect of alternating lines of darkness and light. The man confesses, "I have killed Mr. Villette." From subsequent conversations with his wife and with Fr. Logan, we know the man is counting on Fr. Logan's unwillingness to break the seal of the confessional. When Logan urges him to turn himself in, the man taunts the priest, "It's easy for you to be good. Have you no pity for me?"

Fr. Logan's burdens increase the next day when he, knowing that Villette has been murdered, nonetheless shows up at Villette's home for a previously scheduled meeting. He encounters a police detective, Larrue (Karl Malden), already at work on the murder, explains that he had a meeting, and then leaves. Retreating to the streets where a crowd has gathered, Logan meets an attractive woman and informs her of Villette's death. She comments, "Then, we're free." The detective notices this conversation and, when two girls say they saw a priest in a cassock leaving Villete's home at about the time of the murder, becomes suspicious of Logan. What is interesting about the sequence of events here is that, while viewers are aware that Logan did not commit the murder, they remain suspicious of Logan's involvement with the woman. We wonder whether, given her comment, he did not have reason to want Villette dead. This is often the case in *noir* "wrong man" stories, where the accused is innocent but still feels the pangs of guilt because he had reason to want the victim dead.[57]

Hitchcock briefly increases our suspicion of Logan before clearing him of any serious charges, even if viewers may harbor doubts about the purity of his motives. When Ruth (Anne Baxter), the woman with whom he had spoken, returns home to her husband, the husband questions her accusingly and wonders in despair, "What's a husband to do when his wife is in love with a priest?" However, at Ruth's subsequent meeting with Logan, it becomes clear that while the woman has remained in love with him since the time they dated before he became a priest, Logan is no longer in love with her: "I chose to be what I am. I believe in what I am." The two had been in love prior to his going off to war; during his long absence, she had given up on him and married another man. Upon his return from war, she allows passion to get the better of her, meets him and neglects to tell him that she is now married. They spend the day together and end up caught overnight in a country house during a storm. The next morning, the owner, Mr. Villette, discovers them. A few years later, after Logan is ordained, Villette recalls the episode on his property and begins blackmailing them, threatening to ruin their reputations.

Desiring to clear Logan of suspicion in the murder, Ruth confesses all to her husband, including her continued passion for Logan. She then goes to the police to provide an alibi for Fr. Logan. Prodded by the detective to reveal all the intimate details of her futile love for Fr. Logan, she confesses everything. Only after she leaves does the detective reveal that her alibi is useless. Villette was murdered after the period during which she can account for Logan's whereabouts. When she learns this, she weeps, "So there was no need for my statement?" Her husband corrects her: "You supplied the motive." Adding to her previous exploitation of Logan's good will, Ruth has now aided those intent on prosecuting him for murder.

As the police begin to search for their suspect, Logan walks the streets, something he is often seen doing in the film. Truffaut complimented Hitchcock on the decision to show Logan always walking, a "forward motion that shapes the whole film" and "concretizes the concept of his integrity."[58] His constant motion is also a way of illustrating his loss of direction, the sense that, walk as much as he might like, there is no way out for him. In the most remarkable scene in the film, loss of external direction fuses with internal integrity to create an image of redemptive suffering. In a telling shot, Logan is filmed from above and afar as he walks on a sidewalk. The camera is situated in the front of a church and as Logan passes, the camera catches—and thus superimposes upon Logan—a statue of Christ, carrying his cross and surrounded by Roman soldiers. The *noir* image of the maze is here given new intelligibility as it is inscribed within the redemptive story of Christ's passion. Hitchcock here offers a novel twist on the wrong man as right man theme. In this case, Logan is the right man, not because he harbors guilty motives corresponding to those of the actual criminal, but because he has been mysteriously selected to endure an unjust accusation.

Logan's cross becomes more burdensome after he is taken into custody and put on trial. Ruth's testimony about her relationship with Fr. Logan prompts the suggestion from the prosecutor that she and Logan have been engaged in "a continuous, uninterrupted illicit" relationship. On the stand himself, Logan is asked about the bloody cassock found in his trunk. When he responds that he "can't say" how it got there, the prosecutor speculates whether there is not some "contradiction between his secretiveness and his vocation." Again, the irony is that absolute secretiveness of a certain sort is of the very essence of his vocation.

Although the jury finds him not guilty, the judge goes out of his way to express his disagreement with the verdict. Truffaut notes the similarity to *Vertigo*'s court hearing, the result of which is to clear the defendant of the charges. In both cases, however, the defendant "remains under a cloud because someone in the court may disapprove of the verdict."[59] This is a standard *noir* theme of the justice system as failing to bring about justice even when its verdict is technically correct. As Logan leaves the court, angry citizens surround and taunt him, "take off your collar . . . preach us a sermon." Ignorant of what they are doing, the citizens replay the crowd's bloodthirsty mockery of Christ on Good Friday. Unable to bear the burden of her secret any longer, Keller's wife mutters, "He's innocent." Keller shoots her, and Logan hears her confession as she dies. Now pursued by the police,

Keller flees to a nearby building, where the detective and Fr. Logan follow him. Armed in an adjacent room, he learns that Logan is with the detective and concludes cynically, "So the priest talked. Fr. Logan, my only friend. How kindly he hears my confession. It was too much for you. You're a coward like the rest."

Risking his life yet again for the murderer, Logan walks toward an armed and hostile man. Unwilling to allow Fr. Logan to be killed, the police shoot the suspect just as he aims his gun. As he lays dying, he begs for a priest and Logan gives him last rites. This nifty *noir* thus works its way toward a resolution that is, if not happy, at least clearly just. What is more, unlike many resolutions in *noir*, in Hitchcock's *I Confess*, as in *The Wrong Man*, the public system of justice, while initially at fault, manages to vindicate the innocent, if only belatedly. Although Fr. Logan will likely be plagued by gossip, we can also imagine his holiness being celebrated in ways it never would have been had he not been publicly accused. For Spoto, the consequence of each character being forced into a public confession is that "everyone has been divested of his role or part, and no one can ever be the same again."[60] Certainly the latter claim is true and not incompatible with some degree of public restoration of justice. Indeed, divesting us of our previous self-understanding and our pre-determined public roles is, in certain cases, of the very essence of the sacrament of confession. Moreover, as Spoto also argues, Fr. Logan has undergone a severe purification. Yet, Spoto fails to notice that it is precisely through this very public humiliation that Logan deepens his identification with his true role, his calling, to hear the confession of sinners and act as a vehicle of their absolution. Thus does he act in imitation of Christ who takes the sins of others upon himself.

This is not to say that the path is easy or without lingering regrets but Hitchcock goes a bit further than Greene in the direction of the public restoration of justice. Indeed, in both cases it seems right to say that what tips the balance back toward the community and public acknowledgment of the right order of things is the residual Catholi-

cism in the imaginative worlds of each artist. This has been noted
many times with respect to Greene, for whom the Catholic sacramental
system provides the framework for *The Power and the Glory* and *The
End of the Affair*. As Truffaut has frequently observed and as is palpable
in *I Confess*, the same is true of Hitchcock.

What these artists reveal is a deep compatibility between certain
features of *noir* and a certain type of narrative of redemption.[61] The
implications of this overlooked convergence are perhaps less significant
for *noir* than they are for modern Christianity, which has too often
wanted to ignore the fact that in this life we remain no more than
wayfarers, for whom salvation itself is always tentative. The penitential path to redemption, operative at the margins of film *noir*, never
fully overcomes the isolation of the tragic protagonist. As St. Cyril of
Jerusalem put it many centuries ago, in a passage Flannery O'Connor
fully embraced, "The dragon sits by the side of the road, watching those
who pass. Beware lest he devour you. We go to the Father of Souls, but
it is necessary to pass by the dragon." One of the penances inflicted
on modern souls, at least in the world of religious *noir*, is that it has
become increasingly difficult to identify not just the Father of Souls,
but even the dragon.

PART II

THE RECOVERY OF THE QUEST

— 3 —

Beyond Good and Evil

THE STRAIN OF NOIR FILM on which I focused in the last chapter features dark quests for redemption, whether formulated in religious terms or not. Even where restoration occurs, as in *The File on Thelma Jordon* and *I Confess*, it is incomplete. Most often longing remains unsatisfied and any path toward redemption is tentative and penitential. As some critics have recently noted, religious quest is a neglected sub-genre in the literature on *noir*; conversely, dark tales of religious quest are themselves neglected in treatments of religion in popular culture. As Flannery O'Connor indicates, such dark tales can take on a theological significance: how might contemporary art recover a language of faith in a world where religious vocabulary has become distorted and dislocated from narratives in which it is intelligible?

If classic *noir* resists the attempts of film critics to define it or even to list its fixed elements, neo-*noir* is even more fluid a label. While classic *noir*'s democratic instincts are exhibited in its depiction of a universal human condition of vulnerability from which none can fully escape, neo-*noir* sometimes celebrates characters who transcend the *noir* trap. Such characters may be well-intentioned, even savior figures as in *Dark City*'s hero, or they may be amoral, quasi-Nietzschean superheroes, as in *Basic Instinct* and *The Usual Suspects*. Nihilism, always a threat in classic *noir*—and perhaps more than just a threat in films such as *Vertigo*—becomes almost pervasive in neo-*noir*.

But nihilism is neither the first nor the last word on neo-*noir*. Early neo-*noir* films such as *Chinatown* and *Taxi Driver* do more than flirt with nihilism. But they also, even if paradoxically, suggest that we may still have access to a fleeting sense of justice and order. Moreover, in such crossover genres as the neo-*noir* science fiction film, nihilism is often engaged in such a way as to leave us with tantalizing questions rather than resolutions in one direction or another. Some of these films, for example, *Dark City* and *The Matrix*, go so far as to give us moral superheroes. Yet for all their commitment to noble causes, these heroes sometimes converge with amoral superheroes in one specific respect. Both groups affirm a liberating knowledge or power available only to the few. There is more than hint here of a modern form of Gnosticism that seeks a liberation from the constraints of the finite, vulnerable human body. As Cynthia Freeland astutely observes concerning *The Matrix*, by suggesting "that humans need not be bound by their physical bodies . . . the movie feeds escapist fantasies of a mental reality where the elect few are unencumbered by rules."[1] A return to the limits of the human body and to an anti-reductionist understanding of human desire can be found in the stunning feminist neo-*noir* television series, *Buffy the Vampire Slayer*, a show that recovers and advances classic *noir*'s sense of human life as a quest for redemption. To various strains of neo-*noir* film we now turn.

According to its most trenchant analysts, nihilism involves the dissolution of standards of judgment; there is no longer any basis for distinguishing truth from falsity, good from evil, noble from base action, or higher from lower ways of life. Of the many fertile investigations of nihilism, including those of Dostoevsky, Tocqueville, and Arendt, Nietzsche's remains the most influential. Nietzsche thought nihilism would be the defining characteristic of the twentieth century, an epoch in which "the highest values" would "devalue themselves" and the "question 'why?'" would find "no answer."[2] Nietzsche is most famous for proclaiming the death of God. He certainly does not mean that a previously existing supreme being has suddenly expired; instead, he holds that the notion of God, created by humans to serve a variety of needs, is becoming increasingly less credible. But Nietzsche does not limit the effects of nihilism to religion; it undermines all transcendent claims or standards, including those underlying modern science and democratic politics. The great questions and animating visions—for truth, justice, love, and beauty—that previously gave shape and purpose to human life no longer resonate in the human soul. All moral codes are seen to be merely conventional and hence optional.

For most human beings, decline, diminution, and despair accompany nihilism. The bulk of humanity falls into the category of the last man: "Alas, the time of the most despicable man is coming, he that is no longer able to despise himself. Behold, I show you the last man. What is love? What is a star? Thus asks the last man and blinks. The earth has become small and on it hops the last man who makes everything small." The contented, petty last men create a society that is ruthlessly homogeneous—"everybody wants the same, everybody is the same"—and addicted to physical comfort—"one has one's little pleasure for the day and one's little pleasure for the night; one has a regard for health."[3] These are the passive nihilists, the pessimists, the representatives of "the decline and recession of the power of the spirit."[4]

But nihilism is "ambiguous." If, in one sense, nihilism is the "unwelcome guest," it is also an opportunity, clearing a path for "increased power of the spirit."[5] Active nihilists see the decline of traditional moral and religious systems as an occasion for the thoroughgoing destruction of desiccated ways of life and for the creation of a new order of values. Active nihilists, the philosopher-artists of the future, will engage in the "trans-valuation of values." They stand beyond good and evil and engage in aesthetic self-creation, a project that is an affront to society's religious and democratic conventions, rooted, as they are, in moral absolutes or democratic consensus.

Nietzsche's remedy for the nihilistic epoch, his path beyond nihilism, promotes a particularly virulent form of aristocracy. As he puts it frankly in the chapter "What is Noble?" from *Beyond Good and Evil*:

> Every enhancement of the type "man" has so far been the work of an aristocratic society—and so it will be again and again—a society that believes in the long ladder of an order of rank and differences in value between man and man, and that needs slavery in some sense or another. Without that pathos of distance that grows out of the ingrained difference between strata . . . keeping down and keeping at a distance, that other, more mysterious pathos could not have grown up either—the craving for an ever new widening of distances within the soul itself, the development of ever higher, rare, more remote, further-stretching, more comprehensive states . . . the continual "self-overcoming of man."[6]

Now, it seems clear that Nietzsche would not have welcomed various decadent usages to which his thought has been put, in the service either of anti-Semitism or of various popular anti-heroes.[7] But the problem with rank in the nihilistic era, as with the critique of *ressentiment* as a source of evil, is that nihilism deprives us of a basis for any sort of discrimination whatsoever. Bereft of context, the "pathos of distance" can easily become purely negative; it repudiates and aims to destroy conventional codes. Such a "pathos" is at work in a variety of neo-*noir* dramas, from *Cape Fear* and *Basic Instinct* to *The Usual Suspects*.

For Nietzsche, films that wallow in rather than overcome nihilism, would be decadent. Throughout his career but especially early on, Nietzsche saw art as the key to the overcoming of nihilism. In his first work, the *Birth of Tragedy*, Nietzsche depicts the history of the West as a struggle between two gods, two models of art, and two experiences of the relationship of the individual to the whole of society and nature. The hidden source of Greek society and hence of the West is

Dionysius, the primordial will, the surging force of chaos at the root of all human activity and thought. Dionysius, who is the primal suffering and source of wisdom and creativity of all things, is the spirit of music and is prior to language. Since it eliminates the possibility of individuation, it is void of conscious awareness and hence cannot know its own wisdom. By contrast, Apollo, as the *principium individuationis*, is responsible for the introduction of distinctions between good and evil and among objects. It is embodied in the plastic arts. It thus makes rational comprehension and articulation possible.

Given its dependence on Dionysius, the triumph of Apollo is always tenuous and unstable. If Apollo seeks to dominate Dionysius, it becomes effete, rationalistic, and static. The "entire existence" of Apollo depends "on a hidden substratum of suffering and knowledge revealed to him by Dionysius."[8] Nietzsche writes, "And now let us imagine how into this world, built on mere appearance and moderation and artificially damned up, there penetrated, in tones ever more bewitching and alluring, the ecstatic sound of the Dionysian festival; how in these strains all of nature's excess in pleasure, grief, and knowledge became audible, even in piercing shrieks; and let us ask ourselves what the psalmodizing artist of Apollo, with his phantom harp-sound, could mean in the face of this demonic folk-song."[9]

For a brief but remarkably fertile period, the period of Greek tragedy, the Dionsyian and the Apollonian existed in a kind of harmony. The Apollonian elements in tragedy, the role of speech and individual characters, make possible our indirect apprehension of the primal will, whose confrontation we cannot endure directly. Apollo, who is the source of the maxims "know thyself" and "nothing in excess," individuates and allows for conscious apprehension and expression.

The history of the west is the story of the increasing dominance of Apollo, the crucial stage of which is the Socratic turning away from poetry and music toward the good, the true, and the beautiful. Socratic rationalism is developed further in Christianity and especially in modern science. Christianity, as Nietzsche once quipped, is "Platonism for the people." It democratizes the Platonic teaching that the "really real" resides in a world separate from this one. The bifurcation of reality and the elevation of what is eternal and absolute effectively evacuate this world of meaning. Aceticism in the pursuit of a pure model of truth informs modern science as well. The following out of the trajectory of rationalism undermines itself: "Science, spurred by its powerful illusion, speeds irresistibly toward its limits where its optimism, concealed in the essence of logic, suffers shipwreck."[10] The "limits of theory" engender a "turn to art"; logic "bites its own tail" and gives rise to a "tragic insight."[11] Socratic culture suffers from "the delusion of limitless power."[12] Another way to express science's undermining of itself is in terms of the search for truth, which Judaism and Christianity introduced into the world and which is carried forward most forcefully by science. That very pursuit leads inevitably to the acknowledgment that all these systems are but lies, concealing the chaotic abyss at the root of all things.

By contrast, tragic culture exalts "wisdom over science," seeks a "comprehensive view," and embraces "with sympathetic feelings of love, the eternal suffering."[13] Tragic art serves life and restores health and wisdom to the human soul. Nietzsche urges that we consider science in light of art and art in light of life.[14] This does not entail the rejection of reason but rather its relocation. It can no longer stand apart from the rest of nature as its judge; instead, it is but a part, subordinate to, and nourished by, an extra-rational order of instinct.

The balance and harmony Nietzsche detects in tragedy is, as he himself admits, a tenuous thing, realized rarely in human history. In his later writings, this gives way to some extent to a discourse of excess and violence. Even in *The Birth of Tragedy*, art makes possible our partial and veiled apprehension of the chaos and violence, the primordial suffering, at the foundation of being. One of the problems with which this position afflicts us is that of having to construct an order even as we are consciously aware that order is no more than a construct, that reason is predicated on unreason, justice on injustice, peace on violence.[15] In that context, where nihilism is the basic truth about existence, it is hard to see why any approach to art or philosophy or politics should be preferred to any other. It is hard to see how we could make any meaningful discrimination between better and worse. That would indeed constitute nihilism, which consists not in the absence of happy endings but rather in rendering pointless, even laughable, all human aspiration. Unhappy films can be anti-nihilist, while superficially happy films can be quite nihilistic. The trivialization of purpose is precisely the state that Nietzsche hoped to overcome, but it remains unclear whether his remedy, that of creative self-fashioning, does not immerse us further in nihilism.

Nietzsche's genealogy of nihilism is not the only possible analysis. Famously, Dostoevsky anticipated the consequences of Nietzsche's madman's proclamation, "God is dead." Dostoevsky held that, in the absence of God, all is permitted. Dostoevsky would not concur, however, that Christianity was itself responsible for nihilism. As we shall see in the chapter on science fiction *noir*, Dostoevsky traces nihilism to its roots in Enlightenment liberalism. There is something of an overlap here with Nietzsche's assertion that autonomy and morality are incompatible with one another. Of greater concern to Dostoevsky, however, is the way quantitative, reductionist science inspires a social science that promises to calibrate and satisfy all human desire in the utopian, socially engineered cities of the modern world. Such a project not only entails a totalitarian management of human desire, but also, in its assumption that material causality sufficiently explains human behavior, renders freedom illusory.[16]

Well before Dostoevsky or Nietzsche, Pascal detected the seeds of nothingness in the nascent sciences of his day. The aspiration for absolute certitude sets out to comprehend and master the infinite. This quixotic project involves a forgetfulness of human limits and a subordination of the ethical task to the goal of ameliorating the human condition through the technological mastery of nature. As Pascal learned from Montaigne, he who tries to make himself an angel

ends as a beast. The failure to fulfill the promise of rationalism gives
rise to intractable forms of skepticism and despair. In its flight from
God and nature, modern humanity pursues the false infinity of endless diversion, an infinite nothing (*infini rien*). In partial anticipated
agreement with Nietzsche, Pascal would say that a certain conception
of the divine does indeed give rise to nihilism, but that idolatrous
conception of God is a creation of modern rationalism. The God of
deism, Pascal observes, is closer to atheism than either of these is to
Christianity, which alone proclaims, "God is hidden."

To bestow the victory upon either rationalism or nihilism is, according to Pascal, to assume that we know much more than we do
about the ultimate order or lack of order in the universe. Pascal's moderate skepticism counsels a path between presumption and despair, a
path along which the inquirer grapples with uncertain clues and with
a hope that is always susceptible to defeat. This is a path that seeks to
articulate the emotional and psychological geography of a world in
which we seem to have permanently lost our bearings. Any attempt to
embody such a vision of the human condition in art would be less ambitious than the grand art of tragedy Nietzsche hoped might promote
for national cultural renewal. It would operate in the manner of Pascal's
own fragmentary writing—it would seek to destabilize common assumptions, to shock the audience into a recognition of the disorders
of the human condition, to make the audience aware of its aversion
to truth and invite the audience to engage in a quest for an adequate
articulation of the paradoxes of the human condition.

— 4 —

Neo-Noir

IN 1995, KEVIN SPACEY played the lead role in the neo-*noir* thriller, *The Usual Suspects*, a film that takes to dramatic excess the *noir* motif of human experience as a fabrication of images. It also explodes the classic *noir* assumption that no one wins. Spacey plays Roger "Verbal" Kint, a crippled con man, who walks with a limp and who is the only criminal to emerge unscathed from an exploded boat on a San Pedro pier, where police discover twenty-seven bodies and millions in drug money. With standard voiceover and flashback mechanisms, Kint gives testimony to a police detective, Kujan, about the group of criminals, whose plot was hatched after they were all called in for a police line-up. They are the usual suspects, in a famous line from *Casablanca* that has little to do with this film. One suspect, the secret mastermind, Keyser Soze, is highly unusual—a ruthless, brutal assassin who does whatever it takes to manipulate others and control events. In its celebration of the invulnerable, demonic artist who resides beyond good and evil, *The Usual Suspects* holds out the promise that a certain kind of human being might be able to control fortune, to anticipate and manipulate chance events to his own ends.[1] Much like the duped detective, the viewer is implicated in, and deceived by, Soze's artistry. We are tricked, undoubtedly impressed, and certainly entertained. Yet by unveiling the ruse at the end, *The Usual Suspects* divests evil of mystery and gravity. In this film, the *noir* labyrinth is not woven into the fabric of the world. Instead, entrapment and manipulation, the fallibility of human judgment and the futility of the quest for justice—all these *noir* motifs are now under the control of the artistry of the villain, who transcends and subjects others to the *noir* laws of the human condition. Like the classic comic poet, who appears onstage and winks at the audience before exiting the stage, the artist of darkness lets us in on his joke. Thus does he introduce a new form of *noir* comedy, nihilistic comedy, composed by a demonic poet who specializes in displays of aesthetic self-creation.

As we have seen, classic *noir* avoids overt moral lessons and leaves little room for well-adjusted, happy, virtuous types of Americans. The world of classic *noir* proffers a mannerist vision of disorientation and vulnerability, against which no one is adequately protected. While laced with pessimism and fatalism, *noir* narration, even in the classical period, has proven surprisingly flexible and accommodating, even of redemptive paths. Whatever final affirmation there might be in *noir* is always tentative and made available through the downward path of negation. The suggestion of redemption, where it exists, is penitential, partial, and anticipatory.

By contrast, some neo-*noir* films contain characters who rise above the *noir* labyrinth, not by passing through it but by acts of diabolical will. Impervious to the laws of the human condition, these characters "get away" with lives of criminality. This shift constitutes a movement in the direction of nihilism and a recoiling from the fundamentally democratic world of classic *noir*. The human condition is no longer universal; the *noir* trap is no longer seen as unavoidable. Instead, the trap constrains only those who lack the will power, or "will-to-power," necessary to rise above, and control, conventions. Neo-*noir*'s greatest departure from classic *noir* consists in a turn to aristocratic nihilism.

The most resourceful of these characters are in control of the *noir* plot, using their cunning and artistry to ensnare others. As we shall see in the next chapter, feminist *noir* contains some of the most compelling examples of such characters.

It is not surprising that, with the demise of the production code and a growing skepticism about American institutions beginning in the late 1960s, neo-*noir* films would increasingly fall prey to the temptation to nihilism. Since its inception, *noir* has flirted with nihilism. As I argued in the previous chapter, the most satisfying *noir* productions engage without completely succumbing to nihilism. But the instability of the genre, especially once self-conscious *noir*s begin to be made, makes nihilism a live possibility for filmmakers. The problem is that nihilism dissolves classic *noir*'s tensions and mystery, which are rooted in an insistence on limits, boundaries, costs, and consequences. In his influential *Detours and Lost Highways: A Map of Neo-Noir*, Foster Hirsch goes so far as to identify as a distinguishing feature of neo-*noir* its "cavalier amorality" that can steep viewers in a "depraved point of view."[2] Jean-Pierre Chartier's early and negative reaction, to which we have already drawn attention, to classic *noir* seems to apply more aptly to certain neo-*noir* films. Chartier lamented *noir*'s "pessimism and disgust toward humanity"; void of even the most "fleeting image of love" or of characters that might "rouse our pity or sympathy," *noir* presents "monsters, criminals whose evils nothing can excuse, whose actions imply that the only source for the fatality of evil is in themselves."[3]

We need to be careful, however, not to group all neo-*noir* films under one descriptive category. Hirsch's claim is too sweeping. One of the characteristics of the period of neo-*noir* is the fracturing of what little commonality there may have been among *noir* films of the classic period. The center and boundaries of neo-*noir* are even more elusive than those of classic *noir*. Moreover, the artistic and ethical merits of neo-*noir* films vary widely. Even where neo-*noir* films approach nihilism, they may not fully succumb to it. Before we reach the diabolical super-heroes such as Cady from the remake of *Cape Fear* or Soze in

The Usual Suspects, we encounter a number of artistically more sophisticated and ethically more complex films, such as *Chinatown* and *Taxi Driver*, two of the finest films in the entire history of *noir*.[4] In these films, we can detect the way the approach to nihilism simultaneously opens and forecloses possibilities.

THE GETAWAY

For thinkers such as Nietzsche and Dostoevsky, the phrase, "all is permitted" encapsulates the immediate consequence of nihilism. In this precise sense, classical *noir* was anything but nihilist. Neo-*noir* is quite different; it often accommodates characters to whom "all is permitted." An instructive example can be had in one of the earliest neo-*noir* films, *The Getaway* (1972). At the beginning of the film, Doc McCoy (Steve McQueen) is being released from a Texas prison where he's served four years of a ten-year sentence for armed robbery and is reunited with his wife, Carol (Ali McGraw).

In many respects, *The Getaway* fits the standard form of the heist film, where an ex-con, enjoys only momentarily his release from prison before returning to the business. The release signifies neither progress nor liberation from the past. Prison has served, not to reform, but only to harden the mentality of the convict, who faces the risks of future incarceration with no illusions. In *noir* fashion, *The Getaway* even drops any moment of hesitation or regret or the pull of another sort of life, free from crime. Doc remains entrapped, imprisoned in a past from which he cannot escape. This is a classic *noir* motif, wherein the past bears down upon the present, depriving individuals of freedom and the possibility of change. Doc makes a new start only in the sense that he becomes involved in a different plot to break the law, a new bank heist. He faces all of this with detached resignation. The opening of the film also makes clear that Doc will experience no easy escape, no quick getaway from this crime or his previous life.

After the heist, which involves fairly predictable complications, Doc and Carol face numerous internal and external obstacles to their attempted escape to freedom. Beyond the question of whether they will be apprehended, there is the question whether, if they escape, they will be able to live together in peace. After a culminating bloodbath at an El Paso hotel, only Doc and Carol are left alive. Just at the point where the viewer might expect fate to deal them a cruel blow, they experience remarkably good fortune. Emerging from the hotel, they enlist the services of an old man in a decrepit pickup. He is thrilled, invites them in, and sends his truck hurtling through parking lots and over curbs, as he confesses lightheartedly, "I've been in trouble with the law myself." The discrepancy between Doc and Carol's wanton lawlessness and any minor transgression the old man may have committed comes off as light comedy. They offer the old man $30,000 for his truck and he exclaims jubilantly: "Hope you find what you're looking for. Vaya con Dios. Goddamn!" Decidedly upbeat music plays as Doc and Carol drive toward the Mexican mountains.

The ending of *The Getaway* not only makes light of the traditional happy Hollywood ending but also expresses an aversion to the quasi-tragic endings of classical *noir*. It might seem that the title itself hints at the ending; however, the film takes instructive liberties with the ending to Jim Thompson's famous *noir* story, an ending that stressed the continued strife between Doc and Carol. In Thompson's book, composed during the period of classic *noir*, the title is cruelly ironic, as befits a *noir* tale. Their only means of escape from America and into Mexico requires that they agree to live permanently in an upscale, criminal safe house. In an exchange for protection from the law and other criminals, they agree to pay fees for room and board, fees that slowly diminish the large sum of money stolen from the bank. The safe house is a sort of socialist police state with everyone under the watchful eyes of those in power. It is in fact a prison, a place from which Doc and Carol have no hope of release or escape. The Mexican safe house is so thoroughly and so ruthlessly guarded that they give no thought to going elsewhere. Meanwhile, they live in constant suspicion of one another: "They knew each other too well. They lived by taking what they wanted. By getting rid of anyone who got in their way or ceased to be useful to them. It was a fixed pattern with them; it was them. And in the event of a showdown, they would show no more mercy toward each other than they had toward so many others."[5] By contrast with the book, the film embraces nihilism with a happy face. The film's ending locates Doc and Carol blissfully beyond good and evil, having escaped from the *noir* world of crime and law enforcement and transcended *noir*'s uncompromising insistence on the incompatibility of crime with love and trust. *The Getaway* holds the destiny of its main characters in suspense until the very end; its lapse into soft, comic nihilism is incongruous with the rest of the film.

CHINATOWN

Another early neo-*noir* film, *Chinatown* (1974) reasserts limits, costs, and consequences with a vengeance unknown in previous film, even as it notes the victory of its most nihilistic character, Noah Cross (John Huston), who proclaims that anyone is capable of anything and thus that all is permitted. Set in Los Angeles at the time classic *noirs* were being made in that city, *Chinatown* features a private detective (Jack Nicholson) attempting to unravel a dual mystery, that of a crime and that of a woman. In contrast to *The Getaway*'s simple and optimistic narrative, *Chinatown* illustrates the central thesis of the grandest tragedy of antiquity (*Oedipus Rex*): man's inordinate desire to know leads inevitably to self-destruction. Indeed, the film presents this theme with greater vehemence and more devastating results than does *Vertigo*.

Critics have noted the film's ambitious mythology and its evocations of T.S. Eliot's *The Waste Land* with its "sterile kingdom, dying king, and drowned man."[6] *Chinatown* expands the *noir* setting beyond the city to the surrounding natural world; signaling its distance from classical tragedy, *Chinatown* presents nature, not as an encompassing order that judges and sets right the misdeeds of man, but as an adjunct to the city, which manipulates its resources. *Chinatown* drains of significance the symbols—pagan and Christian, Eastern and Western—that pervade Eliot's poem and preoccupy his anguished and seeking protagonist.

As was the case in *Vertigo*, so too in *Chinatown* the enlightenment desire to control through vision backfires on human beings and precipitates disaster. "We run heedlessly into the abyss after putting something in front of us to stop us seeing it."[7] The passage from Pascal could describe many a *noir* character, but it is nowhere more dramatically realized than in the case of J. P. Gittis (Jack Nicholson), the main character in *Chinatown*. The opening shots of the film are photographs of a man and a woman in an adulterous affair, photographs supplied by Gittis' investigative team. Then a woman enters Gittis' office, introduces herself as Mrs. Mulwray, and asks Gittis to investigate her husband's activities with another woman. Gittis asks, "Do you love your husband? . . . Go home and forget it. You're better off not knowing." In a rather pedestrian and matter-of-fact way, the opening introduces the central themes of looking, seeing, and knowing. Gittis's advice implies that certain kinds of knowledge, the temptation to look and see, can be destructive, that it can be a curse to get what one wants.

As we shall see, *Chinatown* involves a number of the central themes of the tragedy of Oedipus, the great but tyrannical king, whose insatiable desire to know the root cause of the plague afflicting his land entangles him in a dark and forbidden quest for self-knowledge. In this pursuit, Oedipus repudiates religious prophecy and spurns counsels of moderation. The achievement of the truth brings not satisfaction and victory but horror and remorseful self-blinding. In an attempt to outwit a prophecy that their son would kill his father, Oedipus's natural parents give a servant the responsibility to destroy the child but he abandons the boy instead. Oedipus ends up unwittingly killing his father and marrying his mother. The revelation of these harsh truths leads his wife-mother to commit suicide and Oedipus to blind himself. There are a number of overlaps between the story of Oedipus and *Chinatown*: L.A. is experiencing drought conditions, Gittis becomes embroiled in a mystery whose solution he cannot stop himself from pursuing, and an incestuous relationship figures decisively in the plot and in the determination of Gittis's fate. Karl Reinhardt's astute observations about the play, *Oedipus Rex*, apply equally to the film: "What we have to consider is illusion and truth as the opposing forces between which man is bound, in which he is entangled and in whose shackles, as he strives toward the highest he can hope for, he is worn down and destroyed."[8]

Mr. Hollis Mulwray is the chief engineer for the city's board of water and power. Gittis visits a public meeting of the board and hears debate over a proposed dam. The first speaker calls L.A. a desert: "without water, the dust would rise up and destroy us as if we never existed." Mulwray stands to speak against the dam, which, he says, will not hold, just like the last one, whose collapse killed thousands. Gittis's next trip is out to the desert where through binoculars he watches Mulwray speak with a young Mexican boy. Also at work on the case, one of Gittis's assistants brings in photographs of Mulwray arguing with an unidentified man (who turns out to be Noah Cross, Mulwray's father-in-law). Another assistant calls to say Mulwray is with a girl in Echo Park; these photographs land Mulwray on the front page of the city paper and in the midst of a scandal.

Soon another woman arrives at Gittis's office, claiming to be the real Mrs. Evelyn Mulwray (Faye Dunaway): "I never hired you." Irked that he was set up, Gittis tries to find Mr. Mulwray. At the Mulwray estate he pauses at a pond in which he notices a shiny object. Mrs. Mulwray interrupts his attempt to retrieve it and advises him to drop the whole matter. Gittis refuses. When she sends him payment for his work, he complains not about the money, but that she has "shortchanged him on the story." Soon Hollis Mulwray's waterlogged body, dead from what appears to be suicide, is pulled out of a reservoir. At the morgue,

Gittis learns that another dead body, this one a town drunk, was found drowned in a dry riverbed. When Gittis visits the riverbed at night, he is inundated by a sudden rush of water and then has his nose cut by guards of the property. Gittis's theory is that Hollis was murdered because he found out about the illegal pumping of the water.

Affronted by the attack that left him with an obtrusive, cumbersome bandage and with his curiosity aroused by the sense that people are hiding things from him, Gittis continues his investigation. Gittis soon finds out that Hollis Mulwray and Noah Cross, Evelyn Mulwray's father, were business partners in control of the water resources of L.A. County. In his first meeting with Noah Cross, the affluent landowner asks Gittis bluntly, "Are you sleeping with my daughter?" And then issues a warning, "You may think you know what you're dealing with but you don't." Gittis responds, "That's what the district attorney used to tell me in Chinatown." Cross's admonition echoes the one Gittis has issued to the woman impersonating Mrs. Mulwray in the opening scene of the film. Gittis's reference to Chinatown, where he used to work as a cop, foreshadows the end of the film and establishes a narrative parallel between Gittis's current investigation and his previous work in Chinatown.

Narrowing in on the mystery of land, water, and human life, Gittis discovers that most of the land in the valley has been sold in the last few months. The water from the dam, Gittis concludes, was not going to L.A. but to the valley. A certain group has been harassing farmers, buying their land cheap, and then preparing to make big money when water comes to the valley. Noah Cross is behind the entire scheme. Meanwhile, Gittis forges a bond with Evelyn. During an evening together at her place, he confesses that he has not been involved with a woman, since he was working in Chinatown. When she asks what he did there, he responds, "As little as possible." He asks for some peroxide for his cut and, after she expresses shock at how nasty the cut is, she dabs the wound. He notices a black dot in the green in her eye, which she says is a "flaw in the iris, a sort of birthmark." After making love in her bed, they lie next to one another calmly and content-edly. She wonders why he is so reticent to discuss his past, especially his time as a cop in Chinatown. Gittis says he had "bad luck" there. "Trying to keep someone from being hurt," he ended up "making sure she was hurt." "*Cherchez la femme*?" Evelyn comments, "Was there a woman involved?" "Of course." The music moves from romantic jazz to a more ominous tone, as she asks with quiet intensity, "Dead?" A phone suddenly interrupts the conversation and an alarmed Evelyn explains cryptically that she must leave immediately.

This is the pivotal scene of the film, a scene that marks the culmi-nation of Gittis's romance with Evelyn and sets him on path toward the solution of all the mysteries in the case. But the scene is more than transitional; it is a microcosm of the whole film. What we cannot fail to notice is the structural symmetry of the scene, which begins and ends with the two lovers discussing Chinatown and the woman he destroyed by trying to save her. In between these two conversations, they have sex. Thus do we have repetition, foreshadowing, and a symbolic linking of eros and death, both of which seem to be rooted in the desire to know. Gittis's desire to know Mrs. Mulwray sexually parallels his desire to know the truth about the case in which he's now immersed. Erotic desire has the potential to shatter an individual's illusion of self-con-tainment and control. And the flaw in her iris, a birthmark, symbolizes the way her life has been marred by forces outside of her control, forces operative in her very begetting, perhaps in nature itself.

Before she leaves, she learns that Gittis met with her father, Noah Cross. She warns Gittis that he is a "very dangerous man," who might be behind everything, including the death of her husband. She asks him to wait at the house but as soon as she departs, he follows her. He witnesses her restraining and then medicating an emotionally dis-turbed young woman. He confronts Evelyn and accuses her of keeping Hollis's girlfriend hostage. She denies that the woman is being kept against her will, but he counters, "that's not what it looks like." Evelyn explains that the girl is her sister.

After discovering that there is no record that Evelyn had a sister, he confronts her. "Who is the girl?" "She's my sister," Evelyn answers. "You don't have a sister," he shouts as he smacks her across the face and demands the truth. "She's my daughter." Gittis smacks her repeatedly as she alternates sister-daughter responses. Lying in a heap on the floor, she says weakly, "She's my sister and my daughter." He assumes she must be lying when she shifts from one answer to the other and demands that she settle on one or the other, but not upon "both . . . and," an inconceivable answer to Gittis.

The scene is significant. It confirms Noah Cross's warning that Gittis did not know what he was dealing with. The quest for truth—and "Truth" is the title of this scene on the DVD version of the film—can lead to the revelation, not just of things one would rather not know, but of a horrifying, forbidden and destructive knowledge. Once again, a symbol is woven into the story itself, as the discovery of the bifocals foments Gittis's unrelenting—and in this case violent—demand that Evelyn tell him the truth. He must see all.

The scene also reveals Evelyn Mulwray to be an unusually complex female *noir* lead. What one would expect in a standard *noir* is for this interrogation to reveal Evelyn's secret plot, by herself or with another man, to deceive Gittis, to use him as a pawn in a game of her own devising. Her use of the French phrase, "*cherchez la femme*" reinforces this expectation. But Evelyn's secret is intended to protect Catherine, her innocent sister-daughter, and to fend off familial shame. Even more unsettling than the revelation of her incestuous relationship with her father is her response to Gittis's question, "He raped you?" She hesitates, then averts her eyes and gently, sadly shakes her head, "No." To have been violated against her will would be one thing, but to be led by the father she loved to consent—to some extent and for some time—to activities she would come to see as disgusting and repulsive is quite another. He has implicated her in his own perversions.

Evelyn now reveals to Gittis her plan to take her sister to Mexico. Gittis arranges for her and Catherine to be driven out of town and for the three of them to meet in Chinatown. In the interim, Gittis visits Noah Cross and accuses him of killing Hollis. When Gittis wonders what a fabulously wealthy man could possibly want with more land and more money, Cross responds, "the future." Cross adds, "most people never have to face the fact that at the right time and the right place they are capable of anything." Then Cross's bodyguard pulls a gun on Gittis and demands that he drive them to find Evelyn in Chinatown, where the police now wait to arrest Gittis. When they arrive, Cross sees Catherine and mumbles that he is her "grandfather." Asserting "she's mine, too," he struggles with Evelyn. Evelyn pulls out her gun, shoots Cross in the arm and drives off with Catherine. The police fire warning shots and then, as she is nearly out of reach, fire at the car. The horn sounds, the car slows, and a girl screams. As they reach the car to see Evelyn's limp body killed by a bullet that entered the back of her head and exited through an eye, Noah Cross screams, "Oh, Lord" and embraces Catherine, shielding her eyes. Gittis stands motionless, his eyes frozen in a vacant stare. In a whisper, he says, "as little as possible." A cop advises him, "Forget it, Jake. It's Chinatown." The film ends with a cop trying to clear the area. "Get off the streets!" he shouts.

A deeply sympathetic, in some ways admirable, and certainly pitiable, character, Evelyn is not a standard *femme fatale*. Having reversed our expectations once, the film now reverses them again, not by revealing her to be nefarious, but by having her fulfill the destructive role of the *femme fatale* while remaining innocent. Gittis's attraction to her, his desire to solve her secrets, proves his undoing. Evelyn thus performs the function of the *femme fatale* while intending to be the opposite. Gittis is the one who has exceeded bounds in his quest for knowledge; his quest uncovers "an unnatural abomination." Nietzsche sees such an ending as inevitable: "He who by means of his knowledge plunges nature into an abyss of destruction must also suffer the dissolution of nature in his own person."

The conclusion depicts Gittis as perhaps the most victimized of all the *noir* detectives. He had already been taken down a notch or two in the course of the film. The many superficial resemblances between Gittis and the hard-boiled detectives of classic *noir* only serve to accentuate the contrast between them, to underscore Gittis's helplessness and his vulgarity. Not only is he manipulated by others, but the closer he comes to seeming in control of things, to achieving the knowledge he needs to have to solve the case, the nearer he comes to his own defeat. Although Cross praises him for his tough reputation, he mocks him by deliberately and repeatedly mispronouncing his name as "Gits." Then there is the silly bandage he has to wear, something that makes him look weak and absurd. His stating of the police motto regarding Chinatown—as little as possible—indicates that he now recognizes what he should have acknowledged all along, namely, that he was replaying the same tragic scenario from his time as a cop in Chinatown years ago. Chinatown's variety of dialects and its unfamiliar customs throw up insuperable obstacles to understanding and right action. Even an experienced and worldly cop with good intentions cannot succeed there. Whatever one does is likely to go awry; hence, the counsel of minimalism, as little as possible, a more severe counsel and more restrictive moderation than even that enjoined upon, and ultimately advocated by, Oedipus.

For all his similarities to Oedipus, he is markedly inferior to a classical tragic hero, and not just in the obvious sense that he never possessed the grandeur, dignity, or power of Oedipus. His tragic fate is unable to do for L.A. or his audience what Oedipus's self-blinding can do for his nation. Nietzsche has this to say about the regenerative power of the myth of Oedipus: "Sophocles conceived doomed Oedipus, the greatest sufferer of the Greek stage, as a pattern of nobility, destined to error and misery despite his wisdom, yet exercising a beneficent influence on his environment in virtue of his boundless grief."[9] Oedipus continues to speak eloquently about his fate and grief; he is, moreover, still in conversation with others, who express sympathy for his plight. By contrast, Gittis is utterly alone; misunderstood by others, he is reduced to a paralyzing silence, reminiscent of the final frames of *Vertigo*. Because the audience continues to experience the horror of this world and has not entirely lost its bearings, the world of *Chinatown* may partly fit tragedy as Goldmann describes it: "an unbearable world where man is forced to live in error and illusion."[10]

Another reason that Gittis's tragic end cannot function in the redemptive manner of Oedipus is that Oedipus was solely, if unwittingly, responsible for the curse on his land. His self-prosecution and self-punishment exact a severe but satisfying justice. In *Chinatown*, however, the chief culprit is more firmly entrenched in power than ever before. Noah Cross has made the whole of L.A. County into a sort of Chinatown for anyone who would pursue justice and truth. Ruthless and powerful, a matter-of-fact nihilist, he is untroubled by any qualms of conscience and willing to do whatever is necessary to attain what he wants. And he gets whatever he wants. The bleakest part of the ending is not Evelyn's death or Gittis's belated realization that he has once again unintentionally brought devastation upon a woman he loved. The greatest horror comes when Noah Cross takes protective custody of Catherine. How long will it be until she bears a child that is at once Cross's child and great grandchild? And this points up something about the vile narcissism of Cross, whose incestuous abuse is no mere accidental perversion. It defines the very essence of his character. When he confesses to Gittis that he wants to control the future, he is not simply acknowledging a greater degree of ambition than that present in most men, who would be satisfied with much less. He is not interested solely in the financial or the political future of LA. He wants to control the very sources of future life, of generativity—water and female fertility. He wants there to be no future beyond his grasp, nothing other than what he brings to life.

Cross is an inexplicable monster that evades capture and defies comprehension. He is a more troubling character than silly serial killers such as Hannibal Lecter or demonic wizards such as Keyser Soze. He exists in our midst, as a family man, well respected in the community. Cross's victory deprives not only Gittis and L.A. of the prospects for a renewal of justice and order; it also bitterly frustrates the audience's longing for justice. It is instructive to note that the original ending had Noah Cross being killed and Gittis transporting Evelyn's daughter to safety in Mexico, an ending Polanski, the director, altered. It may well be that Roman Polanski intended, as John Cawelti argues, to invoke "deliberately . . . the basic characteristics of a traditional genre in order to bring its audience to see that genre as the embodiment of an inadequate and destructive myth."[11] James Naremore puts the contrast with classic *noir* this way: "The note of failure in classic *noir* . . . was frequently softened by a qualified attempt to assert some kind of justice or return to social equilibrium."[12] Naremore's way of putting it is problematic; he makes it sound as if classic *noir* added a dose of justice or a glimmer of hope in a purely ad hoc way. If that were so, then we should see the ending of *Chinatown* as displaying accurately the true world of *noir*. Yet, as we have seen, the quest, in the face of enormous obstacles, for love, communication, and truthful speech is at the heart of classic *noir*, where failure is not so much a counterbalancing force to the quest in speech, as its provocation. It is failure realized and acknowledged, especially in the face of imminent death, that incites truthful speech. An artistically masterful film, *Chinatown* pushes us further in the direction of paralyzed silence in the face of the frustration of our desire for love, truth, and justice.

TAXI DRIVER

If *Chinatown* at least has the humanity to focus our attention on the pitiful loss of innocence in Evelyn and her daughter and on Gittis's brutal fulfillment of his destiny, *Taxi Driver* relentlessly implicates the viewer in the perverse and psychotic vision of its protagonist, Travis Bickle. More than any other *noir*, *Taxi Driver* sustains an unrelenting identification with the perspective of its disordered main character, whose residual sense of injustice—and he does have a sense of injustice, of the disorders that afflict modern society—can neither be real-

ized nor even clearly articulated in the modern city. The film begins
with a series of shots of a car moving slowly through the streets of New
York at night in fog and rain. The camera moves to a tight shot of the
eyes of the driver. When the camera returns to the street, it gives us the
driver's perspective through the front windshield, beyond which the
streets of New York are a wet blur of lights and colors. Still, the scene
is calm, even serene, a feeling that Bernard Herrmann's mesmerizing
musical score reinforces. But the score moves with disturbing ease
from cool, romantic jazz to dissonant tones, introduced by pounding
drums. As the music makes its transition to more ominous tones, the
camera shifts back to a tight shot of the eyes of the driver visible in
the rear-view mirror.

The camera thus identifies with the viewpoint of the cabbie, Travis Bickle (Robert DeNiro), in whose eyes the city is a classic *noir*
nightmare of the imagination, a decadent and depraved city of loners,
hookers, dealers, thieves, and murderers. Bickle himself is a quintessential *noir* leading man, a veteran of the unpopular Vietnam war, a
dislocated, aimless, insomniac, a natural denizen of nocturnal city
life, whose only career goal is "to work long hours." A former marine
who received an honorable discharge in 1973, Bickle spends his nights
cruising the streets in his car. He figures that a job as a cabbie will allow him to get paid for doing what he is doing anyway.

Incapable of integration into society, Bickle is anonymous and
could live for years unnoticed in the city. But Bickle has longings that
simmer just beneath the surface and can only be suppressed for so
long. The film brings out the sense of impending explosion behind
calm appearances in an early scene where Bickle stops for coffee with
other cabbies. He talks about a cabbie being cut up, then drops an
antacid tablet into a glass of water and stares at the effect. Focusing on
the fizzing, bubbling activity, the camera lingers over Bickle's irrational
obsessions. Bickle then stares stone-faced across the diner at two black
men. Later, he tells a fellow cabbie, "I just want to really do something.

I got some bad ideas in my head." His passions are a twisted mixture of the romantic, the perverse, the military, and the puritan.

A number of early scenes clue us into Bickle's voyeuristic romantic aspirations and his vision of the city in which he lives. In the daylight hours, from the street through the glass walls of an office building, he often watches Betsy (Cybil Shepherd), a young woman working a desk at the presidential campaign offices of Senator Palantine. When he finally speaks to her, he proclaims, "You are the most beautiful woman I've ever seen," and volunteers to work on the campaign. Betsy, a true believer in Palantine's candidacy, finds herself intrigued by Bickle's odd affection for her. Over coffee, she admits that she "feels a connection." He takes her on a date to a foreign porn film, a curious mix of the clinical and the erotic. When Betsy leaves in disgust, the naïve Bickle is genuinely surprised and apologetic. In a voiceover, he explains that he has tried to call and has sent flowers. He then repeats his words slowly as if he's writing them down. The voiceovers, we later learn, are in fact our access to Bickle's diary. This mechanism further accentuates the film's identification with the narrow and peculiar vision of its main character.

The puritanical side of Bickle's personality emerges dramatically when he has occasion to provide cab service for Senator Palantine. After Bickle waxes enthusiastic about Palantine's campaign for President, the Senator brags that he has learned a great deal about America from riding in cabs. "What bugs you?" the Senator inquires. Bickle launches into a tirade on the need to "clean up the city," to get rid of the "filth and scum." He adds, "I can hardly take it. The smell gives me headaches." A liberal whose slogan is "We are the People," Palantine is a bit taken aback but agrees and says, "It's not going to be easy. We're going to have to make some radical changes." Travis concurs, "Damn straight." Later, Bickle sees Palantine on television, proclaiming that "the people are going to rise up." Palantine's words fuel Bickle's fantasies of purification through a violent, revolutionary act.

One evening a young female prostitute (Jody Foster) hops into his idle cab and screams that she wants to get away. But before Bickle can react, her pimp pulls her from the cab and drags her away. Bickle soon encounters the girl again, when he nearly runs her over as she crosses the street. He follows her but squeals off in his cab when she meets a man. In a voiceover, he confesses that "loneliness has followed" him his whole life. Then in a voiceover of a diary entry: "June 8. Life has taken a turn again. . . . Day after day the same thing and then suddenly there is change." At this point, Bickle moves from passive observation to preparation for action.

He buys an arsenal of guns, starts working out, continues to watch porn flicks, wears army fatigues, and prepares himself for some unknown day of combat by standing in front of the mirror, taunting, "You talking to me?" In a June 28 diary entry, he states that his goal is "total organization." The disorder, confusion, and simmering anger within seek a release, a confrontation with some external foe. The film continues to focus on the link between violence and sex. As he watches a porn film, in which heavily breathing actresses moan, "it's getting harder. It's throbbing now," he tells us in a voiceover that the "idea had been growing in" his "brain for some time. True force. All the King's men cannot put it back together again." As the voiceover ends, he is no longer in the theater but at home holding a gun in front of a mirror. The closer Bickle comes to unleashing his inner vision upon the external world, the more intimately does the film enter into his private world, occasionally merging entirely with his fantasy world. Thus does the film implicate the viewer in the perverse attraction and mania of his world.

Having immersed himself in the degrading and dehumanizing underworld of the American city, Bickle now dreams of performing a grand cleansing act of retribution. His first vigilante act involves shooting a black man who is robbing a convenience store. Worried about his unregistered gun, he leaves the store while the owner, complaining that this is the fifth robbery this year, beats the thief with a crowbar.

Back in his apartment, he writes out a card to his parents. Noting that he is no longer able to recall exact dates, he apologizes and expresses the hope that one card will cover his parents' anniversary, Father's Day, and his mother's birthday. He assures them that he is doing "sensitive work for the government," and that he has a steady girl, named Betsy, and signs it, "Love, Travis." Having depicted himself as a conventional success and performed his familial duties, he destroys his television.

Later he returns to the street where he had seen the young prostitute, Iris, and pays her pimp, Sport, twenty-five dollars for thirty minutes, to do, as the pimp says, "whatever" he "wants with her." Once alone, she is all business. Incredulous, he asks, "Don't you remember me? I don't want to make it. I want to help you." She explains that she must have been stoned that night in the cab. When she is sober, she has nowhere else to go. He says he would like to talk further. The next day at breakfast, she explains that her parents hate her. When he berates her for wasting her life with "killers and junkies," she asks accusingly, "What makes you so high and mighty? Have you ever tried looking at your own eyeballs in the mirror?" Of course, Bickle has spent a great deal of time, far too much time, staring at himself in the mirror. He sees himself, not as he is, the product and reflection of the city that transfixes and disgusts him. Rather, he sees himself as he increasingly imagines himself to be, as a savior of lost souls, a warrior capable of purifying the city of evil. The film itself makes it increasingly difficult for viewers to retain their distance, their objectivity; nothing in the city suggests an alternative vantage point from which to appraise his vision.

However much she may have dismissed Bickle's advice, Iris appears to have been affected by it. She tells Sport, "I don't like what I'm doing" and complains that he does not seem to have any time for her anymore. In an unnerving scene, Sport plays a record—easily identifiable as the music for the soundtrack of the film—and dances with Iris. "At moments like these, I know I'm a lucky man, touching a woman who loves me and needs me." This playing of the score within the score invites us to focus on this scene as especially revelatory of the world of the film, a scene of the continued seduction, manipulation, and destruction of childhood innocence. The city, it seems, is the place where dreams turn into nightmares, where affection and love are but instruments for the satisfaction of raw lust, and where human bodies are but commodities in the service of the maximization of profit.

As the scene ends, the soundtrack continues to hold our attention. In yet another marvelous and disturbing integration of music and action, the sound, tone, and setting change abruptly. We hear the sound of a rapidly firing gun and see Bickle at target practice. The sound of the gunfire is reminiscent of the sound of the drums in Herrmann's score, a point that is reinforced when the score itself echoes the sounds of Bickle's gunfire. In a voiceover, Bickle says that he now "sees a clearing." My life "points in one direction. I see that now. There never has been any choice for me." Here the music accentuates and affirms Bickle's sense of his own destiny: a predetermined mission of purgation through violence.

When he reappears in public, he is sporting a mohawk haircut and attending a Palantine rally at Columbus Circle, a place that, according to the senator, is symbolic of a crossroads in history. But a secret service agent thwarts his plan to kill the politician. So, fully armed, he heads to visit Iris. When he encounters Sport, he taunts him and then shoots him. Proceeding to Iris's room, he shoots everyone who stands athwart his path. The rampage ends with the execution of the man having sex with Iris. In one of the most memorable scenes in the *noir* canon, he turns his gun on himself but he has already used all his bullets in his bloody rampage. Having spent both his ammo and his wrath, he sits on the couch, as the police arrive, and then, with eyes wide, points a bloody, dripping finger to his own temple and mimics pulling the trigger three times. A faint smile crosses his face, as he sits back and turns his head toward the ceiling. The scenes of Bickle's carnage are shot in slow motion; and, once Bickle is done, an overhead camera looks directly into his upturned face and then slowly retreats from Iris's room, down the hallway and back onto the streets, now flooded with bystanders. Here the camera pauses to offer a panoramic shot. The slow movements of the camera, its long, lingering, savoring looks at the crime scene bespeak a perverse aesthetic fascination with Bickle's violent rage.

The entire film has a nightmarish quality to it, the sort of deliberately distorted depiction of modern city life that early *noir* inherited from German Expressionism. Both in what it includes and in what it excludes, the film provides a highly selective vision, not just of American life, but of New York City life. These deliberate distortions might provide grounds for seeing the film as simply a fictional exaggeration of one, small portion of the life of one city. And yet the filmmakers seem bent on universalizing that vision, on implicating the rest of America in it. They do not suggest that we are all likely to become Travis Bickle, although they do more than suggest that beneath our conscious lives there are subterranean desires akin to those Bickle harbors. The film implicates us in Bickle's world by underscoring the way American life cannot see or understand Bickle clearly, the way we allow the manipulation of images and the perversion of justice to substitute for truth and justice. How so?

After the scenes of bloody rage, the film provides footage of Bickle in his apartment surrounded by newspaper clips that celebrate his heroic liberation of an innocent young girl from life on the street. It turns out that the man being serviced by Iris that evening was a notorious mafioso. The public has transformed Bickle's bloody rage into a successful battle in the war against organized crime. The media and the American public have confirmed Bickle's vision of himself as a superhero. No portion of American society is separate from the *noir* nightmare, where the release of a violent rage is confused with justice and the acting out of a psychotic fantasy is equated with heroism. In these respects, the film seems to be a sort of leftist response to the right wing celebrations of the vigilante in films such as *Dirty Harry* (1971), *Billy Jack* (1971), and *Death Wish* (1974). Yet, the film's ideological message is convoluted and obscure. It offers no hope for proper political understanding or response.

What makes Bickle so disturbing is his very ordinariness. He is not a self-conscious amoralist or a Nietzschean superman, expressing his superiority through acts of artistic destruction. His mediocrity and his twisted sense of justice, both of which are misunderstood and then celebrated by mainstream American society, bring him closer to us, even as the artistry of the film brings us closer to him. Bickle is the only character who sees and feels the disorder of the city, its wallowing in lust and injustice, yet he is unable to articulate, much less change, it. Iris's parents are effusive in their praise and full of gratitude. But their note to Bickle only exacerbates the sense of entrapment, the sense that a healthy and happy American life is impossible. Into what sort of life has Bickle labored to return Iris? Her parents assure Bickle that they have "taken steps" to insure that she "never has cause to run away again."

At the end, the film depicts an apparently recovered Bickle entering his cab to deliver a passenger, as a reflection of Betsy appears in his rearview mirror. She congratulates Bickle on his success. He responds with self-deprecation and then drops her off. Lest we think all is well or that Bickle's recognition for heroism has made him a new man, Hermann's score once again shifts from harmonious to dissonant. The camera pans to Bickle's eyes in the rearview mirror, unmistakably the same eyes we met at the outset. We have come full circle; in a regular and unending cycle, the city attracts and nourishes characters such as Bickle. Their rage simmers beneath the surface for a time, only to explode into the public arena, where a complex set of forces render it utterly unintelligible to ordinary citizens as well as politicians.

As was true in many classic *noirs*, film is more informative about human character, more penetrating in its analysis of human motivation, than either politics or law enforcement. The film seems to contain a critique of the sort of vigilante justice that became a hot topic in American culture in the 1970s and 1980s. The universally mistaken appraisal of Bickle is a serious indictment of American public life. Only the artist gives access to Bickle's inner fantasies and allows us to see him for what he is. Art delivers a vision, a perspective that would otherwise be unavailable; and yet the art of *Taxi Driver* suggests no way out or beyond, no means by which to transform, the city Bickle naturally inhabits. The paradox of the film is that, if we can make these judgments about it, we must be resorting to some conception of what is natural and healthy independent of the film itself. The film deploys arts of darkness not to shed light but just to show us the darkness; indeed, it is unclear from what perspective the filmmakers hope to make any sort of judgment on the world of the film.

James Naremore suggests that the film is a "Dostoyevskian nightmare of the soul," a "deeply conservative picture about original sin and the absolute evil of modernity."[13] Paul Schrader, who wrote the script for *Chinatown*, described his own psychic state during the time of composition as akin to the mood of Eliot's *The Wasteland*. Pauline Kael has called Schrader a heavyweight moralist with Puritan instincts. This may be right, but if so it illustrates the intractable problem with any crude version of the Calvinist doctrine of total depravity. What Naremore calls "absolute evil," were it to exist, could not be named for what it was, since it would deprive us of any larger frame of reference in light of which we might call something "evil." If we were bereft of any attachment to the good, completely benighted in our understanding of justice, then there would be nothing in us to which an artist could appeal to make us see that things are disordered.

Even in as masterful a film as *Taxi Driver*, nihilistic-tending neo-*noir* threatens to undermine the dialectic appropriate to Pascalian tragedy. Pascal's aim, as we have seen, is not simply to lay out a position in a linear, deductive fashion, but to induce self-knowledge, a self-knowledge to which he thinks we are especially averse. He thus deploys hyperbole to shock his audience into a knowing recognition of themselves and their condition. This much is clear. The complete denigration of reason would lead human beings to despair, which is one of two great evils of human life. The other, opposed evil is presumption. As Pascal writes, "Man must not be allowed to believe that he is equal either to animals or to angels, nor to be unaware of either, but he must know both."[14] Human nature is neither totally depraved, nor capable of achieving the good by its own powers. The largest section of the study of nature has to do with the wretchedness or corruption of human nature. Pascal adduces a plethora of examples of our wretchedness, but our ability to acknowledge these as evidence of our disordered state entails a grasp of what it means for human beings to possess integrity and health. Of course, we possess no more than fleeting glimpses of integrity, health, and natural order, but these are crucial to Pascal's account of the human condition. Does not Pascal concede all this when he states that our greatness consists in our ability to understand our wretchedness? To make depravity the whole picture is to grasp only one part of our duality, to exaggerate our wretchedness and to neglect entirely our greatness. Without a residue of greatness, we would not recognize our condition as wretched.

This point also illustrates the difference between Pascal, Eliot, and Dostoevsky, on the one hand, and Martin Scorsese's film, on the other. The former embed within their work characters and plot lines that suggest alternative paths to that of simple depravity. The sort of dark art practiced by Schrader and Scorsese is trapped between its affirmation of absolute and ineradicable evil and its presupposition that the audience can recognize the darkness for what it is. It simultaneously demands and deprives us of the capacity to name the darkness.

THE USUAL SUSPECTS

Where does neo-*noir* go from here? There is no necessity of course in film taking any particular direction and the sheer variety of modern, including neo-*noir*, films illustrates the indeterminacy of the direction of art in our time. There is, nonetheless, a logical next step in the direction of neo-*noir* films. To see the extent to which nihilism and a celebration of characters beyond good and evil can pervade a *noir* narrative, one need only view another film by Martin Scorsese, his 1991 remake of *Cape Fear*, the original of which was released in 1962. In the original, a lawyer's decent family is unjustly stalked by an ex-con (Cady, played by Robert Mitchum) and must resort to strategies beyond ordinary law enforcement to fend off the threat. In the remake, the filmmaker treats the lawyer and his family as utterly amoral and the ex-con (Cady, played by Robert DeNiro) as a sort of anti-hero who stands beyond good and evil. He has the courage to see through the arbitrariness at the root of conventional morality and to act in opposition to it, to display his freedom and creative independence through horrifying acts of raping, maiming, and murder. Scorsese's Cady is an over-the-top nihilist who alternates between reveling in terror and reading Nietzsche at the local library. In Scorsese's hands, the artistic subtlety and restrained character development of classic *noir* become an unhinged celebration of sadistic sexual terror, itself a source of comic entertainment for jaded audiences.

If Scorsese's *Cape Fear* is an artistically challenged neo-*noir*, it nonetheless suggests the terminus toward which the alliance of *noir* and nihilism tends, the elevation of the anti-hero who stands beyond good and evil. No longer subject to the laws and universal conditions of the *noir* universe, the debased Nietzschean superman marshals these forces to his (or her, as we shall see in the chapter on feminist *noir*) own ends. Indeed, the ultimate embodiment of the nihilistic artist in a *noir* universe would be a character who controlled completely the *noir* story and subjected others to his or her whims. Precisely such a character is at the center of the neo-*noir* caper film, *The Usual Suspects*, a film whose artistic intricacies exploit *noir* motifs more effectively than the remake of *Cape Fear*, or *The Getaway* for that matter.

In *noir*, flashback and voiceover techniques present themselves as aids to the viewing audience. They are purportedly the means by which the viewer reconstructs the past, gaining access to elements of the story otherwise unavailable, and benefits from the clarification of commentary. Even in classic *noir*, however, the use of these techniques was not straightforward. They were often deployed to put the viewer off balance, to provide a vicarious experience of the disorientation endured by the characters populating the *noir* universe. As far back as *Citizen Kane*, the use of multiple flashbacks from different perspectives had the effect of unsettling the linear, narrative expectations of viewers. It asks them to try to piece together an elusive truth about the events and lives captured on screen. However objective and detached the narrator's voice might seem, the will to deceive is always a possibility. Unable to face the truth, a narrator may engage in a complex, and partly unconscious, strategy of self-deception. Conversely, a narrator who is actually in control of the entire plot may use deception to ensnare the viewer. In *The Usual Suspects*, the tools of flashback and voiceover are instruments of a grand and stupefying deception, manifestations of a superior artistry, an artistry at once playful and malevolent. They are the mechanisms of Keyser Soze's will to power.

Soze's artistry expresses what Nietzsche calls the "pathos of distance," the gap separating the superhuman from the merely human. Nietzsche's embrace of nihilism both as symptom of the decadence of a dying Christian worldview and as an opportunity for the great-souled to free themselves from the tyrannical, petty morality of the herd is at root virulently aristocratic. "What has been deified? The value instincts in the community. What has been slandered? That which sets apart the highest men from the lowest, the desires that create clefts."[15] Nietzsche hoped that a new code, an order of rank according to strength, would emerge from the decline of the old morality. An individual's location on the scale of strength would vary in accord with the ability to "admit the necessity of lies," the necessity of destruction as integral to creation. Since Nietzsche also speaks of a hierarchy of laughter, we can surmise that at the top of the scale would reside those who would not just "admit," but gleefully embrace the necessity of lies and violence. Keyser Soze is one possible manifestation of such a man.

Closer to Nietzsche's will-to-power than to Hobbes's diffidence, Soze is a possible embodiment of the the principle of all organic growth: "a living thing seeks above all to discharge its strength—life itself is will to power; self-preservation is only one of the indirect and most frequent results." Although Nietzsche would not likely have admired Soze's fascination with criminality, Soze would seem to be one among many possible embodiments of Nietzsche's will-to-power. As Nietzsche puts it, "life is essentially appropriation, injury, overpowering of what is alien and weaker; suppression, hardness, imposition of one's own forms . . . exploitation."[16]

The film opens with a mystery. A man (Keaton) in a warehouse puts a match to a trail of gasoline spilled across the floor. As the fire begins to spread, another man, whose face we never see, urinates from a balcony one floor above and douses it out. The man then approaches Keaton and shoots him. A huge explosion follows.

We then back up to police rounding up suspects for a lineup, one of whose members, Verbal Kint, supplies a voiceover about how he "didn't belong with this hard core group" of criminals. Especially prominent in the lineup is Keaton, a former cop, who went bad but has recently shown signs that he has turned his life around. All the men from the lineup are held in one cell. With the exception of Verbal, who did time for fraud, they are all familiar with one another. Keaton observes that the lineup must be a set up because "usually it's just you and five dumb guys."

The film shifts back to the present day, to San Pedro, where the cops are assembling and covering fifteen fried bodies from the warehouse explosion at a wharf. There are, we learn, only two survivors. One man, Arkosh Kovash, is in a coma in a trauma/burn unit, while the other is a cripple from New York, named Verbal Kint. When Arkosh awakens, he mumbles unintelligibly in a foreign tongue; the only words spoken clearly are a name that he shouts, Keyser Soze. Once a translator arrives he tells his story. He says there were no drugs on board the ship;

then, his eyes bulge in fear and rage as he describes Keyser as the devil himself. Police begin to work with him on a composite sketch of Keyser. Meanwhile, the police, who suspect that the violence in San Pedro involved a drug deal, interview Verbal. Agent Kujan from customs tries a variety of emotional appeals to get Verbal to talk. "I know you know something. I just want to hear your story. I'm smarter than you and I'm going to get the truth" out of you. But Kujan has no real leverage. Verbal is, as the police chief says, "protected from on high by the prince of darkness." The Governor has weighed in and Verbal has received total immunity. Moreover, Verbal's story "checks out."

Kujan's working theory is that Keaton orchestrated the entire plan and then made it appear to Verbal that he was shot dead so that he could escape undetected. Kujan dismisses the notion that Keaton has gone straight. He describes Keaton as a sort of wizard, who killed even while in jail without leaving any evidence and who, when free, faked his own death but reappeared when it was in his interest to do so. Verbal's response is, "I'm not a rat."

As Kujan presses Verbal to reveal Keaton's involvement, Verbal says that it was in fact a lawyer, named Kobayashi, who brought the San Pedro deal to their attention. At one meeting, Kobayashi arrives and requests that they agree to short-term employment by Keyser Soze, at the mention of whose name everyone, except Verbal, cringes. Kobayashi explains that Soze's "main interest is narcotics" and that a certain Argentinian group has been cutting into his business. So he wants their ninety-one-million-dollar cocaine shipment destroyed when it arrives at port in San Pedro. When they ask why they should oblige Soze, the lawyer enumerates a series of hijackings of money, drugs, and guns that each of the men in the room has performed. All of them, it turns out, have unknowingly stolen shipments under the control of Soze. The only reason "you're still alive," Kobayashi explains, is that "you didn't know" you were stealing from Soze. Keaton says, "You set up the lineup." When the lawyer leaves, a timid Verbal asks, "Who's Keyser Soze?"

When Fenster, one of the members of the group, refuses and parts from them, he is later found murdered at the precise location where Kobayashi told the men they would find his body. Led by Keaton, the group now sets out to get Kobayashi. Verbal comments to Kujan that Keaton had a "cop's mind," which never believes there's an "arch-criminal behind" the scene. Familiar with crime, with its quotidian character and the ordinariness of the motives for even the most brutal violence, cops see through the romantic grandeur of crime as it so often appears in books and films. For them, crime is an everyday event, not deep and perplexing, but banal and superficial. The legends surrounding Soze suggest that the banality of evil thesis may, at least in this case, be in need of serious rethinking. But it is not clear what is fact and what is fiction regarding Soze.

When Kujan asks Verbal why he watched Keaton be killed and did not intervene, Verbal confesses, "Because I was afraid" of Soze. "How do you shoot the devil in the back? What if you miss?" As Kujan is fed incoming information about the murdered Argentinians, he discovers that one of the men had the goods on Soze. He concludes that, since there were no drugs on board, Soze organized the entire thing as a hit on the only man who could finger him for a series of crimes and left Verbal alive to testify that he was dead. "Immunity was your reward. Keaton is Keyser Soze," Kujan exclaims. A teary Verbal says "why me?" Kujan explains, "Because you're a cripple. Because you're weak. Because you're stupid."

Verbal refuses to cooperate with police, saying he's "not a rat" and will take his chances on the street. It turns out that his bail has been posted. As he limps out of the building, Kujan remains in the office discussing the case with the police chief. As he talks, Kujan begins to notice names and places on the bulletin board and on other objects in the office. In horror, he drops his coffee mug. The bottom of the broken mug is inscribed with the words "Kobayashi ceramics." A variety of names and places on the bulletin board figure in Verbal's story. As

Kujan rushes out in search of the cripple, a composite sketch, which matches Verbal, appears on the police fax machine. Kujan is reminded of Verbal's words: "You think you can catch Keyser Soze," but, after he has come "this close to getting caught," you will "never hear from him again." Meanwhile, Verbal pauses on the sidewalk, straightens his gait and gets into a car, driven by the man we have come to know as Kobayashi. Verbal's words provide the concluding voiceover: "The greatest trick the devil ever pulled was convincing people he didn't exist."

If Soze has an overarching purpose, it is the mastery of all persons and events that fall within his purview. His speeches give us glimmers, philosophical fragments, of a position that echoes Machiavelli, a figure much admired by Nietzsche, but a Machiavelli liberated from any attachment to the fame supplied through political rule and national glory. Verbal adopts the Machiavellian maxim that it is better to be feared than loved on the ground that fear is a more sure means of securing compliance from others.[17] This maxim effectively makes the existence of a loving God irrelevant to human life and accounts for Verbal's maxim that he believes in God but fears Soze. Verbal also embraces the Machiavellian thesis that the discrepancy between seeing and touching ("all see what you appear to be but few touch what you really are") allows a crafty leader to manipulate appearances, to seem or appear in one way but to be or act in some other way. Soze here manifests himself in Verbal as the antithesis of the criminal embodiment of the will to power; he appears as a "stupid, weak, cripple."

Soze is the supreme ironist, practitioner of an audacious and nihilistic irony. Walker Percy describes the latter sort of irony as a "locus of pure possibility"; what the ironist will be in the "next moment bears no relation to what he is or what he was the minute before."[18] Percy is glossing Kierkegaard who identifies the "salient feature of irony" as the "subjective freedom that at all times has in its power the possibility of a beginning and is not handicapped by earlier situations. There is something seductive about all beginnings, because the subject is still free, and this is the enjoyment the ironist craves."[19] Having transcended all human limitations, Soze does not "crave" anything; the freedom of the ironist is his rightful possession.

Characters such as Soze constitute a logical terminus in the fusion of neo-*noir* with nihilism. But the surge in aristocratic nihilism is not the only possible route for neo-*noir*. Even where neo-*noir* approximates to nihilism, as in the remarkable films *Chinatown* and *Taxi Driver*, it need not degenerate into self-indulgent parody of *noir*. Instead these films recur to classic religious myths of nature under a curse (*Chinatown*) or to visions of modern society as embodying what James Naremore calls a "Dostoyevskian nightmare of the soul" (*Taxi Driver*).[20] But these films constitute less a revival of the pre-modern conception of the quest than an evisceration of it. They also mimic Nietzsche's conception of art as offering a veiled apprehension of the chaos underlying the Apollonian surface of events. But these films can hardly be said to cover over much of anything; instead, they take us inexorably into the chaos and leave us with no prospect for the revivification of culture through art. Is it any wonder that, in such a context, artists might turn to celebrating the artistic prowess of demonic superheroes?

5

Sci-Fi Noir

F ROM *THE TERMINATOR* TO *AI*, from philosophical debates about whether terms such as "soul" and "consciousness" should be relegated to "folk psychology," to political debates over the ethics of cloning, preoccupation with the nature and implications of technology shapes both low and high culture in contemporary America. In the enormously popular and influential *The Matrix* (1999), the concerns and interests of low and high culture merge. Before it succumbs to the temptations of the comic book superhero genre, *The Matrix* echoes a number of *noir* themes. Both in its plot and its philosophical musings, *The Matrix* draws upon themes and debates that predate the current fascination with technology and artificial intelligence. It also stands in a tradition of futuristic films, many of the most important of which merit the *noir* label. Films such as *Terminator*, *Blade Runner*, and *Dark City* introduce a host of *noir* elements into the sci-fi genre.

Although not as clearly a *noir* film as some other science fiction movies, *The Matrix* contains a number of *noir* themes and offers explicit reflection on the philosophical themes at the heart of sci-fi neo-*noir*. These sci-fi *noirs* replay debates about Enlightenment modernity, debates with which we have become familiar in our investigation of *noir*.[1] The Enlightenment commitment to the mastery of nature through technological progress risks the degradation of humanity, just as an imprudent celebration of individual freedom paradoxically courts a homogenization of all mankind. In these and other ways, liberal modernity is seen as a potential source of nihilism, a human existence devoid of any ultimate purpose or fundamental meaning, where the great tasks of inquiry and the animating quests that inspired humanity in previous ages cease to register in the human soul.

The very notion of a soul (as indicative of a source of animation, of what lives and dies, rather than simply functioning and then ceasing to function) becomes problematic. The quest in sci-fi *noir* aims not simply at the solution of a particular crime or at the discovery of a set of individual identities, but at what, if anything, distinguishes human from machine. The threat of the eclipse of the human by the world of machines predates the rise of modern technology. The coincidence of human and machine follows from the materialistic assumptions of Hobbes's philosophy, according to which man is a machine and human life but a motion of limbs. In spite of Hobbes's attempt to construct a political science upon this assumption, it is at odds not only with naïve human beliefs about the differences between humans and machines but also with Enlightenment assumptions about the dignity and individuality of human persons. Most contemporary sci-fi or futuristic *noir*s struggle with the question of the distinctiveness of human persons, with the theoretical and practical threats of so-called artificial intelligence.

The *noir* sci-fi author and amateur philosopher, P. K. Dick, upon whose stories the films *Blade Runner* and *Minority Report* are based, examines the steadily vanishing gap between the human and the artificial: "Within the universe there exist fierce cold things, which I have given the names of 'machines' to. Their behavior frightens me, especially when it imitates human behavior so well that I get the uncomfortable sense that these things are trying to pass themselves off as human but are not. . . . The greatest change growing across our world these days is probably the momentum of the living towards reification, and at the same time the reciprocal entry into animation by the mechanical. We hold now no pure categories of the living versus the non-living."[2]

In this way, contemporary sci-fi neo-*noirs* make explicit and prominent themes that remained mostly implicit and marginal in classic *noir*: The machine-like character of human life, action, and desire in the modern world, especially in the modern city. Classic *noir* exhibits a fascination with the technology of the city, its mammoth, imposing buildings obscuring the sun, its pervasive concrete eliminating the last vestiges of natural plant life, and its reliance for human communication on artifacts such as the automobile and the telephone. Classic *noir* also underscores the mechanical, deterministic nature of human desire; machine language—"gears meshing" and "traveling straight down the line to the cemetery"—pervades *Double Indemnity*.

Sci-fi neo-*noir* exacerbates classic *noir*'s sense of entrapment in a technological dystopia. Recent films also focus on the political dimensions of the technological dystopia and on the potential link between technology and totalitarian politics. In this respect, sci-fi continues the dialectic of enlightenment and nihilism that I discussed previously. With remarkable perspicacity, Camus saw a link between Sade's radical politics of enlightenment and the common, modern aspiration for absolute freedom under the sway of reason: "Sade's success in our day is explained by the dream that he had in common with contemporary thought: the demand for total freedom and dehumanization coldly planned by the intelligence."[3] Thus does a radical strain of modernity press toward an apocalyptic reversal: enlightenment gives way to darkness, freedom to slavery, and an artificial civilization to the "desert of the real."

The ominous and disorienting sense that through technology human beings have created a world that is now beyond their control is never far from the *noir* film. One of the chief tasks imposed upon the protagonists in sci-fi films is to distinguish the world of machines from that of humans. Various candidates stand out as possible distinguishing marks of the human, the most popular of which is feeling or passion. As J. P. Telotte writes in *The Science Fiction Film*, sci-fi films tend "to lodge a sense of our humanity in feelings, passion, desire—and not in the atmosphere of reason and science that would seem to dominate the world of science fiction."[4] But this proposal, which smacks of nineteenth-century romanticism's reactionary recoiling from enlightenment reason, is not true to the experience of the viewer. Even mildly artistic science fiction engages our emotions and demands that we explore the emotional geography of the story. But it also engages our intellects. The mystery or crisis the science fiction film presents to us requires a strategic response and thus calls upon the full engagement of our rational capacities.

The enduring problem for science fiction is how to capture the distinctively human without allowing technology to set the terms of the debate. However much they might decry the degradation caused by technology, human heroes in sci-fi films sometimes achieve victory by the use of the most technologically advanced heavy artillery available. Critics worry that the genre ends up succumbing to the human nemesis, technology itself. Given the emphasis in these films on special effects and on occasionally the superhero as the one who masters the technological resources in such a way as to restore humans to their place of superiority over machines, critics such as Susan Sontag have worried that science fiction's peculiar mode of arousing and allaying our anxieties inculcates a "strange apathy."[5]

In their recent book, *The Myth of the American Superhero*, John Lawrence and Robert Jewett develop this line of criticism. The authors detect a pervasive myth in American popular culture, a myth that surfaces in the science fiction film. The monomyth, as they call it, is replete with dangerous, anti-democratic messages. The reliance upon a superhero as a rival to corrupt institutions implicitly fosters a "spectator democracy." Sensing the pointlessness of democratic institutions, citizens await the intervention of a "chosen one." Lawrence and Jewett are highly critical of this recurring allegory, which they think embodies a simplistic dualism of good and evil, a naïve faith in human heroes endowed with miraculous powers, and an affirmation of violence as the only effective means of purging society of evil. Underscoring the failure of the Enlightenment to demythologize modernity, the monomyth offers redemption, not through divine agency, but through "superhuman agencies." The monomyth denies the "tragic complexities of human life"; "it forgets that every gain entails a loss, that extraordinary benefits exact requisite costs, and that injury is usually proportionate to the amount of violence employed."[6] In its purest form, the monomyth revives a gnostic conception of human life, which advocates the transcendence of the material world through secret knowledge and celebrates the internal, spiritual journey of the hero.

As perceptive as the critics of the genre are, it is not clear that all sci-fi films fit neatly into the same paradigm or that they are equally susceptible to the same critique. Indeed, science fiction films tend to be the most thought-provoking films coming out of Hollywood; this is in large part because they present the audience with a set of puzzles or questions to be pondered or solved. At their best, they offer a critique of one form of reason in favor of another, the latter of which is the sort operative in the solving of a murder mystery, rather than in the planning of a highly structured bureaucracy. As one of the main characters in *Invasion of the Body Snatchers* (1956) puts it, we need to "stop trying to rationalize everything . . . we have a mystery on our hands." Moreover, sci-fi films often revive the ancient notion of human life as a quest whose success depends on the practice of certain virtues such as truthfulness, courage, loyalty, and friendship. Some sci-fi films even invoke religious conceptions of the quest and theological interpretations of the human condition, though in doing so, they sometimes fall prey to the gnostic temptation to denigrate the body and limiting conditions of the material world. In the post-apocalyptic world of science fiction, there is a desperate desire to uncover or recover a code by which to interpret human experience and in light of which we might guide our actions. Larry Wachowski's description of what informed the making of *The Matrix* is instructive: "We are interested in mythology, theology, and to a lesser extent, higher-level mathematics . . . All are ways human beings try to answer bigger questions, as well as The Big Question. If you're going to do epic stories, you should concern yourself with those issues. . . . We want to make people think, engage their minds a bit."[7] It is striking how neatly certain science fiction films, including *Dark City* and *The Matrix*, invest sci-fi plots not only with *noir* themes but also with the motif of a quest for a lost code of human redemption.

BLADE RUNNER

Before the philosophically ambitious *Dark City* and *The Matrix*, *The Terminator* and *Blade Runner* established the contours of the modern, neo-*noir* sci-fi film. If *The Matrix* marks the high point in contemporary popular culture's fascination with the issues of sci-fi neo-*noir*, *The Terminator* represents the beginning. With its flashing neon sign hanging above the bar, "TECHNOIR" is the name of the dance club where Sarah Connor (Linda Hamilton) has her first confrontation with her nemesis (the murderous, conscienceless cyborg) and her friend and guide (Kyle Reese, a human fighter in the rebellion against the machine domination of humanity). Both have traveled from the future to try to make certain that one possible future, rather than another, becomes actual. Just as the cyborg tries to shoot her, Reese shoots him, grabs Sarah, and pleads with her, "Come with me if you want to live."

Echoing upon the classic *noir* theme of the "wrong man," an incredulous Sarah says, "This is a mistake. I haven't done anything." Reese responds, "No, but you will. It's very important that you live." Reese's statement points up a peculiar twist in futuristic *noir*, a shift in accent from the past to the future. In classic *noir*, the past bears down on the present to circumscribe, if not eliminate, human freedom; the future of the main character in *noir* is often already determined by his past. In *Terminator*, by contrast, it is the future, which in a sense is already past, that bears down on the present and limits one's options. Here Reese explains to Sarah that a choice she will make in the future is currently bearing down on her, limiting her options and demanding that she face harsh realities previously inconceivable to her.

He then explains that what attacked her is not a man but a machine, a terminator, an updated version of a cyborg whose interior machinery is covered by living tissue that makes detection extremely difficult. The machine has no emotion, "no pity or remorse," and "can't be bargained with." He then recounts that at some time in the near future, the US government will come up with the ultimate defense system, a "network of computers trusted to run it all." At some point the computers become "intelligent" and come to see "all humans as threats not just those on the other side." Reese grew up in the post war future, "in the ruins," where the machines have created massive camps for the "easy disposal" of human beings.

The opening of *Terminator*, set in Los Angeles in 2029, gives a glimpse of America in the not too distant future. The city itself is a graveyard, a field of human skulls, reminiscent of certain footage made by liberating soldiers of the Holocaust. A written narrative tells viewers that "machines arose from the ashes of nuclear fire" to begin a "war to exterminate mankind," a war that "raged for decades." The "final battle" will occur, however, not in the future but "here in our present tonight," an evening in 1984. The opening underscores peculiar features of futuristic *noir* films. Prominent among these is a variation on the *Frankenstein* plot wherein humanity's preoccupation with technological progress backfires and engenders the possibility of the destruction of the human race. Mankind's hubris, its ambition to control all things, fuels the construction of ever more sophisticated and deadly technological instruments; eventually the conditions are set for the creation to rebel against its creator. In this case, a nuclear holocaust has apparently animated the world of machines and altered the conditions of evolution. Here the central preoccupations of the modern horror genre converge with those of sci-fi neo-*noir*.

Los Angeles' urban wasteland is also the setting for a battle between machines (replicants) and humans in *Blade Runner*. In its focus on a jaded, anguished detective whose pursuit of lawbreakers takes him through a variety of external, architectural mazes and an internal labyrinth of his own identity, *Blade Runner* is the quintessential tech-*noir*. Set in the year 2019, in the darkest of dark cities, where the brightest lights on the horizon are neon Coca Cola billboards. Even the interiors of buildings are dimly lit and mostly vacant. A giant eye, increasing the sense of claustrophobia and paranoia, watches over the city's inhabitants. The entire city is recycled, trashy, and utterly artificial; having used artifice to exploit nature, artifice itself is now void of beauty and meaning.

The earth is no longer a home; a floating zeppelin promotes a "new life" on an "off-world colony." Having destroyed earth's natural environment, humans have set off to exploit another planet. The Tyrell Corporation has created replicants, "virtually identical to humans," for use as slaves in off-world colonies. In the *Frankenstein* theme that runs through the film, six of the replicants have engaged in a mutiny and returned to earth.

The replicants were created to copy humans in everything except emotions; they perform numerous functions for human beings, including in some cases acting as "pleasure models." There is now a fear that they may be developing emotional capacities. Their successful rebellion against humans indicates not only that they are clever and powerful, but also that they have some sense of injustice. Moreover, if they are returning to meet their makers, then they also have an awareness of themselves as machines. To limit any possible threat the new machines might pose, they have been given only a four-year lifespan. In the meantime, humans have established a police squad of "blade runners," whose task is to seek and destroy renegade replicants. They call this operation, not execution, but retirement.

The film begins with a government investigator examining the "next subject," Leon. The tests are designed to provoke an "emotional response." During the course of the test, Leon becomes increasingly testy. When asked to recall a "good thing . . . about his mother," he balks, pulls a gun, and kills the investigator. In the next scene, we meet Deckard or Dex (Harrison Ford), a former blade runner, who is now being called back into service. Morose and indifferent, Dex is a throwback to the hard-boiled detectives of Raymond Chandler, according to director Ridley Scott. Persuaded to rejoin the force, Dex visits Tyrell and tries out the test for distinguishing human from replicant on Rachael (Sean Young), one of Tyrell's employees. In the course of the test, Rachael asks Dex whether he has "ever retired a human by mistake," to which he responds negatively. After the test, Dex tells Tyrell, "she's a replicant" and asks incredulously, "How can it not know what it is?" This is one of many ironic foreshadowings in the film, which returns repeatedly to the elusiveness of self-knowledge. Also introduced during the early visit to the Tyrell Corporation is the problematic status of memory in a constructed world, the very problem with which *Dark City* wrestles. As Tyrell explains, one of the reasons replicants think they are human is that they have been supplied "with a past, a cushion for the emotions." An astonished Dex replies, "Memories, you're talking memories."

The corporation has supplanted the government and turned everything into a commodity, to such a degree that it has become quite difficult to discern creator from creation, producer from product. As Tyrell puts it, "commerce is our good." The corporate motto is "more human than human." The world of *Blade Runner* represents the final stage in what P. K. Dick calls "the momentum of the living towards reification and at the same time the reciprocal entry into animation by the mechanical."

Meanwhile, Rachael visits Dex and protests that she is not a replicant. She supports her claim by producing a collection of family photos.

In a rather cruel analysis, Dex flips through the pictures, then lists her memories and concludes that these memories are "implants, not yours but somebody else's." Rachael weeps and thus exhibits the sort of emotional response once thought to be the peculiar prerogative of human beings. A remorseful Dex tries to retract his analysis by stating that he was just joking. Once he is alone, he sits down at his piano, on which stand his own family photographs. He plays the piano and then drifts off into a sort of "reverie" during which he has a dream of a unicorn in a lush green landscape, an image that stands out in a film void of rural, natural settings. This is one of the few moments in the film that suggests a possible return to the natural over the constructed, innocence over corruption, a hope that the ending of the film mercilessly snatches away.

After a gun battle with replicants, Rachael and Dex are back at his apartment, where Rachael asks Dex whether he will hunt her if she runs away. He assures her that he will not. In a note of reciprocity between blade runner and replicant, he acknowledges, "I owe you one." At this point he moves from facing her to standing beside her and just behind her; for a fleeting moment Dex's eyes glow, just as Rachael's and those of the other replicants had done numerous times before. In this way, Scott gives the attentive viewer a clue to the identity of Dex, a clue that will be confirmed at the end of the film. The film actually reinforces this suggestion immediately, as Rachael asks him whether he's ever taken the replicant identity test. Then, repeating his actions, she examines his pictures and sits at the piano to play. The scene ends with Dex and Rachael in a passionate embrace.

After a lengthy battle scene with a rebel replicant, Dex meets Gaff, a seemingly all-knowing Chinaman who makes tiny tin foil origami figures. He asks Dex, "I guess you're through?" "Finished," Dex admits. Aware of his affection for Rachael, Gaff states, "It's just too bad she won't live, but then again who does?" Dex meets Rachael and the two of them exchange promises of love and trust; just as they are about to depart, Dex discovers an origami figure of a unicorn and immediately recalls Gaff's words, "It's just too bad she won't live, but then again who does?" Dex pauses for a moment, nods knowingly and then heads off to escape with Rachael.

The ending confirms what the careful viewer may have suspected for some time, namely, that Dex is himself a replicant. How else to account for Gaff's knowledge of Dex's private dream reverie of the unicorn? This ending is from the Director's Cut, released some ten years after the original film hit theaters; the original contained a number of elements, including a Dex voiceover, eliminated from the Director's Cut. The most significant change has to do with the ending. The theatrical release avoided the confirming evidence of Dex's replicant status and added a happy ending, a scene of Rachael and Dex together in a wooded refuge. The ending of the Director's Cut is more in keeping with the film's desultory mood and tone of impending doom. The film recasts classic *noir* themes in a sci-fi context, themes about limitation, loss, the fleeting experience of love and self-knowledge. Its suggestion that the unanticipated resolution of the private investigator's quest is the realization that he is identical in nature to the enemy he had been pursuing throughout is vintage *noir*, a tragedy of the ordinary man. Or so it seems.

P. K. Dick's worry about the encroachment of the machine and the vanishing of man resurfaces here and presses upon the viewer the following questions. What is the appropriate response to the revelation that Dex is not human but a replicant? Is it shock and a shudder of horror? If so, what is the basis of this reaction? Clearly it involves surprise at Dex's ignorance and absence of self-knowledge; it also involves the realization that Dex himself belongs to the very category of beings he had pursued and ruthlessly executed. But does it involve more than this? Does it involve a horror at the fusion of the human and the machine? Or terror in the face of our inability to discern any surface difference between the mechanical and the natural? If so, what should we make of our response? Does it put us in a tragic bind, where we continue to search for a difference that we are confident must exist? Or is it just an infantile delusion about the grandeur of our own species? An irrational narcissism? *Blade Runner* provokes, but leaves unanswered, these questions.

In its tone, atmosphere, plot, and ending, *Blade Runner* is perhaps the most *noir* film in the sci-fi canon. Its chief competition is *Dark City*, a less well-known film with spectacular *noir* visuals and a plot that anticipates *The Matrix*. Its opening voiceover informs us that at first there was only "darkness," but then came the Strangers, a "race as old as time itself." The Strangers mastered the "ultimate technology," the ability to "alter reality by will alone." They call this ability "tuning." But their race is dying and, in search of a "cure for mortality," they traveled the universe, eventually discovering human beings. As he speaks, the camera descends into the dark city, with its strong, imposing vertical buildings, around which there are only narrow passages, grids that cars traverse in a robotic fashion.

As we see a clock ticking toward midnight, everything suddenly stops, with all human beings now asleep. This is followed by a series of shots, first an overhead shot of eyes opening, then an off-angle shot of a lamp swinging in a pendulum motion. Then a man with a trickle of blood on his forehead awakens in a tub, emerges, and knocks over a gold fish. He quickly scoops up the fish and puts it in water, finds a key, a suitcase, and a post card of Shell Beach. The man receives a phone call from a Dr. Schreber (Kiefer Sutherland), whose nervous, halting voice is recognizably that of the opening voiceover. The doctor urges him to leave immediately because the Strangers are on their way to capture him. As he talks on the phone, the man notices a naked, dead girl, whose body is decorated with a nautilus design, on the floor of the apartment. As he departs room 614, he flees an approaching group of men and hurries down the steps. In the hotel lobby, the desk clerk calls him Mr. Murdoch (Rufus Sewell) and tells him he left his wallet in an automat. At the automat, Murdoch retrieves his wallet; on his way out of the building, cops eye him suspiciously and interrogate him until a stunning blond intervenes and distracts the police. The woman, a prostitute, escorts him to her apartment, where she undresses, as he searches his wallet and discovers his name is John. He remarks that her profession "seems dangerous" and leaves without having sex with her. Back on the street, he sees a billboard ad for Shell Beach, and then has his first battle with the Strangers, whom he surprises by his ability to counter their tuning with his own ability to tune. The strength of his opposition prompts an emergency strategy session in the underground cave of the Strangers, whose similarity to one another gives them a clone-like appearance.

As all this has been going on, two other plot lines have been developing. Dr. Schreber contacts John Murdoch's wife, Emma (Jennifer Connelly), to discuss John. She admits that she has not seen her husband in three weeks and that he left after learning of her affair. Schreber explains that John is suffering from amnesia and comments, "wherever he is, he's searching for himself." At the same time, Inspector Bumstead (William Hurt) arrives to investigate the murder of the girl, a prostitute, found in Murdoch's apartment, the sixth prostitute in a pattern of homicides whose signal is the nautilus design left on their naked bodies. But Bumstead wonders, ""what kind of killer stops to save a goldfish?"

When Murdoch meets his wife again, she explains that it was her affair that led to their separation. Uncertain about whether he could be the killer of the prostitute, he says he went to the apartment of the other prostitute to test himself, to find whether he was capable of such of act. He concludes that he doesn't know who he is, but "I'm still me and I'm not a killer." Emma says she believes him and, when Bumstead arrives and tells her move out of the way so they can arrest John, she blocks his path and John escapes. Bumstead comments, "No one ever listens to me." John makes his getaway in a cab, whose driver he asks about the route to Shell Beach. The driver recalls with enthusiasm his own trips to the seaside locale, begins to give directions, and then cannot remember the last few roads.

A similar case of forgetfulness afflicts Bumstead's colleague on the police force; Walenski has been driven to near madness by one of his cases. When Bumstead visits his home, he finds him drawing circles and nautilus figures frantically over all the walls in his house, mumbling about the past, about how there's "no way out." He asks Bumstead whether he thinks about the past, to which Bumstead responds indifferently, "As much as the next guy." Walenski has clearly been doing a lot of thinking about the past, thinking that quickly reaches an impasse. It is as if "I've just been dreaming this life, that I'll wake up and be somebody else, somebody totally different." Trapped in an incomprehensible maze whose comprehension is nonetheless his obsession, Walenski is a character straight out of classic *noir*, whose quest for knowledge brings him ever closer to self-destruction.

We are gradually informed about the odd relationship between the Strangers and Dr. Schreber, a human whose knowledge of medicine and of humanity has made him useful to the Strangers. The Strangers are performing experiments on humans, imprinting them nightly with a different set of memories to discover the key to the human soul and to human individuality. Schreber explains that Murdoch resisted the imprint. Later, Schreber, speaking before the underground assembly of Strangers, taunts them: "weren't you looking for the human soul? Perhaps you found what you were looking for and now it's going to bite you." This is one of many interesting twists in *Dark City*, a film that uses creatively the resources of two traditions, sci-fi and *noir*. Here the novelty consists in the reversal of the *noir* trap; Schreber warns that the one in control of the maze, the Strangers, will end up ensnared themselves.

When the Strangers finally catch up with Murdoch, they offer further explanation of their plan. The Stranger boasts, "we made the city."

They have been using "stolen memories," which they have "revised and refined" to try "to learn what makes" someone "human." In a final boast, the Stranger proclaims, "we use your dead as vessels."

By the end of the film, Bumstead, Schreber, and Murdoch are working together to solve the mystery of Shell Beach, in search of which they head in a tiny canoe through the canals of the city. Just at the point in an ordinary action film where one would expect a violent, high-speed car chase, *Dark City* gives us a boat ride, during which the characters learn from Dr. Schreber about the extent to which human history is now a construct of the machinations of the Strangers. We now learn that the dark city is not the natural or original home of human beings. "The Strangers abducted us and brought us here." All human beings have now had "dozens" of lives and the originals have been permanently erased. In an example that touches directly upon Murdoch's fate, Schreber states, "Will a man with the history of a killer continue" along this path or "are we more than the sum of our memories?" The Strangers are interested in the soul, the "key to individuality" because they have "one group mind" with "collective memories." So the recent decline of the species is a decline for all at once.

Their aversions, Schreber explains, include not only water but also light. So foreign is human individuality to their kind that they "needed the help of an artist" to assist them in "understanding the intricacies of the human mind." Schreber is that artist. The Strangers forced him to erase all his memories except for those related to his skills as a doctor. Murdoch asks, "What about me?" Schreber replies, "Your entire history is an illusion." Bumstead asks, "They brought us here, from where?" Schreber says no one can remember what we "once were . . . or might have been . . . somewhere else." This is a hyperbolic form of a classic *noir* dilemma, a dilemma that thrusts us into the crisis of radical post-modernism, which repudiates the existence of an original or exemplar in light of which we might understand images. The situation of Murdoch and Schreber calls to mind a vertiginous statement from Derrida: "a mirror of a mirror . . . a reference without a referent, without any first or last unit."[8]

Schreber's comments about the impossibility of retrieving the past, of distinguishing original from copy, or false from true memories would seem to undercut the very possibility of the quest. The film at once confirms this nihilistic conclusion and veers away from its paralyzing implications. The quest is indeed stymied, just as the trio eventually reaches the sign for Shell Beach, the goal of their search. The sign is just a poster over a thick wall of bricks. They begin to hammer away at the wall as the Strangers arrive with Emma as a hostage. Breaking through the wall brings a shocking discovery of empty, dark space, into which Bumstead and a Stranger fall and float away. The city is but an island floating aimlessly through space, with no hope of return to a natural homeland or of a resolution to the question of whether there is any trustworthy set of memories that might guide human life.

The scene calls to mind a chilling aphorism of Pascal: "the silence of these infinite spaces fills me with dread."[9] Intent on a happy ending for humanity, *Dark City* has no time for dread; instead, it devotes its energies to the celebration of the powers of the super-human intellect and the quasi-divine creative imagination.

When the Strangers threaten to harm Emma, Murdoch surrenders. He is taken to the underground, where the parasitic Strangers demand that Schreber imprint their collective memories into Murdoch. Instead, Schreber switches the memories and imprints Murdoch with the remainder of the life history—a purely constructed life history, it is important to note. These memories include an education concerning Murdoch's crucial role in liberating humanity from the Strangers. Part of the imprint contains instructions from Schreber. You can find "strength within yourself and prevail." You can "take control of their machine" and rule them. The "world can be what you make it" so long as you "concentrate." Murdoch does just that and, in the climactic battle scene, his tuning skills prove superior to those of the Strangers.

After the battle, Murdoch learns that Emma, having been reprinted, is now "Anna," and her previous memories are irrevocably lost. Deprived of their position of superiority, the Strangers now coexist with humans. In a conversation with one of them, Murdoch points to his head and comments, "you went looking . . . in the wrong place" for the key to the human soul. In its elevation of the heart over the head, *Dark City* calls to mind the classic film, *Metropolis*, directed by German expressionist filmmaker and former architect, Fritz Lang, an émigré who went on to make a number of seminal *noir* films. Resemblances can also be detected in the structure of the city itself and in the central theme of a battle between individualism and collectivism. *Metropolis* is a worker's city, under the power of Moloch. The workers seek inspiration from a woman named Maria, whom they honor with a sort of religious devotion. Maria promotes peace and brings to the workers the revolutionary teaching that the heart is the necessary mediator between the brain that plans and the hand that builds. By inference, we can see that the hierarchical class structure of *Metropolis* moves without mediation between the brain of the ruling class and the hands of the workers. Meanwhile, the son of the leader of the ruling class witnesses the poor conditions of the workers and complains to his father, from whom the son becomes increasingly estranged.

Worried that Maria is fomenting a dangerous rebellion among the workers, the leader kidnaps her and orders the construction of an artificial Maria who preaches a message of violent uprising. The message will supply the leader with an excuse to put down the uprising and institute an even more totalitarian system of government. A mob mentality grows among the workers and they begin to destroy even their own members. But the real Maria manages to escape, to defuse the violence, and to reconcile father and son, ruler and worker. She does all this through the implementation of her teaching about the mediating role of the heart. This was the feature of Lang's film that received the most derisive response from critics when it was released, with H. G. Wells excoriating its "silly clichés and platitudes."

At the end of *Dark City*, Murdoch uses his tuning ability to refashion the city according to his own desires and designs. He makes water flow and brings sunshine and a glorious coastal vista. At the end of an ocean pier, he meets Anna (Emma), introduces himself, and they walk off together in the direction of the freshly created Shell Beach. The ending of the film is on surer ground in its symbolism than its plot. At the symbolic level, the film suggests that humanity is distinguished by its relationship to a natural world, to water, to sunlight, and to an organic pattern of birth and growth. The quest for Shell Beach represents the drive to recover a connection to water and sun, the sources of birth and life. The spiral growth pattern of the nautilus shell, an image of which is drawn on the bodies of murdered girls in the opening of the film and which covers the walls of Walenski's home office, permeates nature and art; the logarithmic spiral or the golden section points to a universal intelligibility in the growth of natural beings and beckons humans to recover some sort of natural order.

The prominence of water, especially as the setting for Murdoch's liberation from the control of the aliens, suggests a level of religious symbolism in the film. Much like Neo (Keanu Reeves) in *The Matrix*, John, who bears a significant Christian name, is a sort of messiah figure, the one chosen to lead his people out of tyranny and into freedom. But the Christian symbols here seem to register a gnostic vision, in which pure knowledge enables select individuals to overcome the limits of the mortal body and become quasi-divine. The film's concluding scenes accentuate Murdoch's ability to "concentrate hard enough," an ability that has to do exclusively with the mind and thus to belie Murdoch's claim that the Strangers were looking in the wrong place when they sought to mimic human intelligence. The ending forgets the tragic lesson of Walenski, the character destroyed by his quest for his knowledge. Murdoch represents, not so much a reaffirmation of the human, as a transcendence of it, especially of its fragile and vulnerable bodily condition. Cynthia Freeland's criticisms of *The Matrix*, to which we shall turn shortly, seem equally trenchant with respect to *Dark City*. Both films suggest "that humans need not be bound by their physical bodies. The movie feeds escapist fantasies of a mental reality where the elect few are unencumbered by rules."[10]

On one level, the film disavows the possibility of a return to childhood, a repudiation that is evident both in the scene where Murdoch realizes that the filmstrip his uncle shows is "all lies" and in the depiction of the child Stranger as the most sinister of the Strangers. Yet, on another level, it affirms a rather naïve conception of free spontaneity. What Murdoch constructs at the end is less a return to something real, distinct from what has been constructed for him, than a version of wish fulfillment. Recall Schreber's words: "the world can be what you make it so long as you concentrate." Well, why this world rather than another? In light of what does one create? Murdoch is forced to create out of fragments that have been constructed for him. The ending wallows in an optimistic and self-congratulatory existentialism, the sort of shallow existentialism that Porfiro, in a famous essay, inaccurately applied to classic *noir*. In "No Way Out: Existential Motifs in Film *Noir*," he argued that what halts the encroaching nihilism in *noir* is the "experience of freedom," in which human beings "literally create good and evil."[11] The problem with the ending of the film, as with Porfirio's thesis, is that it fails to come to terms with the Nietzschean analysis of nihilism, with the deep incompatibility between freedom understood as unfettered autonomy, on the one hand, and morality or dignity, on the other. As Nietzsche trenchantly observed, once freedom is liberated from all external constraints, there is no basis for distinguishing between better and worse, noble and base, or even between free and unfree.

Once again, neo-*noir* finds its way back to aristocratic nihilism, veiled from us here by Murdoch's apparently good intentions. There remains a huge gap between the superhero Murdoch and the rest of ignorant humanity, including Emma-Anna. Humanity remains under the control of a sort of dictator, but this time an apparently benevolent one. The capacity for superhuman, intellectual creation is distinctive not of humans but of the Strangers, who call this ability the "ultimate technology." The film thus suffers a devastating philosophical lapse at the end. The filmmakers appear to be utterly oblivious to the incoherence at the heart of their plot. Superhero wish fulfillment undermines the possibility of a consistent, *noir* narrative. In this respect, as in others, *Dark City* anticipates the mythic universe of the *Matrix*.

THE MATRIX

It is a mark of the thoughtfulness of films such as *Blade Runner, Dark City*, and especially *The Matrix* that they call to mind some of the most astute philosophical analyses of the tragic dilemma of humanity in a technological utopia. Consider, for example, the reflections of the Russian novelist, Dostoevsky, whose *Notes from Underground* anticipates many of the issues addressed in sci-fi films.[12] *Notes*, a work in which Nietzsche claimed he could hear "the voice of blood," is a satirical diatribe against a certain strain of western Enlightenment thought that had begun to infiltrate Russia. An amalgam of humanitarian socialism, romanticism, utilitarianism, and rational egoism, N.G. Chernyshevsky's *What is to be Done?* is the target of Dostoevsky's polemics. Chernyshevsky's text, which Lenin credited with reinforcing his own revolutionary propensities, develops the utopian ideas of the French socialist, Fourier.[13] Dostoevsky's underground man rails against the utopianism of the Enlightenment designers of the modern city, who claim that their applied social science will enable them to tabulate, regulate, and satisfy every human longing. In a protest against the "rational" reconstruction of society, the underground man opts to live in his sordid underground cell. The underground man suffers from a paralyzing hyperconsciousness. Whereas the "healthy man of action" sees no difficulty with the laws of nature as applied to human life (indeed he finds them consoling), the overly conscious individual realizes the incompatibility between the mechanical determinism of natural science, on the one hand, and human deliberation and choice, on the other. The hyperconscious individual confronts the "stone wall" of the laws of natural science and the result is psychic "inertia."[14] He expounds: "Science itself will teach man ... that in fact he has neither will nor caprice...and that he himself is nothing but a sort of piano key ... ; and that, furthermore, there also exist in the world the laws of nature; so that whatever he does is done not at all according to his own wanting, but ... according to the laws of nature."[15]

The goal of social science is to establish a logarithm for human desire and choice and to predict the future course of human life. Thus, there will "no longer be any actions or adventures in the world."[16] Given this conception of science and of what is considered rational, the underground man's protests can be nothing but negative, a repudiation of reason, health, and science in the name of an irrational freedom. So he opts for passivity over action, isolation over community, and spite over the rational pursuit of happiness. But even this is self-defeating; as he notes, the "spite in me (according to the laws of nature) undergoes a chemical breakdown."

To the attentive reader, however, the underground man offers more than a dark negation of Enlightenment social science. He points out contradictions inherent in the Enlightenment project. The chief contradiction, the one that preoccupies the underground man and is the source of his unrelenting and paralyzing dialectic, concerns freedom. Enlightenment theorists promise liberation from various types of external authority: familial, religious, and political. But an unintended consequence of the implementation of Enlightenment theories is the elimination of freedom. How does this happen? One source of the elimination of freedom is the method of the nascent social sciences, which admit as real only what is verifiable according to the criteria of mathematical-mechanical natural science. Another source is Enlightenment naïvete about the ease with which theory can be translated into practice. The implementation of the theory requires both the correction of human nature and the radical restructuring of society; thus is the compulsory and violent nature of the project made clear.

The gap between theory and practice evinces a deeper difficulty with the Enlightenment project. In attempting to detect and regulate human desires, in treating man as a rational egoist, Enlightenment theorists have miscalculated. They suppose that what profits a human being is transparent to rational scrutiny and that all evil will diminish with education and political reorganization. But they overlook not only the fact that increased violence and desire for blood often accompany so-called progress in civilization but also that human beings have a deeper sort of desire, a desire for "truly independent willing." To exhibit their own freedom, the underground man insists, they will deliberately choose that which is harmful and self-destructive. Here the underground man anticipates Nietzsche's claim that human beings would "rather will nothing than not will." As is often the case in Nietzsche, so too in *Notes From Underground*, nihilism is not an end in itself but a protest or preparatory moment. Negation, it is hoped, will give way to affirmation. Thus the underground man confesses that he does not want to remain an "anti-hero" who merely inverts and rejects the theories of his contemporaries. It is "not at all the underground that is better, but something different, completely different, which I thirst for but cannot ever find. Devil take the underground."[17]

The paralysis, spite, and nihilism that the underground man embodies are not alternatives to Enlightenment theory; on the contrary, they are its logical consequences. As he taunts his opponents at the very end: "I have merely carried to an extreme in my life what you have dared to carry even halfway."[18] The pursuit of transparent understanding engenders blindness, as enlightenment progress breeds the *noir* anti-hero.

The Enlightenment, rationalist project raises questions that pervade sci-fi *noir*s, questions about what is real, what is human, and to what extent freedom and self-knowledge are possible. As the underground man describes it, the Enlightenment project for society is an extension of modern mathematical physics, based in the reductionistic assumption that whatever is real is susceptible to quantitative analysis. Given such assumptions, the problem of human freedom and self-knowledge becomes acute. A related problem informs the openings scenes of *The Matrix*. As Morpheus (Laurence Fishburne) comments in one of his first conversations with Neo, "we're inside a computer program" where you have only a "residual self-image." He then asks, "How do you define the real? . . . electronic signals interpreted by the brain." The world of the Matrix is a world of "neural interactive simulation." The "anatomizing of man," as Dostoevsky's underground man calls it, dissolves the very possibility of human self-knowledge.

Whether or not it is actually underground, the cramped Nebuchadnezzer has the same feel as the underground man's cell. With its technological gadgets and their capacity artificially to affect human consciousness, the ship, operating on a "pirate signal" that "hacks into the Matrix," is a lesser version of the Matrix itself. But it has neither the naïve, unreflective self-confidence enjoyed by the human constructs of the Matrix, nor the sense of omnipotence and autonomous control of the agents of the Matrix. Rooted in the "desert of the real," the rebel band struggles to ascertain clues about humanity's past, to gain a clearer understanding of what their task is in the present, and to recover a positive orientation toward the future.

Opting for the "desert of the real" over a constructed but more comfortable "reality" has its costs. There is, first, the unsettling fact that what one has taken to be real is in fact merely a fiction, that, as Morpheus explains, the "world has been pulled over your eyes to blind you to the truth," that you have been enslaved in the prison of "your own mind." Just as in Dostoevsky, here the false sense of freedom is accompanied by an illusory sense of our own unity, self-control and dominion over the future. A more adequate conception of freedom grows from a sense of uncertainty and internal division and leads to a more complex appreciation of humanity. Morpheus asks Neo whether he has not had the sense that "something is wrong in the world," a sense that you "cannot explain but feel." We must begin with a sense that something is awry, which, if investigated further, will initiate a quest. As Morpheus puts it, "it's the question that drives us—what is the Matrix? The answer is out there and it will find you if you want it to."

"The answer is out there" calls to mind "the truth is out there," the slogan of the popular and long-running television series, *The X-Files*. Although the central plotline of *The X-Files* concerns the control of the earth by alien rather than artificial intelligence, it shares much with *The Matrix*. Both stories play upon fears that some inscrutable and malevolent power—be it aliens, complex machines, the government, bureaucracy, or technology itself—has surreptitiously substituted a fictional world for the real world. But the situation is even worse than this, for the enslaving tyrant is not a clearly identifiable, external force, which we have only to identify and then find the means of eliminating. Instead, the power is exercised in and through us, constituting in large measure who and what we are. The great danger—the one that can naturally generate nihilism—is that, having lost our grip on the real, we shall forever wallow in a world of illusion. If there are not sufficient clues to find our way out of the constructed universe, we risk a debilitating psychic vertigo, a loss of any sense of who and what we are and where we're headed. In such a situation, a situation familiar to viewers of *noir* films, the investigation of the roots of our dilemma risks becoming a parody of the quest for truth. (It is significant that *The X-Files* couples "the truth is out there" with other slogans such as "trust no one" and "believe the lie".) As Adrienne MacLean puts it,

Scully and Mulder are literally and figuratively alienated, penetrated, and probed to the molecular level by omniscient and omnipotent forces who have infiltrated like television and, now, computers, virtually everything in our lives. . . . Scully and Mulder trust each other. . . . Yet everything they think they know is wrong. Television has taught them the arts of insight but not how to formulate a point of view. It has sent them on a quest for

identity, but taught them also never to trust what they find. . . .
The media-driven milieu of *The X-Files* suggests that the whole
world is now the same place, all of its accessible, all of it at once
sage, dangerous, restricting, liberating.[19]

Although MacLean's claim that the quest motif on *The X-Files* is
utterly fruitless is open to debate, her description nonetheless captures
a very real possibility for the show's characters. Given the similarities
in plot between *The X-Files* and *The Matrix*, the characters in the
film would seem vulnerable to the same fate as the characters on the
television show. Indeed, narratives that begin with such radical claims
about human alienation, about our inability to distinguish truth from
fiction, reality from the construction of a wily artifice, run two, diametrically opposed risks: that of never finding a way out of the trap
and that of offering superficial solutions, what the literary and cultural
critic Mark Edmundson calls modes of "facile transcendence."[20] Neither strategy overcomes nihilism: the former immerses us in it, while
the latter provides only the illusion of escape. How does *The Matrix*
fare on this score?

There is much evidence that the film wants to avoid these two
poles; its alternative path is especially evident in its treatment of the
issue of human freedom. The notion that our lives have been constructed for us is particularly irksome to our sense of freedom and
personal control. As Neo says in his response to Morpheus's question
about whether he believes in fate: "No . . . because then I wouldn't be
in control." That Neo is operating with an impoverished conception
of freedom is clear not only from this conversation with Morpheus
but also from the Oracle's gentle mocking of him on this issue. As he
prepares to leave her, she tells him he can forget the hard truths that
she has revealed to him: "You'll remember you don't believe in fate.
You're in control of your own life." But what Morpheus calls fate is
not the same as the elimination of freedom perpetrated by the Matrix. Morpheus's notion of fate eclipses the divide between a shallow conception of freedom as complete control over one's life and a

thoroughgoing determinism. In the references to Neo as the One for whom Morpheus has been searching all his life, there are suggestions that fate is actually a sort of providence. A prophecy of the Oracle, Morpheus explains, predicts the "return of a man who will be free of the Matrix." The relationship, however, between whatever powers of fate or providence may be operative and the power of human choice is left prudently understated. The best example of the film's ambiguity on this issue occurs in the scene where Cypher is about to "unplug" and thus kill Neo. He mockingly asserts that if Neo is the One, a miracle will disrupt his plans and keep Neo alive. Immediately, another member of the resistance kills Cypher.

Of course, very few ever entertain the paradoxes of freedom. Dostoevsky's underground man dwells on the contradictions of freedom in the utopian world, contradictions that the character Cypher embodies in *The Matrix*. In a pivotal sequence in the film, Cypher turns traitor and begins unplugging his colleagues in the resistance. When he is discovered, he admits that he is returning to the Matrix, that he's tired of doing what Morpheus tells him and that the Matrix is "more real." Morpheus himself has predicted that many are so "hopelessly dependent on the system that they'll fight to protect it." Cypher consciously chooses to relinquish willing, to abandon freedom for comfort, security, and an absence of struggle.

Morpheus explains that the Matrix is a "computer generated dream world" whose goal is to keep human beings "under control." Their project is to "change the human being into a battery." Here we find a striking parallel to the theorists satirized by Dostoevsky, who liken the human being to a "piano key," a reference Dostoevsky may well have derived from Denis Diderot, the French materialist Enlightenment philosopher. In 1769, Diderot wrote, "We are instruments endowed with sense and memory. Our senses are piano keys upon which surrounding nature plays, and which often play upon themselves."[21]

Later Agent Smith confirms and amplifies Morpheus's description of the Matrix's project. He speaks of the "billions of people just living . . . oblivious." Smith admits that the first Matrix design, which attempted to construct a human world devoid of suffering, was rejected by humans. He concedes one of the underground man's points, namely, the necessity of suffering for free beings. "Humans," Agent Smith observes, "define reality through misery and suffering." But Agent Smith and his cohorts share the utopian designers' view of natural, human life as an affliction, even an illness. As Smith puts it, "human beings spread like a virus . . . and we're the cure." This echoes the belief, which the underground man imputes to his enemies, that, in order to realize the dictates of reason, human nature itself must be corrected. Like all utopian theorists, Agent Smith has a naïve faith in progress. He states, "It's evolution, Morpheus, evolution; the future is our world."

Another parallel emerges concerning the absence of self-consciousness and self-knowledge. According to the underground man, the theorists deprive not only others but also themselves of self-knowledge. If they had any self-awareness, they too would be afflicted with inertia. Morpheus tells Neo, "the Matrix can't tell you who you are." Is there also the implication that a deficit of self-knowledge played some role in humanity's original act of hubris, which gave birth to artificial intelligence (AI) in the first place? In his description of the source of the Matrix, Morpheus strikes a note of utopianism: he relates that in the early twenty-first century "all humanity is united" and in unison creates AI.

In this, *The Matrix*'s depiction of humanity and its creation mimics the classic structure of the horror genre, with *Frankenstein* as prototype, where the creative ambitions of science generate a creature it cannot control and who turns against its maker. But in *The Matrix,* the creature, AI, having gained the upper hand, seems doomed to repeat the errors of humanity. The Matrix itself is now engaged in a utopian scheme of social reconstruction. What is the way out of this cycle?

The answer has much to do with complex conceptions of freedom that the character Neo moves toward in the course of the film. Yet it is on precisely this score that the conclusion of the film is highly ambiguous. Part of the problem is that in many ways *The Matrix* opts for the typical, Hollywood action-film ending, with the superhero taking on a slew of evildoers. Of course, the sophisticated technology of *The Matrix* renders its denouement more creative and more subtle than the ending of films in the *Die Hard* or *Terminator* genre. Still, the film has been rightly celebrated more for its special effects than its crafting of plot and character. As Neo comes to transcend the constraints of the ordinary human body and begins to exercise powers possessed by comic book superheroes, improved technique overshadows the quintessentially human traits that Neo has had to develop to prepare to wage war against the Matrix.

Until the final contest with the agents, Neo seems quite vulnerable, resisting and then only gradually accepting his role in the fate of humanity. Even when he elects to risk everything to battle against the Matrix, the outcome remains uncertain. In the pivotal fight with the Agent in the subway, he is shot and apparently dead. Trinity (Carrie-Anne Moss), revealing the Oracle's prophecy that she would fall in love with the One, insists, "you can't be dead because I love you." She kisses Neo, and when he revives, she chides him, "Now get up." Although we have had hints all along of a growing attachment between Neo and Trinity, the relationship is insufficiently developed to carry this sort of dramatic weight. And this is a serious flaw in the film. Why? The way to overcome the threat of nihilism in *The Matrix* is through the recovery of distinctively human traits and ways of living. Central among these traits is the sense of human beings as distinct individuals capable of loyalty, love, and sacrifice. Whereas the characters of Neo, Trinity, and Morpheus are complex, different, and complementary, the agents of the Matrix are impersonal, generic, and interchangeable. Is not this the significance of the name "Smith" for the agent who spends the most time on screen?

It is odd, however, that the human characters come increasingly to resemble the agents of the Matrix in crucial respects. They abandon ordinary human clothes for slick, black wetsuits and don the shades worn by agents. As in *Dark City*, the superhero's success at counteracting alien powers requires that he transcend the constraints and limitations of the human body. Once revived, Neo manifests super-human powers. He stops bullets and defies the rules of gravity; defying also the solidity of bodies, he dives inside an agent who then explodes. As Cynthia Freeland astutely notes, Neo, his cohorts, and fans of the film seem to have forgotten that Neo's actual body remains inertly hooked up to machines in the desert of the real. "Ideally, to be consistent, *The Matrix* ought to enable viewers to recognize and reject the seductive illusions of movies"; instead, the film "celebrates not freedom from the Matrix, but the indulgence in exciting filmic simulations. . . . We viewers are urged to escape illusions, but hypocritically so, by a film that works hard to seduce us with its own remarkable visions."[22]

Having won a crucial battle with the agents of the Matrix, Neo warns them that he will reveal all things to all people and then they will enter an uncertain and unpredictable world. As he puts it, "I know you're out there, afraid of us, afraid of change. I'm going to show them . . . then we'll have a world without you, without rules, without boarders, and without boundaries . . . where anything is possible. Where we go from there is a choice I leave to you." Here Neo ignores all sorts of complications: he underestimates not so much the continued opposition of the Matrix as the likely resistance of complacent, still-enslaved humans. The lesson of Cypher seems to have been forgotten. This raises certain pressing questions. Has the more complicated account of freedom that the film spends a good deal of time developing been sacrificed to a shallow conception of human freedom as autonomous self-creation? Does the film succumb to the facile transcendence criticized by Edmundson? Neo's prophecy echoes the situation of humanity, described by Morpheus, at the end of the twentieth century, when a united humanity emjoyed its peak of creativity and gave birth to artificial intelligence. Is Neo unknowingly promising yet another utopia?

As we know from the next two entries in the trilogy, Neo's trials are far from over. We have a litany of battle scenes, quests, philosophical discussions, and debates over strategy. At its philosophical best, the film tries to sharpen our sense of the options: a debased, mechanized humanity, void of the aspirations characteristic of what is best and most noble in our traditions versus a humanity that has recovered a sense of purpose, a sense of the goods for which we ought to be willing to fight and die. The most important plotline in *Matrix Reloaded* and *Matrix Revolutions* occurs in silence and deep within the soul of Neo; it involves not so much his wrestling with options as his growing realization of who he is and what he is called to do. As his core group awaits his direction, he disappears, only to reappear to tell them that he must take a ship to the Machine World, an apparently suicidal course of action that Neo concedes is "difficult to understand." Those gathered immediately divide into the skeptics and the true believers in Neo. The scriptural echoes—his withdrawal to be alone, his plan to go directly into the midst of his enemies on a ship named "The Logos," the presence of traitors, and the accentuation of faith in a person—multiply as the film moves toward its climax.

Throughout all three films, *The Matrix* is something of a mishmash of symbols and myths. It mixes a superficial dash of Eastern or Jungian opposites, as in the Oracle's assertion to Neo that Mr. Smith "is you, your opposite, your negation," with a bit of the blind-seer theme from Sophocles's *Oedipus*. But what is surprising about *Revolutions* is the clear ascendancy of Christian imagery: the suffering servant, the One who conquers evil by enduring it, light overcoming darkness, and especially, in the final apocalyptic battle between Neo and Smith, the cross.

Initially threatening, then given to dry humor, Mr. Smith ultimately functions as a sort of devil figure to Neo's savior. Proclaiming, "This is my world," Smith comes out as a nihilist philosopher, a despiser of both human flesh and human aspirations. He describes the human body as "nothing . . . a piece of meat," so "fragile" that it is not "meant to survive." In his final encounter with Neo, he asserts that "the purpose of life is to end," that the ideals of truth, love, and peace that inspire

Neo are "illusions" and "constructs," futile attempts at "justifying an existence without purpose."

In their reflection on religious themes in *The Matrix*, Chris Seay and Greg Garrett detect the pervasive influence of "Gnosticism," an early Christian heretical sect. Gnosticism, which teaches redemption of a select few through intellectual awakening from a state of somnolence or forgetfulness, "supplies some of the clearest sources of myth in *The Matrix*."[23] They describe the final battle of the trilogy thus: "Neo's death at the hands of Agent Smith—his crucifixion, if you will—represents the final moment of awakening in the film, and the ultimate gnosis. Neo becomes the One ... As a result of this final awakening, Neo becomes a creature of pure light that bursts apart Agent Smith from within."[24] As Joseph Campbell has observed concerning the Orphic mystery cults, the accent is not upon "the purely phenomenal aspect of one's life" but on the "spiritual, the deep, the energetic, the eternal aspect." It denigrates the body as a kind of tomb, an obstacle to knowledge.

Now it might seem that Mr. Smith, who rails against the human body, is more gnostic than Neo is. Neo is indeed attracted to the physical body of Trinity; they express their love in bodily ways, even engaging in a bizarre public orgy in Zion during the second film. But, as Cynthia Freeland has noted, there is a deeper and more sophisticated way in which *The Matrix* denies the frail, human body. This is evident in the film's preoccupation with virtual reality and in its marking Neo's progress by the increased invulnerability of his body.[25] Unlike the forms of redemption in the classic films of Greene and Hitchcock, Neo's experience of transcendence exhibits no sense of continued limits or ongoing penitence or loss. Indeed, Neo is a fully realized divine action hero. Stymied in its fundamental quest to solve the riddle of the distinctiveness of humanity in the technological age, *The Matrix* trilogy succumbs to the gnostic temptation to identify humanity with that which transcends the body. Both *Dark City* and *The Matrix* are striking examples of film with uplifting endings that nonetheless court the shallow nihilism that often afflicts neo-*noir*.

6

Feminist Neo-Noir

QUEST FILMS IN THE SCI-FI MODE may not succeed, but they often attempt to supply what Edmundson thinks we need in contemporary popular art: stories that confront and encompass the evils of our time in a hopeful narrative. As we have seen, some of the most imaginative popular dramas of our time combine elements of *noir* with themes of religious quest. Perhaps the most notable of all such tales is *Buffy the Vampire Slayer* (*BtVS*), a television series that, along with *Beverly Hills 90210* and *Dawson's Creek*, helped initiate the teen revolution in television programming. While *BtVS* shares Hollywood's fascination with contemporary teen life and is replete with demons bent on world destruction, its moral horizon is more complex than that of the standard teen fare on film and television. *BtVS* infuses contemporary youth and feminist plotlines with classic *noir* themes to create a compelling and ethically nuanced feminist *noir* drama. It also depicts its characters struggling to recover a lost code of good and evil and longing for a kind of redemption. *BtVS* thus illustrates the fertile dramatic possibilities in the linking of *noir* stylistics and themes to the quest for a lost code of redemption.[1]

With its focus on a female, teenage superhero, *BtVS* exhibits a convergence of contemporary feminist themes with the themes of the deprivations and possibilities of teen life. It depicts contemporary family and teen life as rife with sexuality and violence, even violent sex; it depicts both male and female characters as equally liberated and equally ensnared in traps devised by themselves and others; beyond all this, it depicts the shape of human life as a quest, as involving what Andrew Delbanco calls the "unslaked striving for transcendence." To appreciate the cultural achievement of *BtVS* as a teen, feminist neo-*noir*, it will help to consider other feminist neo-*noir* productions, from *Body Heat* to *Basic Instinct*, the latter of which Camille Paglia celebrates as an incarnation of Sadean art.

I have already noted a trend in contemporary film toward a depiction of evil itself as the highest form of aesthetic self-expression, indicating a character's transcendence of the petty, conventional morality of ordinary citizens. In previous chapters, I have also detected a surprising link between the liberationist themes of modernity and the celebration of amoral superheroes who stand beyond good and evil. In *Forbidden Knowledge*, Roger Shattuck traces this tendency to "an eerie post-Nietzschean death wish." He writes that the "death wish seeks absolute liberation, knowing that it will lead to absolute destruction—physical, moral, and spiritual. For some, apocalypse exerts a strong attraction."[2] In *Nature and Culture: Ethical Thought in the French Enlightenment*, a book that contributed to the scholarly elevation of the Marquis de Sade, Lester Crocker asserts that Sade was the "first to face the failure of rationalism" and the first to construct a "complete system of nihilism with all its implications, ramifications, and consequences."[3] Perhaps the most significant and artistically impressive example of this quest for absolute, nihilistic liberation can be had in the feminist neo-*noir*, *Basic Instinct*, a film that takes to its logical term certain tendencies latent within neo-*noir*. But the embrace of amoral self-creation is not the only possible outcome of the fusion of neo-*noir* with feminist themes; the juxtaposition of *Basic Instinct* with *BtVS* illustrates the resilience of classical *noir*'s accentuation of limits and costs, even as *BtVS* advances a remarkably developed and explicit ethical sensibility, tied directly to the conception of human life as a quest.

Before they became famous for *The Matrix*, the Wachowski brothers made a clever little *noir* thriller, entitled *Bound*, a film that features two lesbians, an ex-con (Corky) and the longtime girlfriend (Violet) of a mafia money launderer (Caesar). The women become lovers and hatch a complex heist plan; as is always the case in *noir*, things do not go as planned. Caesar discovers what they have done, ties up Corky, and interrogates both women as to the whereabouts of the money. When in disbelief and anger he asks Violet, "What did she [Corky] do to you?", Violet responds, "Everything that you couldn't." He accuses her of ingratitude; she counters that she is now using him the way he used her: "It's all business." Proving themselves superior in cunning and violence to the male characters in the film, the women manage to make off with the money and deflect the attention of the mob away from themselves. Sitting in their getaway car, Corky asks, "Know what the difference is between you and me?" When Violet says, "no," Corky smiles, "Neither do I." They hold hands and kiss as the soundtrack plays Tom Jones singing, "She's a Lady."

The film, which contains some nifty plot twists, is in many respects representative of feminist neo-*noir*, with the female characters exceeding the men in calculation and especially in their appetites for money and sex. No qualms of conscience keep them from doing "whatever it takes," as the pathetic male victim says of the female character in *Body Heat*. Neo-*noir femmes fatales* often prove deadly to men but rarely to themselves. In this respect, the opening scene of *Bound* is deliberately misleading; it features a bound Corky with voiceover commentary about making choices, paying costs, and wanting out. When a flashback takes us into the past and the beginning of the plot, we assume that the final frames of the film will return us to a trapped Corky. But the film has a happy ending, reflecting in some measure the conclusion of a romantic comedy. To achieve this ending, the film must turn inside out a fundamental tenet of classic *noir* about the incompatibility of crime with love and trust.

The liberation of the *femme fatale* is a consequence of neo-*noir*'s nihilistic turn, a transition that opens the possibility of celebrating the *noir* anti-hero as an individual beyond good and evil, a ruthless, intelligent, and creative individual who is not only free from the rules of *noir* but controls and manipulates them to his or her own ends. Just as was true of some of the films discussed previously, so too in feminist neo-*noir*, the presence of the nihilist transcending conventional limitation often serves to undermine the *noir* plot. The prototype of the feminist neo-*noir* is Kathleen Turner's sultry and calculating Matty from *Body Heat* (1981), a film that helped spur the revival of *noir* over the last twenty years. Andrew Spicer identifies *Body Heat* as the film that marks the transition from modernist to postmodern film *noir*.[4] In the latter stage, neo-*noir* was already established, its motifs and style recognizable by critics and audiences. According to Spicer, postmodern *noir* involves a "fundamental shift in the conception of artistic production in which creativity is no longer conceived in terms of pure invention but rather as the re-articulation of preexisting codes."[5]

The accent on "re-articulation" makes feminist *noir* possible in the first place. Although critics, even feminist critics, differ over the status and depiction of women in *noir*, classic *noir* films are not often identified as feminist. Re-articulation issues an invitation for the writing of more explicitly ideologically driven *noir* scripts. Although less clearly embracing the feminist superwomen motif of *Body Heat*, *Thelma and Louise* is a feminist neo-*noir* bent on delivering a message. The film features female characters in flight from masculine sexuality, equated simplistically with violence against women. The film is caught, as are its main characters, between the logic of the *noir* plot and a desperate desire to make ideological statements of feminist liberation. The link between *noir* fascination with sadomasochistic sex and nihilistic feminism comes to fruition in *Basic Instinct*, a *noir* murder mystery with a main character who does not flinch from translating into practice the most radical elements of Sade's theories.

One of the definitive films of neo-*noir*, *Body Heat* opens with a soft jazz soundtrack and flickering flames. In the midst of the flames, the silhouette of a naked woman appears. The flames eventually transform into an inferno of a burning building in a coastal Florida town, as a naked Ned (William Hurt) watches the fire from a hotel room where he has just had sex with a prostitute. He jokes that the fire is probably arson, "one of my clients." The next morning we see a haggard and feeble Ned in court facing off against his friend and prosecutor, Lowenstein (Ted Danson). He ends up being chastised by the judge for his pathetic defenses of low-class clients.

A sleazy, marginally successful defense attorney, Ned's life is irrevocably altered by a chance meeting with Matty (Kathleen Turner), who saunters past him and catches his eye at an outdoor concert. Ned pursues her, strikes up a conversation, and quickly finds himself in a torrid affair with a woman whose body temperature runs a "few degrees higher" than normal. She explains, "It's the engine, I guess." The town, known for its cool breezes, is in the midst of a heat wave. As Oscar, a black police detective, tells his buddies, Ned, and Lowenstein, in the midst of a heat wave, persons start to believe that "the old rules don't apply."

Among the film's many echoes of *Double Indemnity*, the most obvious is Matty's eagerness to discuss her husband's will. She complains about a prenuptial agreement that makes divorce financially costly and stipulates that, in the event of his death, half of his estate should go to his sister. She blurts out, "I wish he'd die. He's horrible, ugly." When Ned makes an allusion to "what we're both thinking," Matty cuts him off, "talk is dangerous. It can make things happen, make things real."

After the inevitable murder, Ned finds himself more deeply ensnared by the wiles and plotting of Matty, who ends up framing him for the murder, successfully faking her own death, and escaping to a tropical paradise. In jail for murder, an incredulous and nearly psychotic Ned concocts seemingly preposterous stories about what happened. He rants, "Maybe we never really knew her real name. Maybe she was living as another girl from her past. When the girl shows up, she threatens to expose Matty. Then Matty discovers a way to get both of us. It's so perfect, so clean." The last two scenes show Ned receiving in the mail a copy of Matty's college yearbook, where her picture appears under an entirely different name, accompanied by the caption: "Ambition: To be rich and live in an exotic land." The final scene is Matty on an exotic beach, with a male companion who comments, "It's hot." The scene, which suggests that the next man in her life feels the heat Matty exudes and may be her next victim, underscores Matty's victory. It confirms Ned's statement about her ability to do whatever was necessary to achieve her desires. Matty is the archetype of the neo-*noir femme fatale*, a sort of Nietzschean superwoman, who is deadly to men but not to herself.

As is true in classic *noir*, in *Body Heat* there is an alliance between sex and death. As Ned half-knowingly comments when his friends urge him to stay away from Matty, "maybe she'll try to f--- me to death." But Ned is insufficiently aware of the truth of this statement until it is too late. Even as his skepticism about Matty grows, he is unable to learn from his experience or to free himself from the labyrinth of Matty's sexual allure. He admits to her at one point: "experience shows I can be convinced of anything." By constructing the maze, Matty is not herself trapped within it; she satisfies her desires without experiencing any cost or consequence. She is a bridge between the classic *femme fatale* and the new wave of male nihilistic supermen such as Keyser Soze.

For the feminist super-hero of *Body Heat*, sex is an effective tool or weapon in a world where male desire can be twisted and turned to produce not just sexual pleasure, but whatever women want. Entries in feminist *noir* are often credited with liberating female characters from the tyranny of male sexual oppression. As we have noted in other contexts, liberationist themes are not naturally at home in *noir*; if they are not handled adeptly, their presence can cause *noir* implosion, an example of which is *Thelma and Louise*. Its status as a *noir* film rests on its central storyline: the flight of its eponymous characters from the law after an unplanned act of murder in self-defense. With its "no-way-out" plot, the film appears to capture better than *Body Heat* classic *noir*'s sense of entrapment without recourse or means of escape. Yet, the film strives to be a tale of feminist liberation. It evades *noir* in its heavily didactic tone and its bitter aversion to male sexuality on which it simplistically blames all that ails modern women.

The story begins innocently enough. In an act of mild rebellion against the brutish, abusive male boors with whom they spend their lives, Thelma (Geena Davis) and Louise (Susan Sarandon) set out for a drink and some music. Announcing that she "wants to let her hair down," Louise gets drunk and spends the evening dancing with a particular guy. Reluctant to let her leave, he follows her into the parking lot, and, when she rebuffs his advances, he forces himself upon her and starts to rape her. Just then Louise arrives with a gun and forces the man to back off. As he retreats, he taunts the women, "Bitch . . . suck my c---." Louise shoots him dead and comments, "You watch your mouth, buddy." To Thelma's suggestion that they call the cops and explain that he was raping her, Louise counters, "You were in there dancing with him all night. Who'll believe this was rape?"

In a less than credible plotline, Louise forges an escape plan that will take them to Mexico. Along the way, Thelma discovers "the call of the wild." Louise later tells her, "you've always been crazy. You're just getting your first chance to express yourself." In contrast to classic *noir*, where crossing the line is at once intoxicating and productive of increased anxiety and fear, *Thelma and Louise* depicts it as an act of straightforward exuberant liberation. In the simplistic dualism espoused by the film, pervasive male power is incorrigibly evil, while girl power is good. In the culminating scenes, Louise eludes a horde of police cars as she drives like an experienced professional driver through the desert, while the feeble male cops slam into one another or roll their cars. As Foster Hirsch comments, *Thelma and Louise* is so driven by a feminist mantra about the evil that men do that it presents a "cartoon version of real-world grievances" and ends up painting itself into a "corner from which the only solution seems to be killing off characters who have become steeped irreversibly in *noir*."[6]

Then, in the finale as police surround them at the edge of the grand canyon, their drawn guns symbolize the intrepid phallus, hunting down women to kill them, as the women fly jubilantly into a giant orifice (the cosmic vagina?). This moment marks the completion of Thelma's process of awakening; not Louise but Thelma insists, "let's not get caught. . . . let's just keep going." They kiss and hold hands as the car becomes airborne over the canyon. We never see the car crash; we only see it flying freely in the air. The camera gives us a retrospective clips of their journey, clips carefully edited to present only happy moments. Clearly the filmmakers want us to see the ending as a victory for its feminist, anti-heroes, Thelma and Louise.

In stark contrast to the politically correct, feminist cheerleading of *Thelma and Louise* is the blatantly transgender, sadomasochistic *noir* thriller, *Basic Instinct*, a film that opened to howls of protest from feminist and gay groups. The film illustrates Freud's succinct description of sadism, wherein the "death instinct twists the erotic aim in its own sense and yet at the same time fully satisfies its erotic urge."[7] Freud's rather pedestrian description of Sadism hardly does justice to Sade or to *Basic Instinct*, the most radical and most significant feminist *noir* ever made. Sade espouses a grand, demonic view of nature that severs any possible connection between happiness and the so-called virtues. Some have argued that Sade's thought is the logical term of the moralism of Kant, whose authoritative definition of Enlightenment is that individuals dare to reason for themselves, no longer subject to external authority. If one holds, as Nietzsche does, that "autonomy" and "morality" are mutually exclusive notions, then the path from autonomy to amoral self-creation is not a long one.[8] For Sade, daring to reason for oneself could be genuine only if one reasoned for and from one's most powerful and most perverse desires, the satisfaction of which is incompatible with a universal, common morality. Egoism is the only natural code of conduct in accord with nature; there is "no possible comparison between what others experience and what we sense."[9]

In distinctly Hobbesian language, Sade insists that we "come into the world as enemies" and live in a state of "perpetual and reciprocal warfare."[10] He also holds to the same sort of materialistic physics as that advocated by Hobbes: "nature is naught else but matter in motion." The bridge from Hobbes's radical defense of a mundane conclusion on behalf of political order to sexual sadomasochism as a way of life is a romantic celebration of excess and transgression. Happiness, according to Sade, is "by way of pain"; the key faculty here is imagination, which plays a crucial role in the quality of desire and the degree of its satisfaction. The overstepping of boundaries "inflames" the imagination; hence, those who would make progress in enlightenment must strive to bend the imagination "toward the inconceivable." This is precisely what Michel Foucault—the most perceptive contemporary reader of Sade—sees in his books: "the insane delight of love and death in the limitless presumption of appetite," "the possibility of transcending . . . reason in violence."[11] For those bold enough to follow Sade's precepts, Hobbes's focus on violent death operates less as a restraint upon, than as an incitement to, the passions.

Precisely such stimuli are operative in the opening scene of *Basic Instinct*. The viewer's initial experience is one of disorientation as the camera provides an upside down shot of a couple having sex, reflected in a ceiling mirror. As the camera allows our vision to gain its bearings, we realize that the couple is in a well-appointed bedroom. In what we soon learn is a San Francisco apartment, a man lays on his back on a bed while a blonde female, whose face remains covered throughout by her thick mane, mounts him and ties his hands to the bedposts. The camera briefly slides behind the bed to reveal the man through the bedposts, a shot that hints at his helplessness and imprisonment. As the sex reaches a crescendo, she reaches over to her side, grabs an ice pick and begins stabbing the man furiously in his neck and torso. The woman occupies the male position on top and penetrates him with a phallic knife; for her, the violence marks the climax of sex.

In its shocking opening, *Basic Instinct* states with unprecedented boldness a thesis often more subtly operative in *noir*: primal urges simmer just beneath the surface of civilization, which is no match for these passions once they are unleashed. These are the fundamental or "basic" instincts over which societal conventions lay a distracting veneer. As Max Horkheimer and Theodor Adorno observe, Sade is more interested in the social than in the intellectual consequences of the Enlightenment. The thoroughgoing materialism of modern science and its correlative egoism in ethics undermine every form of human solidarity, from familial to national bonds. His heroes embody "neither unsublimated nor regressive libido but intellectual pleasure in regression, *amor intellectualis diaboli*, the joy of defeating civilization with its own weapons."[12]

In *Basic Instinct*, the weapons of civilization are wielded by male police officers, who arrive at the crime scene the morning after the murder. The victim is Johnny Boz, a retired rock star who became civic-minded and was close with the mayor. A veteran homicide detective, Nick Curran (Michael Douglas), begins working the case by visiting the home of Boz's girlfriend, Catherine. At the home, a blonde greets them, calmly learns the news of Boz's death, and, adopting a masculine posture, stands defiantly athwart their path. In the first of many cases of mistaken identity, she admits, "You're looking for Catherine. I'm her friend, Roxy." She refers them to the beach house, where the police find Catherine sitting calmly in a chair looking out over the Pacific Ocean. Facing the water with her back to the cops, she never even rises to greet them; during the entire interview, she barely averts her eyes from the ocean. She flicks her cigarette and nonchalantly asks, "So, how did he die?" When asked about their relationship, she explains frankly, "I wasn't dating him. I was f---ing him." She says she was not in the mood last night so they were not together. Before the cops leave, Curran asks, "Are you sorry he's dead?" and Catherine responds, "Yeah, I liked f---ing him." Her icy manner and unhesitant use of vulgar language catch the cops off guard; indeed, the camera, located behind Catherine, presents her as reclining in regal comfort, while the angle of the shot makes the cops look as if they are hanging precariously over the cliffs and ocean.

Back at police headquarters, Nick Curran makes an obligatory visit to the department psychiatrist, Elizabeth "Beth" Garner, his former lover, who—it will turn out—knew Catherine prior to the time she met Nick. What he learns about Catherine increases his unease and piques his interest. She is a millionaire heiress, a Berkeley grad with a double major in psychiatry and literature, and now a very successful novelist, specializing in psycho-killer mysteries. Her latest book, *Love Hurts*, just happens to focus on a retired rock star whose girlfriend kills him with an ice pick. Police figure that either she planned the murder herself and is using the book as a sort of alibi or—since no one would be crazy enough to perform the exact murder described in her own book—someone else is trying to "incriminate her." When they discuss whether to bring her in for questioning, the district attorney argues that she has no motive and they have no evidence to use to threaten her. Nick assures them, "She won't hide behind a lawyer."

Her boldness continues to keep Nick at bay. He notices that Catherine has a large amount of data about him, which she has collected for a new book, of course. She even knows information from his confidential police records. When she asks him bluntly why his wife committed suicide, Nick becomes irate. As he storms out, Catherine begins kissing Roxy and laughingly says, "You're going to make a great character."

Nick's suspicions only increase when he learns that Catherine's parents, to whom she owes her initial fortune, died under suspicious circumstances. She once wrote a novel, called *The First Time*, about a boy who kills his parents just to see whether he could get away with it. Noteworthy in this story and in Catherine's life is the absence of any evidence of childhood trauma to explain or mitigate the evil acts of the child or adult. Like the child in the book, Catherine envisions evil deeds as experiments in living, experiments that test and refine one's independence and artistic creativity. She transforms life into art. Everything, including sex, is instrumental. In an interview with *Parade* magazine, Sharon Stone observed that Catherine never "really cared about sex at all. That's why it was so easy for her to use her sexuality—it had no value."[13] Thus does a perverse form of gnostic transcendence emerge even in a transgendered celebration of sexualized violence.

Untethered self-creation instrumentalizes everything, since what it must continually repudiate is the very notion of an end or standard that might limit, shape, or inform the autonomous power of choice. In severing any link between freedom and nature and in asserting an absolute autonomy, the most popular contemporary conception of freedom ends up treating the human body as a raw datum, devoid of meaning.[14] No longer understood as ensouled, the body becomes a mere assemblage of parts, some of which can be manipulated to produce momentary pleasure; sex loses its moral, even its human, significance; it involves, as Walker Percy's *Lancelot* puts it, merely "cells touching cells." Liberal politics and conservative economics conspire together to turn the "body" itself into a sort of "product, made delectably consumable."[15] The consequence for our understanding of sex is predictable. What is left is a "dispirited description of the working of a sort of anatomical machinery—and this is a sexuality that is neither erotic nor social nor sacramental but rather a cold-blooded, abstract procedure."[16]

The accentuation of aesthetic self-creation in *Basic Instinct* at once provides a response to a common criticism of the film and raises another difficulty that neither the critics nor the defenders of the film have considered. The common objections, which gave rise to virulent attacks on the film when it was first released in theaters, concern the alleged misogyny and homophobia of the film. In her commentary on the DVD version of the film, Camille Paglia rightly counters that these objections miss the mark. Paglia celebrates the film for its unflinching depiction of the potential link between sexual desire and violence and for celebrating bold, artistic and androgynous female characters such as Catherine and Roxy. Indeed, the film depicts their way of life as sexually alluring, aesthetically captivating, and interestingly complex. It does not denigrate them.

Paglia uses *Basic Instinct* as an occasion to express her own philosophical position on eros and violence. Elsewhere, she asserts, "wherever sexual freedom is sought or achieved, sadomasochism will not be far behind. Romanticism always turns into decadence."[17] She argues that "sex is power and all power is inherently aggressive." Mainstream liberal sexual liberation "misses the blood-lust in rape, the joy of violation and destruction. An aesthetics and erotics of profanation—of evil for the sake of evil, the sharpening of the senses by cruelty and torture."[18] Of course, freedom and power are only for the few, not the timid, petty many. The film's elevation of Catherine results in a version of aristocratic nihilism advocated most directly and courageously by Nietzsche and by Sade. Catherine is, in Nietzsche's terms, an active nihilist who sees the bankruptcy of conventional moral codes, not as an occasion for despair, but as an opportunity for aesthetic self-creation. Nietzsche's description of the bold is apt: "headstrong, sudden, improbable" with an "utter indifference to safety and comfort." Such individuals have a "taste for cruelty" and take a "terrible pleasure in destruction." These character traits, according to Nietzsche, are the preserve of the very few. Pascal himself captures the attraction and grandeur of a certain form of evil when he writes, "A certain kind of evil is as difficult to find as what we call good. . . . An extraordinary greatness of soul is needed in order to attain to it as well as to good."[19]

Paglia focuses on the way Catherine's sexual prowess unsettles the patriarchal hierarchy and the way her bisexuality disrupts conventional gender roles. But there is a new hierarchy in the film, with Catherine at the apex. She is the only fully liberated individual in the film; others, such as Roxy, Beth, and increasingly Nick, approach but never quite reach her insouciant embrace of the incoherence and violence that underlie all apparent order and civilization. Catherine's knowledge does indeed liberate those capable of receiving it from the constraints and repressive political structures of the conventional social life. But there is no suggestion that this teaching is for everyone; the few, the very few, are the only ones who will receive and live it. As one of Sade's characters puts it, "Nature's laws prescribe to yield to the strong." Or again, "cruelty is simply the energy in a man civilization has not yet altogether corrupted; therefore, it is a virtue, not a vice."[20] Catherine's relationships are all instrumental to her creative pleasures. As Gus, Nick's only friend and confidante on the police force, warns him: "Everybody she plays with dies."

Discovering evidence that Beth may have been involved with Catherine during college and that either or both may be implicated in another murder, Nick is now suspicious of both women. He is now embroiled in a labyrinth of dual and dueling *femmes fatales*. The mounting suspicions about Beth lead Nick to return to Catherine with an open mind. He tells her that he has thought up a new ending for her book: the detective falls for the wrong woman but does not die. She says, "it won't work; somebody has to die." Then she dismisses him curtly, "Goodbye. I've finished my book. Your character's dead." In a concluding sequence that contains obligatory plot-twists and enough ambiguity to leave us wondering whether anything has been solved, a now-murdered Beth is judged to be the culprit in the murder with which the case began.

Nick and Catherine are now free to resume their peculiar romance. In bed together, the music turns ominous a number of times during and after they have sex, especially when Catherine's arm seems to stretch toward the floor in the direction of an unseen object. At one point, with her arm in an awkward and concealed position, Nick's expression turns anxious and fearful. As she turns toward him, hugs him, and reveals her empty hand, the tension is momentarily released. But then the music grows to a powerful crescendo, as the camera pans to the floor and leaves the viewer with the image of an ice pick lying under the bed.

Despite its celebration of the Nietzschean superwoman, a figure decidedly alien to classical *noir*, the film ends on a satisfyingly *noir* note. It leaves us with a set of unanswered questions. Who was the real killer? Were there multiple killers? The presence of the ice pick does nothing to reassure us that Catherine is no longer a threat. Is she planning to continue her string of fictional tales becoming true crime dramas? What are we to make of her expressions of emotion, her pleas for affection? Are these genuine or mere performances? And what about Nick? Clearly Catherine remains a potential threat, but that has always been at the core of his attraction to her. The question is whether, having survived two *femmes fatales* and been instrumental in the death of each, he is now in a position to survive playing Catherine's deadly game.

BUFFY THE VAMPIRE SLAYER

As fitting and tantalizing as its ending may be, *Basic Instinct* saddles us with the problems of the aesthetics of evil mentioned at the outset of this chapter. For all its artistry, it remains trapped in a shallow liberationist model of aristocratic nihilism. As we shall see shortly, a way out of this trap, which returns us to the themes and dramatic logic of classic *noir*, can be found in the television show *Buffy the Vampire Slayer*, a show whose depiction of evil, sexual desire, and the quest merits the *noir* label. Indeed, *BtVS* provides an instructive link between the large and enduring themes of *noir* and the new sub-fields of teen and feminist *noir*, even as it subsumes both of these within a narrative of human life as a quasi-religious quest. In its affirmation of a noble calling for its main character, *BtVS* transcends the limitations of *noir*, as it is commonly and more precisely construed.

As is true generally in *noir* but especially in feminist neo-*noir*, the family is in a bad way. Such an assumption about the family has become commonplace and rather tiresome in the vast majority of Hollywood films. At best, the family retreats to the margins to allow youth to take center stage. At worst, it is identified as the principal source of evil, the root of trauma and betrayal, depriving children of innocence and hope. Where adults are present, they appear as repressive authority figures, clueless buffoons, or grown-up adolescents. The blurring of the basic distinction between children and adults has made the task of educating children, of raising them to be mature, responsible adults a thoroughly confused affair. This is true not just of film but television as well. On the two most influential teen shows of the late 1990s, *Dawson's Creek* and *BtVS*, the family is in bad shape. What is peculiar about these shows is the way they capture (in the figures of their main characters, Dawson and Buffy) adolescent longing for something more than what is given in our culture. The shows do not fare equally well, however, in their attempts to transcend and reshape the current cultural climate. Where *Creek* fails to transcend the insular self, *BtVS* succeeds.

On *Dawson's Creek*, teenage fantasy is a driving force in the series. Given the perpetual flux of human passion in the series, mild suspicion about the rekindled romance is in order. Infidelity is a perpetual possibility in this world; not just in the sense that commitments are tenuous and passions unpredictable, but also in the sense that this is what gives the show its vitality, what motivates characters and captivates viewers. The dramatic structure of romanticism dictates an endless series of conflicts, both external and internal, and a perpetual uncertainty about relationships. Since they possess no larger framework, no overarching vision of human life and its purpose, the characters are largely self-absorbed. They are also extremely articulate. The teenagers talk like characters twenty to thirty years their senior; they have mastered therapeutic language and are attuned to the significance of the least alteration in their psychological landscape. The swirl of conflicting emotions and the excessive, at times, paralyzing self-consciousness—these are the essential ingredients of the show's romanticism. For all its longing for something more, *Dawson's Creek* fails to provide any vision beyond that of the desires and aversion, pleasures and pains, of individuals. Despite the superficial frivolity and good looks of the *Dawson* youth, the underlying picture of human life is that of teenagers "locked in a soul-starving present," where meaning "narrows to the vanishing point of the self alone," as Andrew Delbanco puts it.[21]

While *BtVS* shares *Dawson's Creek's* appreciation of the predicament of contemporary teenage life, it suggests a larger moral horizon in light of which individuals might understand themselves—a horizon typically lacking in standard *noir* narratives. *BtVS* creator Joss Whedon has said the insight for the show came from the idea of reversing a standard motif in horror films, where a terrified and helpless girl is pursued and eventually butchered by a monster. Whedon's thought, "what if the girl turned, faced the monster, and killed it?" The contrast between Buffy's vapid life as a teenage girl and her realization of her vocation is evident in the first exchange between Buffy (Sarah Michelle Gellar) and her watcher, someone sent to train and advise the slayer in her confrontation with demonic forces:

Buffy: You're not from Macy's are you? 'Cause I meant to pay for that lipstick.
Watcher: There isn't much time. You must come with me. Your destiny awaits.
Buffy: I don't have a destiny. I'm destiny free. Really.

But Buffy has a destiny, a calling. She is "the chosen one," selected to fight demons, especially vampires, and protect the human world from being overrun by the powers of darkness. It has often been noted that Whedon's choice to feature a teenage girl as the leading public warrior against evil subverts a number of Hollywood conventions. But this is only the most obvious reversal of convention in the series. Even where it adopts current Hollywood motifs, *BtVS* does so in unexpected ways. Buffy's town of Sunnydale sits on top of the Hell Mouth and Buffy herself is the cheerleader turned demon slayer. In subverting the superficial tranquility and alleged normality of American life, *BtVS* adopts a strategy now common in Hollywood. But *BtVS* does not rest in these dark negations of American optimism, however. Instead, it treats the purported normality of American life as blocking from view a cosmic battle between good and evil. In its focus on the duality of American culture, especially in teen life, *BtVS* echoes a central motif of *noir*.

BtVS also shares some of the standard Hollywood cynicism about the family. Buffy comes from divorced parents; adults, with few exceptions, do not figure prominently in the series. Where they do appear, they are either clueless or instruments of evil, as is the case with the principal of Sunnydale High and the town's Mayor. While it follows the pattern of displacing the family from its central social role, *BtVS* does not leave its characters to wallow in a cultural and moral vacuum. On *BtVS*, the teen characters indulge in the same sort of personal rivalries, disappointments, jealousies, and animosities, as do their counterparts on other shows. But when the greater good of protecting the innocent is required, personal problems must be put aside. The themes of friendship, which is more than mere mutual agreement, and love, which transcends egoistic lust and involves self-sacrifice, are powerfully portrayed in *BtVS*.

The show is not all seriousness about the grand conflict between good and evil, however. It combines action and humor in unconventional, entertaining, and instructive ways. Early in the series, Buffy discovers that Angel (David Boreanaz), a handsome, nocturnal young man who has been assisting her in her slaying duties, is a vampire who has regained his soul. She objects to the suggestion that they might become partners, "You are a vampire, after all. Or, do you find that offensive? Should I say 'undead American'?"

The visual highlights of every episode are the expertly choreographed action sequences with Buffy and friends battling the forces of doom. But the depiction of violence on the show is not to be confused with the aesthetics of evil mentioned earlier. The problem is not with violence itself, but with how violence is used, by whom, under what circumstances, against whom, and for what purposes. In the aesthetics of evil, courageous resolve signifies the superiority of the evildoer to the timid mores of ordinary Americans. On *BtVS*, courage is never an end in itself. Instead, courage is necessary to protect innocent life; often this will require the use of force. As Buffy is about to face a powerful demon, Xander asks, "what are you going to do?" She deadpans, "I thought I might try violence." Whenever Buffy experiences ambivalence about her vocation and the sacrifices it entails, a good fight helps her to recover her sense of purpose. Buffy and her friends affirm in every episode the existence of things that are worthy of defense and sacrifice.

Yet Buffy's fulfillment of her calling as slayer is not a straight or easy path; in *noir* fashion, her destiny is often unclear. In later seasons, her path nearly becomes a lost highway. The opening episodes of the 2001 season set a dark, despairing tone for the life of the slayer. Buffy's town of Sunnydale, the cosmic center for the battle between good and evil, is bereft of its slayer, who died in the previous season's finale, sacrificing her own life to avert yet another impending apocalypse. Buffy's friends, affectionately known as the Scooby Gang, are disconsolate, their only hope being a tricky spell that might resurrect their dead friend. When the charm works, Buffy's friends are miffed at her lack of gratitude. Unable to tell them the truth, Buffy manages a feeble expression of thanks for being rescued from her awful existence beyond the grave. As she leaves them, she runs into Spike (James Marsters), a vampire and her longtime nemesis, now deprived of his vampire skills by a high-tech experiment. Buffy confesses to Spike that her experience of death was akin to paradise; having been "torn out of there by her friends," she experiences life on earth as a living hell. Among the darkest moments ever on *BtVS*, the scene portrays Buffy's sense of entrapment in an alien and hostile world, her isolation from those who know her best and care for her most, and her uncertain quest to discover her place and purpose. It also foreshadows her decline into a self-lacerating, sexual alliance with Spike.

The dark themes of *BtVS* call to mind film *noir*. Operating as a counter to the superficial and optimistic visions of the American dream, the characteristic styles and themes of *noir* constitute a "set of conditions producing amazement," symptomatic of "meaning's multiplicity and elusiveness." *Noir* productions depict their characters as trapped in a kind of labyrinth or maze in which they attempt to decipher clues to the resolution of their quest and signs of exit. *Noir* offers "a disturbing vision . . . that qualifies all hope and suggests a potentially fatal vulnerability."[22]

Yet *noir* rarely involves a simple repudiation or denial of properly human longing. In its accentuation of darkness and mystery, its rejection of standard characters and clear-cut happy endings, *noir* counters the naïve American and Enlightenment faith in inevitable progress and transparent objectivity. At their most ambitious, modern conceptions of progress presuppose that we have a clear idea of where we are, where we are headed, and precisely how we are to reach the goal. A related Enlightenment theme is that of freedom from the bonds and superstitions of the past, a detachment from tradition, history, and religion. *Noir* productions are not typically religious nor are they particularly nostalgic, but they do depict the past as bearing down upon the present. Memories and forgotten events from the past haunt and afflict human beings, circumscribing, if not utterly destroying, their possibilities in the present and their hopes for the future.[23]

Previously noted themes and assumptions of the *noir* universe bear repeating in this context. Although the properly human desires for truth and love are rarely, and never completely, fulfilled, longing itself is not mocked but rather seen as noble and admirable. The quest theme is prominent in *noir*. Always tenuous and often deadly, the quest of classical *noir* is twofold: "to solve the mystery of the villain and of the woman."[24] Thus, the quest can be about something more than the mere discovery of who did what to whom. It is also a search for love, communication, intelligibility, and truthfulness. As one critic aptly puts it, in its attempt at achieving a "talking cure," *noir* seeks to "formulate our place in the cultural landscape" and thus it is a "genre of life."[25] However much classic *noir* raises questions about the purpose of human life, about the elusiveness of love and justice, it does not typically embrace nihilism. There are no superhuman anti-heroes in the world of classic *noir*; no one escapes the limits of the human condition. Nietzsche's vision of a superman standing beyond good and evil and transcending the petty conventions of morality by aesthetic self-creation finds no place in classic *noir*, a world where every aspiration is qualified, constrained, and limited by circumstances and by others beyond the control of any particular individual.

The mythic structure and leitmotifs of *BtVS* reflect *noir* themes: the central role of the labyrinth and the quest, the influence of history and memory on the present, and the repudiation of Enlightenment autonomy and progress. Despite these similarities, there is no neat overlap between *BtVS* and classic *noir*. One difference concerns the setting of the productions. The definitive films of the classic *noir* era are set in cities. Both in their visual depiction of the city and in their narratives of city life, they put in question the vision of the city as modern utopia. According to the precepts of scientific rationalism, the city was to be the place where desires could be tabulated and satisfied, where human life would become transparent to inspection and amenable to rational management. Moreover, *noir* often depicts those who play key societal roles in the city as morally compromised or at least as seriously tempted by vice of one sort of another, usually lust or greed. In this respect, the *BtVS* spin-off *Angel* is a more typical *noir*. Set in LA, with most of the action at night, in a city run by a corrupt, greedy corporation of lawyers, *Angel* also reflects the detective story lines so prominent in *noir*. But the *noir* pattern of transforming the American dream into a peculiarly American nightmare is present in *BtVS* as well. On *BtVS*, suburban paradise is but a storm drain over the sewer of hell.

A similar and very creative reversal of Enlightenment assumptions about knowledge and happiness is evident in the role of the library in

Buffy's public school. Giles (Anthony Head), Buffy's watcher, someone sent to train and assist the slayer in her task, sets up shop in the safest place in any high school, the library. The vacant library plays upon the motif of high school as a place where both students and teachers avoid learning, where teachers process students and students just do time between childhood and the freedom of college. Under Giles' supervision, the library is the place where a forgotten wisdom about good and evil can be collected and studied. In a clear defiance of Enlightenment assumptions of the library as instrument for the progress of society through the dissemination of the latest scientific knowledge, Sunnydale's library shelves are filled with musty ancient manuscripts in a variety of now-dead languages, texts that are themselves labyrinths in need of deciphering, interpretation, and application.

Another difference between classic *noir* and *BtVS* has to do with the overt feminism of the latter. Although classic *noir* has given us some of the most complex parts for women in Hollywood history, most female leads were subordinate in the plot line to the male leads. Some neo-*noir* films, such as *Body Heat* (1981), often identified as initiating the period of neo-*noir*, and *Thelma and Louise* (1991), break with these conventions and reverse the standard *noir* relationship between males and females. As we noted above, these films violate fundamental assumptions of classic *noir*, even as their excesses run counter to the dramatic restraint of that era. In one case (*Thelma and Louise*), the story is overly moralistic and in the other (*Body Heat*), flatly amoral. More explicit than classic *noir* about the sexual desires and activities of its protagonists, the films nonetheless provide shallow, reductionist visions of sex. In *Body Heat*, Matty's sexual allure is all performance and her high-octane sensuality is "fatal to her male victim but not to herself."[26] Conversely, *Thelma and Louise* reduces sex to a form of male sadism, the only rational response to which is for women to fight physically for their rights not to be raped by male predators.

BtVS certainly deserves to be called feminist *noir*. Buffy replaces the standard male lead of classic *noir*. Here the female crime fighter is on her own quest to solve mysteries, concerning the crime, the fidelity of her male assistants, and her own identity. Buffy has inevitably been linked with male figures (Giles, her watcher, Xander, her friend, Angel and Riley, her lovers, and Spike, her nemesis and sex tool), who often assist and sometimes thwart her quests.

But *BtVS* is feminism in a different key. It is a contemporary feminist drama cast in a classic *noir* mold. *BtVS* avoids both the preachy moralism of *Thelma and Louise* and the amoralism of *Body Heat*. *BtVS* is always tinged with a tragic, often sorrowful, sense of limitation, of the vulnerability of all human longing, including feminine longing. It avoids reducing women to mere victim status, labeling men as evil or stupid, or granting the feminine icon status. *BtVS* also reckons with the consequences of vice, especially of violations of truthfulness, friendship, and love, in ways reminiscent of classic *noir*. The series, as Whedon insists, is all about "girl power," but it is not in the grip of illusory feminist theories of autonomous freedom or unbridled self-creation. *BtVS* is the greater counter to the mainstream feminist, and optimistic American, mantra: "You can have it all!"

Like many classic *noir* films, *BtVS* portrays human life as a quest, whose success depends largely on our ability to decipher uncertain clues and on the dubious help of others. It thus counters Enlightenment themes of transparent certitude with shadowy mystery and of independent autonomy with inescapable dependency. *BtVS* presents human life itself as part of a cosmic labyrinth, a universal battle, whose outcome for individuals and for humanity is perpetually in doubt.

For all its probing of themes excluded from other Hollywood genres, classic *noir* has a deeply conservative strain, affirming a clear set of limits to human desire and aspiration and a warning of the dangers of transgressing boundaries. *BtVS* repeatedly affirms a clear structure to the cosmos, a sense of boundaries that cannot be crossed without dire consequences. At the end of the 2002 season, Willow's wiccan lover, Tara, is accidentally killed by a stray bullet intended for the slayer. Willow, whose use of magic has increasingly served her own aggrandizement, deploys all her powers to avenge Tara's murder. Buffy comments: "we can't change the universe . . . if we could, magic wouldn't be changing Willow the way it is. There are limits to what we can do. Willow ignored that and now the powers want to hurt her . . . to hurt all of us."

Implicitly affirming the classical teaching on vice as intrinsically corrupting of the perpetrator of evil, Buffy worries that, if Willow continues down the path of vengeance, she will "cross a line." For all of its allure, evil itself is, as Angel confesses at one point, "simple." Demons themselves have no soul. As Giles puts it, "a vampire isn't a person at all. It may have the movements, even the personality, of the person it takes over, but it is a demon at the core. There's no halfway." As Angel, the vampire with the soul, says, "No conscience, no remorse . . . it's an easy way to live."

Some see the metaphor of the soul, particularly of the vampire with a soul, as illustrative of ambiguities about good and evil, perhaps as teaching that all is ultimately gray. But this confuses the teaching of *BtVS* about good and evil with the question of whether characters can be neatly categorized as good or evil in a peremptory fashion. *BtVS* presents a spectrum of good and evil, along which the position of individual characters is never permanently fixed. Nor is it immediately evident in each case confronted by the Scooby Gang what the right response is; but doubts about whether we have ascertained what is good or evil in this circumstance, even doubts about whether we will be able to do so does not entail nihilistic skepticism about good and evil. Before the battle against evil, the quest often involves an anguished inquiry into what is good and evil in the present circumstances.

As is true of the complex characters in *noir*, so too on *BtVS* the complexity of humanity is as much curse as blessing. Indeed, the story of Angel's recovery of his soul illustrates precisely this point; along with the soul, comes a conscience, a sense of remorse, and an insatiable desire to atone for his sins. As he confesses, "You have no idea what it's like to have done the things I've done and to care."

With some regularity, both *BtVS* and *Angel* edge beyond the motif of entrapment and hint at the possibility of redemption. The 2001 and 2002 seasons ended on precisely this note: first, with Buffy offering her own life in place of her sister, Dawn, and then with Xander, the carpenter, subjecting himself to Willow's wrath as a way of deterring her from destroying the world. In these and other scenes, *BtVS* gestures powerfully in the direction of redemptive suffering.

Interestingly, the 2002 finale contained a systematic reversal of conventional gender roles. The female leads (Willow and Buffy) are the chief protagonists who appear as warriors, seeking resolution through a violent attack on their opponents. Meanwhile, the male characters (Giles and Xander) play roles on the margins of the drama, until crucial moments when they confront Willow. But even then, they see that the use of direct force is futile. They opt for another response to evil and allow themselves to be subjected to unjust violence in an appeal to the residual humanity latent in Willow's soul. Although *BtVS* never rules out and often insists on the use of violence to fend off threats to the innocent, the show depicts a higher, more active, and more noble way of fighting evil: the sacrificial offering of oneself.

Giles calls this a higher magic or power, superior not only to the dark magic deployed by those bent on vengeful destruction, but also to the ordinary and virtuous use of violence to fend off evil and protect the innocent. So, for example, Buffy's slaying powers prove no match for Willow, whose comment that "there's no one with the power to stop me now," greets the return of Giles from England. Giles responds with his usual reserve, "I'd like to test that theory." Giles proves no more successful than Buffy at combating Willow's ever-growing wrath and bellicose skill. When Willow drains all the power from Giles and leaves him for dead, the most able combatants have been rendered useless.

Willow, Giles warns, is "going to finish . . . the world," as the only way, she later admits, to "stop the pain." Just as she begins to put these plans in motion, Xander, Willow's best buddy from high school, a guy never known for his courage, arrives. Willow mocks his presence and his weakness. But Xander is not here to fight Willow; instead, he wants to be with his old friend as she destroys the world, a destruction that will have to be visited upon him first of all. As she lacerates Xander's flesh, he is undeterred. The combination of his pitiful willingness to endure her wrath and his protestations of friendship and love causes Willow to relent in a torrent of tears.

Meanwhile, Giles recovers and explains how Xander saved the day. Since Giles knew that he would be defeated by Willow and that she would steal whatever power he possessed, he had himself infused with a different kind of magic, the "true essence of magic," which revived whatever "spark of humanity she had left in her." The residue of humanity was precisely what allowed Xander's appeals to be heard. The true essence of magic has to do with sacrificial love, with a willingness to lay down one's life, not just for the innocent but also as a way of bearing the sufferings of others, even of converting those who have begun to cross the line.

Of course, Angel is the great example of a character seeking redemption. In one of the early episodes of his spin-off, an enemy traps Angel and tortures him as he probes Angel's soul. He repeatedly asks Angel what he most wants; unsatisfied with Angel's responses, he warns him to tell the truth because he will know if Angel lies. Angel responds, "I want forgiveness."

One of the best plots in the series juxtaposes Buffy with another slayer, Faith, who becomes tempted by the prospects of using her slayer powers for her own ends. Her unrepentant murder of an innocent person signals her alignment with malevolent powers. When Faith crosses a line by slaying an innocent human being, Buffy is aghast. Faith accuses Buffy of being uptight and dismisses any repercussions of the act. The two become enemies. At one point, a spiteful Faith uses a spell to exchange bodies with Buffy. Once she inhabits Buffy's body and her life, she realizes that Buffy's goodness and the love and admiration it elicits from others are genuine. Unable to bear this knowledge, she rushes to Angel, curses herself as "nothing, a disgusting, murderous bitch," and begs Angel to kill her. The story of Faith illustrates two related *noir* themes: the intractable limits that the human condition places upon human acts and the way the pursuit of certain kinds of knowledge destroys rather than perfects the knower.

For Buffy, the lesson of Faith is that the slayer must resist temptations to power, lust, and jealousy in herself. This is not to say that Buffy always avoids vice or that she is uniformly enthusiastic about her lot in life. The show often highlights the tensions between Buffy's personal aspirations as a teenager and the requirements of her duties as slayer. The working out of the conflicts between personal aspiration and duty is one of the abiding sub-plots in the series. In fact, no contemporary television show depicts the necessity and nobility of self-sacrifice in more realistic or more attractive terms. Over time, Buffy's character and destiny have become more intimately intertwined as she has discovered at a deeper level that being a slayer is who she is and what she wants to be. Buffy's realization of her destiny is not a matter of conformity to an abstract and impersonal code of duty; rather, it is for the personal good of others, indeed for her own good. The show provides a subtle and supple depiction of the way conspiring with evil forces, by commission or omission, deprives one of humanity.

But redemption, like complete justice, seems always to be postponed in the *noir* worlds of *Angel* and *BtVS*. Angel has a long and tortuous path to travel before he recovers his humanity, while Buffy's return from the dead has only exacerbated her anguish. She now lives with the burdensome memory of paradise lost. A later episode features a despondent Buffy, desperately seeking to escape from a life she now detests. She retreats into a fantasy world, where her parents and psychiatrist treat her slayer world as a delusion of grandeur from which they hope she will return to her normal life. Buffy becomes torn between the two worlds. She ultimately opts for life as a slayer, but a final shot of a catatonic Buffy in a psych-ward leaves us wondering whether the entire *BtVS* series might simply be our window on Buffy's imaginary cosmos. Now, that's *noir*.

The 2001-2002 season witnessed the near shattering of Buffy's identity. The show has always focused on the question and problem of Buffy's identity, with early episodes addressing the obvious tensions between the demands of Buffy's calling as a slayer and her desire to lead a normal teen life. Even in these episodes, deeper questions about the identity and mission of the slayer were raised. In a later episdoe, Willow's most piercing criticism of Buffy touched on Buffy's own loss of purpose: "You hate it here as much as I do. . . . You know you were happier in the ground." Alluding to Buffy's sexual escapades with Spike, Willow taunts her need to "screw a vampire to feel" anything.

Being plucked out of heaven to return to earth, failures in love and romance, the death of her mother—all these weigh heavily upon her, creating doubt and resentment. If early on in the series, Buffy seemed at times to be cursed by the inordinate burden of her duties as the chosen one, she seems increasingly cursed by an absence of a sense of what she has chosen or might choose to do. She is also afflicted by memories of what has or might have been. Buffy's *noir* labyrinth is increasingly an interior maze of her own soul.

The most demoralizing sub-plot in the 2001-2002 season concerned her sadomasochistic sexual relationship with the vampire, Spike, previously a most vicious enemy. Being drawn inescapably to the sort of love that can only bring one harm and perhaps even destruction is a central motif in *noir*. The sexual relationship with Spike brings shame and a desire for secrecy. Although Spike shows glimmers of affection and is occasionally helpful to Buffy, their sexual chemistry is characterized mostly by violent genital stimulation. Toward the end of the season, as Buffy seeks to come to terms with what she is doing with Spike, she admits that she has been "in love with the pain" and that she has just been "using" Spike. To her repeated assertions that "it's over," Spike responds with knowing skepticism and then with a violence that culminates in attempted rape.

Of course, Buffy's love for men has always been tinged with elements of sadomasochism, a result of her own deeply competitive, physical prowess and the superheroes to whom she is naturally attracted. Prior to the preeminently sadomasochistic relationship with Spike, Buffy's boyfriends, most notably her first and greatest love, Angel, had been admirable, noble sorts, whose lives were committed to visions of justice and sacrifice. But Buffy's love for Angel underscores the contingency of love and human identity, their susceptibility to radical reversal. During the second season, Buffy and Angel become an exclusive couple, and on Buffy's sixteenth birthday, in an episode entitled "Surprise," they consummate their love. The next day, Angel is full of mocking wrath, a stand-in for the predatory male, who reveals his true and truly vile self only after he gets what he wants.

But Angel's true self is more elusive and complex than this. His life illustrates the importance of history for *BtVS*, its embrace of the *noir* theme of the past's continued resonance in the present. Angel's life dates to mid-eighteenth century Galway, where a simple bite from a vampire named Darla granted Angel membership among the undead. Known not so much for the number of his conquests as for the peculiarly cruel manner in which he inflicts evil, Angel becomes one of the most notorious vampires in history. After Angel kills the daughter of a gypsy family, the gypsies plot revenge. In a flashback to events unfolding in the Romanian woods in 1898, we witness the gypsies cursing Angel with the return of his soul, whose presence will bring back his memory and his conscience. He will thus be tormented by the memories of his innocent victims and "know true suffering." To keep the ensouled Angel from experiencing the pleasures of which humans are capable, the curse includes a caveat. If Angel ever experiences a moment of true pleasure or happiness, he will immediately be deprived of his soul and revert to his vampire ways.

But the curse is also a potential blessing. When Angel appears in Manhattan in 1996, a fellow named Whistler meets him and tells him that "he can become a person." He then guides Angel to observe a novice slayer named Buffy Summers. Whistler's suggestion is that Angel can begin the process of redemption by assisting the slayer in her assigned duties. Angel complies and an unusual friendship is born. But Angel's experience of happiness activates the rider to the gypsy curse. He loses his soul and then sets out to torture and destroy the slayer.

Thus, *BtVS* replays themes about eros, sex, and love from classic *noir*, where sexual desire is typically seen as incompatible with conventional American life, where acting on that desire is always accompanied by unanticipated consequences and rarely brings the happiness or even the pleasure sought. When Angel finally regains his soul and returns to the margins of the human world, he agrees with Buffy that their love is impossible and departs for LA.

The last installment in the Buffy-Angel chronicles was entitled "I Will Remember You," a crossover episode in which Buffy travels to LA to chastise Angel for secretly returning to Sunnydale and spying on her. Angel's visit was prompted by word that Buffy was in grave danger and his secrecy by his unwillingness to stir up old passions and memories. As Buffy and Angel engage in verbal sparring, a demon appears to attack them. When the demon's blood splashes on Angel, he is magically returned to a human state, with a heartbeat and an enormous hunger, both for food and for sex. But like Sampson without his hair, Angel is now useless as a warrior against evil. Meanwhile, Buffy, distracted by her enjoyment of the love that had for so long been forbidden and by her worries over Angel's vulnerable state, is losing her sense of duty as a slayer. So, Angel returns to the oracles, creatures that call to mind the Fates of ancient Greek mythology, and works out a deal to return himself and Buffy to their prior states. The oracles agree to wipe out the previous day. The catch is that, while Buffy will have no memory of the blissful events, Angel will privately bear the burden of recollection. The end of the episode depicts Angel explaining this deal to a teary-eyed Buffy as they count down the seconds to the moment when the oracles will erase the past and forever alter their future. If in this episode, Angel appears once again as a sort of male protector of Buffy, it is also the case that the conclusion leaves Buffy once again alone, enduring the isolation proper to many a *noir* character.

With the explicit depiction of the sexual activities of Buffy and Spike and the lesbian romance of Willow and Tara, *BtVS* seems quite contemporary, even indulgent. Sexual desire has always been a staple of *noir*. In its insistence on the inevitable and usually destructive consequences of sex, *BtVS* once again reflects classic rather than neo-*noir*. *BtVS* is certainly feminist in its reflection of relaxed social constraints on the sexual activity of women. But it eschews the amoral sexual domination of women over men (*Body Heat*) and the flight from male sexuality (*Thelma and Louise*). Indeed, it is deeply skeptical about the very notion of sexual liberation. On *BtVS*, there is no free sex; consequences, usually unpleasant, always accompany sex.

Although they contained some of the least dramatically successful episodes of the entire series, the final shows of the series were noteworthy precisely for their focus on the transformation of Spike. At the heart of Spike's transformation is his transcendence of sexual desire understood as mere physical pleasure, an understanding that reduces one's partner to a mere instrumental status. After the attempted rape, Buffy keeps Spike at a distance, but the season's final episodes had Spike expressing in both word and action a love for Buffy independent of his own possession of her. How many shows could make dramatically credible the moral regeneration of an attempted rapist?

What contributed to the dramatic credibility was the surprise return of Spike's soul. For the vampire, lacking a soul or conscience, evil is simple, as Angel explains in one episode. In a remarkable episode, a disoriented Spike living in an abandoned crypt explains the return of his soul to a deeply skeptical Buffy. He blames his current state of torment on his love for Buffy. The exchange ends with Spike standing in front of a crucifix, saying "and she shall look upon him with forgiveness and everyone will forgive and love . . . and he will be loved." He then drapes himself over the cross which sears his flesh; a teary eyed Buffy watches as smoke rises from his body. This is one of the most dramatically striking uses of Christian symbolism in contemporary popular culture, more potent than anything on offer in explicitly religious television shows such as *Touched by an Angel* or *Seventh Heaven*. The themes of sacrificial suffering, of bearing one's cross, of the invocation of the merciful Madonna, and of the fires of lust transformed into the purgative fires of redemption—all this is compressed into a single scene.

This is not to say that *BtVS* is a consistently or fundamentally Christian series. Its symbolism is an undifferentiated amalgam of Christian, pagan, and even new age sources. What is clear is that *BtVS* illustrates the fertile dramatic possibilities in the linking of *noir* stylistics and themes to the quest for a lost code of redemption.

Much of that lost code concerns sexuality, the problematic complexity of which is palpable on *BtVS*. The show is remarkably and refreshingly frank about the way sexual desire often conflicts with other human desires and goods, renders individuals susceptible to self-deception and vulnerable to the pain of being used for another's pleasure, and the way it tends toward excess and potentially lethal destruction. If, as critics have insisted, *noir* is an attempt to articulate our place in a confusing social and cultural landscape, then it would seem that in the contemporary *noir* world of *BtVS* nothing is more uncertain or more volatile than our sexual mores.[27]

Of course, much of contemporary art, literature, and film is precisely about this sort of issue. But *BtVS*'s feminist *noir* with a difference sees something else, our desperate need to see our erotic attachments to others in something more and other than merely genital terms. In this, *BtVS* revives a classical sense of eros, however tragically unfulfilled that desire may remain. It recovers eros as a longing for beauty, for wholeness, for discovering one's place both within the grand sweep of cosmic history and within the specific human community in which one finds oneself. In its treatment of sexuality, as in its depiction of so many other themes, *BtVS* distinguishes itself as a dramatically successful and intellectually captivating feminist variation on the narrative of the dark quest.

PART III

THE RELIGIOUS QUEST

7

Questions about One Thing

I N FOCUSING, as I have been doing, on dark tales of the quest, I
do not suppose that all quest films are *noir* or that *noir* is to be
defined in terms of religious quest. Indeed, as I have moved from
classic *noir* into neo-*noir*, what little shared sense of the meaning of
noir there may initially have been has become increasingly elusive.
Although there are in some cases points of contact between what film
critics call *noir* and the dark tales of religious quest that I will now
consider (the most striking of which is *The Passion of the Christ*, the
story of a man whose "only companion is darkness"), I will be using
the term *noir* in a colloquial and non-technical sense.

From *American Beauty* to *Magnolia*, from the films of M. Night
Shymalan to Gibson's *Passion*, some of the most provocative films in
recent years are dark tales of religious quest. In the group of films to
which I now turn, a pre-eminent theme is that of divine providence,
whether events and lives are ultimately matters of chance or a divinity that shapes our ends, however much we may be unable to identify
precisely who or what is giving shape to the narrative arc of our lives.
As I have already noted, dark tales of religious quest have important

theological implications in our culture. Their possible contribution to theological discourse, at least to the raising of questions that transport viewers to the cusp of the religious, remains underappreciated. If the dark and disquieting manner of formulating religious issues is troublesome to us, we should recall that perhaps the greatest work of Christian art ever composed, Dante's *Divine Comedy*, begins not with a direct ascent to God but with a descent through Hell, followed by a penitential path through purgatory. This is not to say that the popular films I will examine speak with one voice, let alone an orthodox Christian voice; nor is it to say that they are invulnerable to artistic, ethical, or theological objections. It is simply to say that they constitute a noteworthy strain of contemporary film. Indeed, part of what makes them noteworthy is that they provoke questions and objections of various sorts.

The consideration of films that depict, in divergent ways, possible providential responses to the apparent purposelessness of the human condition will also afford us the opportunity, in the final chapter, to examine in greater detail Pascal's account of our *noir* condition. As I have already noted, there are at least two "Pascals" operative in the literature. There is, first, Goldmann's Pascal, the Pascal whose account of the human condition we have found enormously illuminating as a commentary on the alienated condition of man in the world of classic *noir*. But there is a second Pascal, a more complete Pascal, who does not leave us with the tragic quest of the *noir* protagonist, but who proposes a specific path through the *noir* trap. Even here, in Pascal's affirmation of a Christian "answer" to our condition, he continues to insist upon the hiddennes of God and continues to commend the individual who "seeks with groans."

AMERICAN BEAUTY

The reign of the adolescent self, beholden to nothing other than its fleeting preferences, is relatively secure in Hollywood. To rephrase Andrew Delbanco, in much of contemporary culture the vision of the good shrinks to the vanishing point of the fleeting passions of the adolescent self. Childhood disappears even as it begins and adulthood recedes beyond the horizon. Yet it would not be accurate to suggest that Hollywood is universally committed to a naïve celebration of un-tutored, teenage appetites. As we have just seen, a popular television series such as *Buffy the Vampire Slayer* depicts its heroes as drawn into an order of events beyond their imagining, events that impose upon them certain non-negotiable obligations. The costs and consequences of human choices are on full display, as the main characters embark on quests not just to solve crimes but also to experience a kind of re-demption. Characters are caught up in a cosmic battle, in which they strive to discern their place, to determine their "calling," and thus does the series raise the question of a providential shape to human lives.

A recent film like *American Beauty* faces squarely the hollowness at the heart of the idolatry of youth. Oscar winner for best picture in 1999, *American Beauty* constitutes the most prominent depiction of the American dream turned nightmare, of the family as trap. Similar themes can be found in another film from 1999, Paul Thomas An-derson's celebrated *Magnolia*, which features dysfunctional families whose members aspire not so much to escape from their families as to achieve reconciliation and be relieved of a burden of guilt they can no longer bear. Anderson's subsequent film, *Punch-Drunk Love*, which bespeaks the violence simmering just beneath the surface of ordinary American life, goes further than *Magnolia* in the direction of deliver-ing redemption for its main characters. Indeed, *Punch-Drunk Love* has the feel of *Fight Club* (another 1999 film featuring a dark subter-ranean quest) retold as a romantic comedy. None of the characters in these dark quests is able to find a vocabulary adequate to the frustra-tion of their desires. They share naïve, romantic assumptions about childhood innocence or about its mirror image, unhinged adolescent mayhem. None of these difficulties afflict another quest film, *Thirteen Conversations About One Thing*, a film that treats many of the same issues: alienation, the seemingly futile search for happiness, the apparent pointlessness of human life, and the possibility of redemptive second chances. It also includes violence and desire (*eros*) but its understated, rather than hyperbolic, examination presents more accurately the debilitating consequences and roots of violence. The film also manages to depict *eros* in something of its original form, as a longing for wholeness through a discernment of one's place within the larger scheme of things. *Conversations*, which addresses these issues in a much more subtle way than any other recent film, moves its viewers to the cusp of the religious as characters inquire about the narrative shape of their lives and ponder the mysterious overlapping of individual lives. Before turning to Anderson's films and *Conversations*, we will consider *American Beauty*, an influential suburban family *noir*. Beyond its dramatically compelling illustrations of the twin nihilisms of suburban, consumerist paradise and of endless youth, *American Beauty* offers a reflection on the resources for transcendence and redemption.

American Beauty begins with the sound of the whirring shutter of a home video camera. In his bedroom, Ricky Fitts is making a home video of his teenage girlfriend and neighbor, Jane Burnham, who states, "I need a father who's a role model, not some horny geek who's going to spray his shorts whenever I bring a girlfriend home from school.... Someone really should just put him out of his misery." Apparently joking, Ricky offers, "You wants me to kill him for you?" Jane stares grimly at the camera and responds, "Yeah, would you?"

In real time, this scene occurs somewhere near the middle of the film, but its transposition to the opening provides an anticipatory glimpse of the violence just beneath the surface of this suburban, American family. By beginning with the making of a home video, the film also evinces something of its self-conscious artistry, its attention to the ideals to which contemporary film might aspire, the essence of which is embodied in the advertising slogan for the film: look closer. The character whom the film invites us to examine most closely is Lester Burnham (Kevin Spacey), whose retrospective voiceover succeeds the opening exchange between Ricky and Jane. Lester introduces himself to the audience by announcing that within a year he will be dead. But, as he confesses, "he's dead already."

Not technically a *noir* film, *American Beauty* does overlap with *noir* in a number of respects: in its use of flashback and voiceover; in its focus on a character who is already dead (*D.O.A.*); in its assumption that the source of American alienation is somehow connected to the infiltration of consumerism into the very heart of intimate relations; in its theme of an apparently doomed quest; and in its setting of the final, crescendo of violence at night in rain. *American Beauty* is also a deeply, if not entirely coherent, religious film that, according to at least one perceptive Christian film critic, can help viewers see "the world as it truly is: resplendent and suffused with a radiant, implacable love that shows itself in the exquisite beauty of the very fabric of the created world."[1]

But that is not where the film begins. Instead, productive consumerism and banal sexual desire are on display in Lester's life. A sort of lackey for the advertising industry, disrespected by his wife and his daughter, Lester will soon be shocked from his living death by the body of Angela Hayes (Mena Suvari), his teenage daughter's cheerleader friend. Awakened by her beauty as he watches her cheer during a high school basketball game, Lester begins to undergo a transformation—of sorts. He soon befriends Ricky, the drug-dealing son of his new neighbors. Ricky is a classmate and at this point still would-be lover of Lester's daughter, Jane. Both dad and daughter are drawn to Ricky's confidence and independence from societal expectations. Freed from conventional constraints, Lester himself negotiates a lucrative retirement package just as he is about to be fired from his job, by threatening to trump up a charge of sexual harassment against his boss. Coining his own version of Janis Joplin's "Freedom's Just Another Word for Nothing Left to Lose," he informs his stunned supervisor, "I'm just an ordinary guy with nothing to lose." He begins working out in order to "look good naked." He also starts smoking pot supplied by

Ricky, and, just for the fun of it, takes a job flipping burgers at a fast food joint, Mr Smiley's.

Through it all, Lester fantasizes about Angela, but she is never naked in his fantasies; though devoid of clothes, she is draped in blood-red roses. In settings dominated by neutral colors, the blood-red roses—both those that appear in the fantasy sequences and those that Lester's wife, Carolyn (Annette Benning), prunes with maniacal detail in her garden and uses to decorate her home—stand out. Lester is too preoccupied with his new-found adolescent freedom to ponder the symbolic significance of the roses. Yet he does have a sense that he has begun some sort of quest, that he has (to borrow Walker Percy's phrase from the *Moviegoer*) shaken the malaise and is now onto something. "It's a great thing," he observes with a smile, "when you realize you still have the ability to surprise yourself. It makes you wonder what else you can do that you've forgotten about."

Meanwhile, Carolyn, whose pruning shears match her gardening clogs, continues to be absorbed in her career as a self-lacerating real estate agent. A prime example of what Tom Wolfe once called a "social x-ray," Carolyn pumps herself up for a day of work by repeating the mantra, "I will sell this house today." After a grueling day of cleaning and unsuccessfully presenting the house to potential buyers, she weeps in humiliation and then smacks herself as she rants, "Shut up! You weak! You stupid! You baby!" When she accompanies Lester to watch their daughter cheer, she musters a great deal of enthusiasm to compliment her daughter's performance, "Honey, I'm so proud of you. You know, I watched you very closely. You didn't screw up once." She, too, develops a sexual interest in someone other than her spouse, the self-described real estate king of the town. They begin a brief but torrid affair, whose peak moment occurs in a mid-day tryst at a local hotel where she gets the royal treatment from the King. Her joy is both skin-deep and short-lived. She continues to torment herself with self-improvement tapes. Her most self-confident moments occur during her gun lessons, at which she is receiving increasingly high marks. When she and the King inadvertently stop for lunch at the drive-through window of the very burger joint where Lester works, Carolyn is, as one of Lester's teen co-workers puts it, "*so* busted." An amused and triumphant Lester tells her, "this means you don't get to tell me what to do ever again."

As Lester casts off one conventional expectation after another, Carolyn becomes more shrewish and domineering. Lester is happy to play the naughty, rebellious adolescent to his wife's matronly oppressor. At one point, Carolyn enters the living room, where Lester sits comfortably, barefoot, drinking a beer and operating the remote control on a toy car. When Carolyn asks whose car is in the driveway, Lester responds, "Mine. 1970 Pontiac Firebird. The car I've always wanted and now I have it. I rule!" What we expect is another battle between adult and child. But, as Lester looks at her, he sees her in a different light and asks, "Have you done something different? You look great. . . . When did you become so joyless?" Lester sits next to her on the couch and kisses her, asking playfully, "Whatever happened to that girl, who used to fake seizures at frat parties when she got bored . . .? Have you totally forgotten about her? Because I haven't." As he leans in to kiss her neck, the beer bottle in his hand tilts and nearly spills. Seeing this, Carolyn becomes indignant: "Lester, you're going to spill beer on the couch." Lester backs off, stands, and says: "So what? It's just a couch." Carolyn counters, "This is a $4,000 sofa, upholstered in Italian silk. This is not just a couch." Lester pounds the couch and retorts: "This isn't life, it's just stuff and it's become more important to you than living. Well, honey, that's just nuts."

The hostility in the family, the public life of unadulterated consumerism, and the violent sexual urges plaguing the hearts of the adults in this film confirm a thesis of Wendell Berry. "Beginning with economic brutality," Berry argues, "we have reached sexual brutality."[2] Berry criticizes conservatives for their simultaneous and contradictory promotion of conservative standards in the area of sexual morality and of a so-called free economy. But that economy brutalizes both nature, treating it as raw material out of which to create "products," and persons, treating them as consumers whose freedom is realized in market preferences. Conversely, liberals who often disdain capitalism but who decry as fascist any conception of right ordering of sexuality end up tacitly advocating the same conception of the person and of choice as that operative in capitalism: the private preferences of individuals.

Lester's attempt at reunion with his wife is an indication that he wants something more than the mere satisfaction of his preferences, though he may not yet recognize it. Yet it now seems clear that Lester's quest will not involve a return to domestic bliss. In fact, the tone of the film becomes even more ominous, especially in the scenes from the Fitts' residence, where Ricky's military father—the most crudely drawn and predictable character in the film—becomes increasingly threatening and violent. But Ricky is the film's moral center. He sees and records on his video camera what the filmmakers hope we will see. At one point, he shows Jane a video of a floating baggie, which he describes as dancing for him and affording him the following insight: "There is an entire life behind things and this incredibly benevolent force wanted me to know that there was no reason to be afraid, ever. Video is a poor excuse, I know, but it helps me remember. I need to remember. Sometimes there's so much beauty in the world, I feel like I can't take it. And my heart is just going to cave in." Ricky associates seeing with remembering and both of these with the heart. Indeed, the most accurate diagnosis of the malaise that afflicts the families in *American Beauty* is hardness of heart. For Ricky, the heart is kept alive and nourished by looking closer, by glimpsing a benevolent power behind things; conversely, a rightly affected heart makes this vision possible. The heart is, as Pascal argues, an organ of perception. What the heart perceives is not so much the providential orchestration of events in and through temporal moments; rather, by adopting a stance of receptive stillness, it discerns a constant order behind things.

Toward the end of the film, Lester is just about to realize his version of the American dream: the sexual conquest of a teenage beauty.

But he relents, after Angela, who had previously bragged about her sexual exploits, admits that she has never done this before: "This is my first time . . . I thought I should tell you, in case you wondered why I wasn't better." Realizing perhaps that there is still innocence in the world and now aware that he did not want what he thought he wanted, Lester covers her naked breasts and gently hugs her. When she leaves the room, Lester picks up an old family picture, taken in happier days when his daughter was still young and he and his wife still in love. As he smiles contentedly at the picture, he is shot through the back of his skull, which oozes rose red blood. In his final voiceover from beyond the grave, Lester reiterates Ricky's words about gratitude for the beauty of the world and for his apparently insignificant life. Conceding that he could be justifiably upset at the way he died, he adds, "It's hard to stay mad when there's so much beauty in the world. Sometimes I feel like I'm seeing it all at once and it's too much. My heart fills up like a balloon that's about to burst. And then I remember to relax and stop trying to hold onto it. Then it flows thorough me and I can't feel anything but gratitude for every single moment of my stupid little life."

What Ricky sees from the beginning, and what Lester comes to see at the end, is that America has been looking for beauty in all the wrong places. Ricky finds what his heart desires, or at least a cessation of desire, in what American society shuns: the insignificant, the ugly, the useless, the dead, the inactive, in images of floating baggies, dead birds and homeless persons. Given Ricky's fascination with dead things and Lester's resignation about his own death, we can also surmise that the superficial American conception of happiness and beauty, the endless pursuit of material well-being, the "joyless pursuit of joy," is rooted in an aversion to death, the futile attempt to escape one's mortality through diversion.

In *American Beauty*, the American quest for happiness is rooted in flight from mortality. Consumer society is a colossal diversion from confronting death. As Pascal puts it, "we run carelessly into the abyss, after we have put something before us to prevent us seeing it."[3] Unable to cure death or disease, Pascal observes, men cease thinking about such things. Our condition is characterized by endless diversion: "The only thing which consoles us for our miseries is diversion, and yet this is the greatest of our miseries. For it principally hinders us from reflecting upon ourselves. . . . Diversion amuses us and leads us unconsciously to death."[4] Pascal proposes that our diversion is a result of our sinful alienation from God, to whom we can be reconciled only through the gift of faith and humility, through seeing with the heart.

In spite of the benevolent vision at the end of the narrative, the film lets Lester off too easily. It bestows upon him a vision of transcendence, an escape from the twin nihilisms of consumerism and perpetual adolescence, only to remove him from the scene. Lester's insight has clearly liberated him from the resentment he felt toward his family. By killing him, the film avoids the difficult questions: How could someone with Lester's history and habits live in harmony with that vision? How could the vision be embodied in a specific way of life, here and now in America? Or, to put it more concretely, how could Lester even begin to repair things with his daughter and his wife? The only character who manages to live the vision is Ricky, but his mobility and freedom presuppose an affluence made possible by what the film makers apparently think is the only acceptable form of capitalism, drug-dealing. Ricky's plan to escape from his oppressive father and catatonic mother is to take Jane to New York, where they will live off the money he has amassed selling drugs.

American Beauty is a deeply frustrating film, entertaining and prurient, ambitious and pretentious. It is hypocritical about capitalism and not just in the generic way so many Hollywood films are. They mock capitalism while shamelessly exploiting the economy to maximize their profits. The hypocrisy is present in the film itself, not only in the character of Ricky, but even in Lester, whose entertaining quest to recover his lost youth, his railing against the advertising industry, is made possible by his having negotiated a lucrative retirement buyout.

Without that generous financial package, he too would have had to find a real job and be submerged once again in the malaise. Given the film's unwillingness to reckon with consequences, one is tempted to esteem its guiding vision—captured in the byline "look closer"—as nothing more than a soft, Americanized version of Buddhism.

In many ways, the film embodies the incoherence at the root of much leftist criticism of capitalism. A more consistent critique of capitalism as source of brutality can be found in Wendell Berry's essay "Sex, Economy, Freedom, and Community." Berry argues that giving free reign to capitalism wipes out local communal life, leaving individuals isolated and powerless in the face of large, impersonal forces. The proper, mediating role of the community is lost and individuals, liberated from local traditions and communal expectations, are increasingly subject to the whims of national bureaucracies and international markets. One of the problems with the "family values" espoused by conservatives is that it often leaves the nuclear family to itself, isolated amid an increasingly hostile economic and social order. Family values are also quite compatible with what Tocqueville identified as one of the great vices of modern politics: individualism. Tocqueville contrasted egoism, which elevates the satisfaction of one's own desires above all else, with individualism, which is a "a mature and calm feeling" that disposes each person to "draw apart with his family and friends" and "willingly leave society to itself."[5] The attempt to escape into personalist enclaves will not work, however, because the dominant language of the overarching culture infiltrates even the spheres of family intimacy. The consequence of this sort of individualism, according to Berry, is the loss of the sense of marriage as anything other than a contract between two isolated individuals: "If you depreciate the sanctity and solemnity of marriage, not just as a bond between two people but as a bond between those two people and their forbears, their children, and their neighbors, then you have prepared the way for an epidemic of divorce, child neglect, community ruin, and loneliness."[6]

MAGNOLIA

"An epidemic of divorce, child neglect, community ruin, and loneliness," is a pretty good description of the world depicted in another critically acclaimed film from 1999, Paul Thomas Anderson's sprawling *Magnolia*, which is also a tale of dysfunctional, suburban family life. Unlike *American Beauty*, *Magnolia* never entertains the prospect of a recovery of a vivacious adolescence. The abuse of children is so pervasive, the destruction of innocence so effective, that the youthful aspiration for pleasure-seeking freedom is undercut at the outset. *Magnolia* depicts a number of overlapping stories of families, in each of which the focus is on the father figure, his narcissism, his infidelity, and his abandonment of his family in time of need. The cycle of abuse and regret promises that each generation of sons will repeat the sins of the fathers. And yet the film holds out the possibility of repentance, forgiveness, and reconciliation, a possibility predicated, not on mere human capacities, but on a violent and bizarre act of divine intervention. With characters alternating between self-assertion, vengeful anger, and desperate longing for reconciliation, *Magnolia* is another ambitious example of the quest for redemption in American *noir*. Preoccupied with chance and coincidence, the film contains a shadowy vision of contemporary American life—with most scenes at night in the midst of torrential rain and with characters dominated by passions of lust and greed.

The film begins and ends with a narrator's ruminations on chance and design in the universe and thus invites viewers to consider whether *Magnolia*'s partially intersecting sub-plots and their dramatic resolutions constitute mere chance or represent some sort of providential design. The film's case for providential design is at once prominent and underdeveloped. There is nothing here that approaches an older comic vision of benevolent providence, bringing good out of evil, reconciling opposed characters, averting tragedy while introducing a happy ending, or elevating characters to a state beyond their merits.[7] The possibility of such large scale transformation is minimal in a world where characters are so thoroughly ensnared in patterns of self-destructive and self-deceptive behavior, behavior that bleeds into the lives of others and saps them of hope and love.

The mantra of the film, "we may be through with the past but the past is not through with us," captures the theme of entrapment. At one point that motif is entwined with the biblical motif of the sins of the father being visited on his children, with explicit reference made to *Exodus*. The two themes are inseparable in the life of T.J. (Tom Cruise), the national spokesman for a new men's movement, "Seduce and Destroy," which promotes male independence from, and dominance of, women. In explicit language, T.J. mocks the subordination of men to women and to their demands of responsibility and monogamy: "I won't apologize for who I am. I won't apologize for what I want. I won't apologize for what I need." T.J. harbors a secret hatred of his father, from whom he has been estranged for many years. His angry repudiation of his father generates an amplified repetition of his father's behavior toward women. T.J. has become a spectacularly successful version of what he loathes.

As critics have noted, the film contains a critique of patriarchy. But the use of other persons as instruments of personal pleasure or gain is not the exclusive province of male characters. T.J.'s father, Earl, is currently married to a much younger woman, Linda, for whom financial issues, rather than romance, are of preeminent concern. But watching Earl's health decline has prompted Linda to rethink her marriage. Unable to function without a steady flow of prescription drugs, Linda becomes increasingly unhinged as she desperately seeks a kind of redemption. Even as she longs for relief from the guilt of her self-indulgent life, she lacerates herself and takes a kind of perverse pleasure in self-inflicted suffering. She visits the family lawyer and informs him that she wants to be excised from Earl's will. Concerned at her distraught state and her irrational request, the lawyer asks on what basis she could ask for such a change in the will. She confesses that she never loved Earl and married him solely for his money. When she adds that she cheated on him, the lawyer observes that adultery is not against the law. Linda proceeds to describe her sexual activities with other men in graphic detail. She weeps as she explains that the realization of his impending death has prompted the first stirrings of love in her soul. She wants to make amends, to gain forgiveness.

Meanwhile, Earl, in and out of deep sleep, offers a series of confessions to his male nurse, who has been trying to contact T.J. to reunite him with his father before he dies. Earl reminisces about his first wife, how he cheated on her and left her to face cancer with only the help of their young son. In the midst of talking about how hard and long life is, he proclaims, "don't let anyone tell you not to regret." Earl's deathbed plea on behalf of regret is the film's ethical complement to the theme that the past is not done with us yet. To think that one could live free of regret or remorse for the vicious, harmful deeds of one's past is a naïve illusion, the very self-deception at the heart of Earl's son's philosophy of male power.

Modern and especially masculine forgetfulness of the past is an effort to proclaim an individual's autonomous control over the future. In the *noir* universe of *Magnolia*, liberation from the past is not possible; it will find and overtake you. As Georg Lukacs puts it, "the present becomes secondary and unreal, the past threatening and full of danger, the future already known and long since unconsciously experienced."[8] Just when you think you can escape from yourself, from your history, you run right into yourself. As was true in *American Beauty*, in *Magnolia* familial and romantic bonds have been so perforated, individual souls so scarred, that it is difficult to imagine any reliable way forward for these characters. In an interview concerning her role as Linda, Earl's wife, Julianne Moore said, "I found the part [of Linda] very arduous. It's really very difficult to try to find a way to make you understand her, because she doesn't understand herself.

She isn't what she appears to be, she isn't what she wants to be. She's at a place of real turbulence."[9]

The same could be said of nearly every character in the film. The characters twist and turn in the abyss of their personal dramas of damnation and redemption. They have a sense that some sort of judgment is upon them, that sins of the past demand a reckoning, and that the ultimate shape of their lives hinges upon the fulfillment of their longing for reconciliation and forgiveness.

One plotline culminates in a conversation about child abuse that seems at once frank and evasive, a conversation reminiscent of Todd Solondz's depiction of pedophilia and its impact on a father-son relationship in *Happiness*. In the case of *Magnolia*, the father is a television star, host of the popular kids' game show, "What Do Kids Know?" A sickly man, he collapses during a live broadcast and returns home to have a candid talk with his wife. When the topic shifts to his estranged daughter and why she despises him, the father admits that that he thinks that she thinks that he abused her. As if this indirection were not enough, he responds "I don't know" to the direct question about whether he did abuse her. The wife accuses him of indulgent self-deception; alone with the burden of his guilt, he contemplates suicide.

The game show host is representative of the parents in this movie, none of whom can comply with the plea of one of the children, a successful game show contestant pushed by his unfeeling father, "Dad, you have to be nicer to me." But then that plea itself may be part of the problem with the film. *Magnolia* suffers from an impoverished vocabulary of virtue and vice, success and failure, hope and despair. In place of supple descriptions, it substitutes a naïve romantic vision of the dichotomy between the innocent child and the alienated adult. The question is whether these characters have the requisite self-knowledge to make a meaningful confession and to begin to alter their lives through penitence and change of habits.

The difficulty with the characters in *Magnolia* is that they lack a vocabulary to articulate their own alienation. They lack the narrative resources to begin to describe their lives differently, the indispensable prerequisite to transformation of character. Charles Taylor tries to put his finger on the reason for this:

> In his depiction of real families in *Magnolia*, Anderson has fallen back on pop-psych banalities about abandonment and the inner child. This is a movie that climaxes with an act of God which acts as a kind of gateway to healing and forgiveness, and which (if I read it correctly) appears to suggest that a child has the gift of prophecy. When you hear a character say "It's a mistake to confuse children with angels," you realize that, on some basic level, Anderson is refuting that statement. He wants us to see children as innocents, and adults as nothing more than the protective shells of those damaged children. The movie's revelations of traumas and betrayals feel as if they spring out of something very personal for Anderson. But the revelations that parents aren't perfect because they act like human beings seems like the kind of thing a filmmaker of his sophistication should have grasped long ago.[10]

Taylor is right about the limitations to the dialectic of innocence lost versus innocence longed for, the romantic celebration of the child versus the inherent corruption of adult civilization. But what are we to make of the vigorous divine intervention at the end of the film, the violent storm followed by the cascade of giant frogs from the heavens? The entire city is inundated, windows are shattered and cars, destroyed. Given the film's reference to *Exodus*, a scriptural interpretation suggests itself: Yahweh's plagues upon the Egyptians. God works in and through the violence of this world. God's initial intervention seems destructive and accusatory, rather than healing and affirmative. But it alters or accentuates the movement of each of the plots in the film and suggests a possible drawing of human individuals out of their private worlds of desire, self-analysis, and grief and into some larger, more comprehensive story. Of course, the shape of that story remains elusive at the end.

PUNCH-DRUNK LOVE

The path of redemption through a love that overcomes violence is traced in Paul Thomas Anderson's *Punch-Drunk Love*, which infuses a romantic comedy with themes from *Fight Club*. In what has to be the oddest pairing of a director and lead actor in recent memory, *Punch-Drunk Love* unites Paul Thomas Anderson, director of *Boogie Nights* and *Magnolia*, with that embodiment of juvenile humor, Adam Sandler. Though more coherent, and blessedly more concise, than *Magnolia*, the film retains *Magnolia*'s mood of arbitrariness and stresses the difficult, desperate, and nearly inarticulate search for affection and love in a hostile universe.

Barry Egan (Adam Sandler) works selling fancy toilet plungers out of a nondescript warehouse in the same San Fernando Valley setting that provided the backdrop for *Magnolia*. Barry seems passive, deferential, and timid, but there are fearsome passions lurking just beneath the surface. Anderson constructs an environment that mirrors the division between Barry's external serenity and internal strife. When, at the beginning of the film, he walks out of his office and toward the street, the early-morning stillness is abruptly broken by a horrendous truck rollover and the sudden arrival of a van that leaves a small piano or harmonium by the side of the road. The rupturing of apparent serenity by unanticipated violence is the basic narrative pattern of the entire film.

The alternation in mood between isolated hostility and harmonious romantic love can be seen in a number of ways in the film, especially in the musical score. From cacophonic noise to notes of romance, the sound of the film effectively keeps the viewing and listening audience off balance by interspersing silence with violent staccato and hints of harmony. The small piano whose precise instrumental identity no one can name and which no one ever really plays is of course symbolic of the possibility of human concord. Befitting the dominant themes in the movie, the piano arrives purely by chance and in the midst of inexpli-

cable violence. The color scheme of the film, shot in widescreen Pan-
avision, highlights the omnipresence of California sunlight. The light
fosters different moods in different scenes; at times, it fosters a mood
of oppression, while at other times, particularly when it highlights the
radiant blue suit that Barry wears, it suggests luminous joy.

Oppressive is perhaps the best description of Barry's family of
seven sisters, who harass him with jabs about his past and his social
awkwardness. At a family party, they discuss him in condescending
terms as though he were not even present. He then disappears, only to
reappear smashing plate-glass windows. More unnerving than Barry's
outbreak of violence is his family's reaction. They do not register horror, or fear, or alarm; instead, they react the way one might to the
inappropriate speech of a teenager.

Barry's lone hope is Lena Leonard (Emily Watson), a friend of one
of his sisters who becomes inexplicably attracted to him after seeing
a family picture with Barry in it. The element of chance calls to mind
Magnolia. There, as here, Anderson suggests, "without coincidence—
spatial, temporal—there would be no tales to tell, no relations between
people whatsoever." There is a telling scene in the middle of the film
where Barry takes Lena out to dinner, where his playful awkwardness turns somber when Lena, in a gentle and jesting tone, mentions
a story she's heard from Barry's sister about him smashing a sliding
glass door with a hammer. Barry calls his sister a liar, excuses himself,
enters the bathroom, and tears it apart. When his destruction comes to
the attention of the manager and he is asked to leave, it seems as if his
violence has destroyed his best chance for friendship and love. But as
he and Lena exit the restaurant, the music turns playful and romantic
and their mood lightens. Yet another truck passes them—this one a
moving van with the word "Relocation" scrawled on it. This is a pivotal
scene. Both Barry and Lena want "relocation" or, in the case of Barry,
just "location," since he is a sort of nowhere man. Barry's desire to be
rescued from his current life is comically suggested in his enormous

collection of pudding, the labels of which can be turned in for frequent flyer miles and be "redeemed" in six to eight weeks.

Barry's pathetic loneliness, dislocation, and vulnerability are on display throughout the film. After smashing the window at the party, he says to one of his relatives, "I don't know what's wrong with me because I don't know how other people are." His gullibility and vulnerability are especially evident in the early scene where, while cutting out coupons from a magazine, he chances upon an ad for phone sex. He calls the number and, after providing far too much financial data to the operator, is soon talking to "Georgia." Her repeated attempts to talk dirty are rebuffed by an apparently indifferent Barry (or Jack, as he asks to be called so she will not "know it's me"). To her salacious, anatomical questions about his state of arousal, he responds, haltingly, "I don't know . . . I'm not in bed and I have my pants on."

The innocent encounter with Georgia haunts Barry for the rest of the film, as she hounds him with phone calls demanding money. It turns out that Georgia is the front-girl for a scam artist (Phillip Seymour Hoffman) who bribes wealthy men by threatening to reveal their phone-sex activities to family and friends. Georgia and her boss decide to send the "brothers" to teach Barry a lesson, and thus begins a series of violent encounters in which the lives of both Barry and Lena are at risk. Just as their romance begins to blossom, he is beaten, escapes, and is chased through the streets by violent thugs. These scenes are marvelously filmed, as the expression on Barry's face captures simultaneously his desperation and his determination. But the direct confrontation with brutal aggression also provides Barry with an opportunity to take control of his life.

There is much to admire in the film, not least Adam Sandler's performance. Anderson's directorial achievement is astonishing, exceeding that of *Magnolia*. *Punch-Drunk Love* works directly and relentlessly on the central nervous system of its audience. This is especially evident in the musical accompaniment, which is percussive rather than or-

chestral and which ties the viewer up in knots of tension that yearns
for release.

The film induces in viewers a sense of Barry's desperate longing,
of the arbitrary violence that lurks around every corner, and of the
slim, but nonetheless real possibility of affection and love. The ending
rather nicely hints at Barry's achievement of redemptive love. It does
not quite demonstrate the thesis that love conquers all; it leaves us
with the ominous specter of arbitrary violence. It does, however, make
a compelling case, more persuasive in this respect than in *Magnolia*,
for love's capacity to come upon us unaware, particularly in the midst
of hostile threats.

Despite their attempts at reviving a quest for redemption, all the
films I have discussed thus far in this chapter suffer from similar weaknesses. They all fall prey, to some degree or another, to a certain kind
of romantic myth, a celebration of childhood innocence in a civilized
world, where corruption of soul is a necessary accompaniment of any
measure of adult complexity. Another way to express the defect is to say
that these films are strongest and most entertaining in their negations,
even if these too can at times be sophomoric. *American Beauty* spends
most of its time mocking corporate suburban American and wallowing
in teen hedonism, even though it manages to craft a language of the
vision of the heart as an alternative to these twin nihilisms. Still, that
language is never clearly embodied in the lives of the characters and
so the film's answer is less than persuasive. Anderson's films, *Magnolia*
and *Punch-Drunk Love*, are the most Rousseauian of all. Verbal inarticulacy is the order of the day for the characters in these films, whose
expressions of self-knowledge and love are either rife with profanity
or involve a childlike simplicity that renders the characters less than
credible. To its great credit, *Punch-Drunk Love* manages at least to
make inarticulacy and our stuttering attempts at communication into
a thoughtful and captivating central theme.

THIRTEEN CONVERSATIONS ABOUT ONE THING

None of these weaknesses afflicts *Thirteen Conversations About One Thing*, a subtly crafted and intellectually rich film, directed by the relative newcomer, Jill Sprecher, based on a script she co-wrote with her sister. The central issue of the film, the quest for happiness in a world of apparent randomness, calls to mind Pascal, who writes, "All men seek happiness. There are no exceptions. . . . This is the motive of every act of every man, including those who go and hang themselves. . . . Yet all men complain: old, young, strong, weak, learned, ignorant . . . in every country, at every time, of all ages, and all conditions."[11] As in Pascal, so too in this film, the puzzle is not so much about happiness as it is about an inexplicable paradox at the heart of the human condition. It seems we cannot *not* want happiness—and yet we can never achieve it. Is this fact significant, more than a mere fact, perhaps a clue to the grand mystery? Or is it just an inexplicable, perhaps regrettable, fact? Even if the film tends toward a pessimistic answer, it leaves the possibilities open and leaves us transfixed by the question.

The freshness and thoughtfulness of the film consist precisely in the subtle way in which it provokes reflection about the shape and destiny of individual human lives. The philosophical issues are rarely formulated directly or abstractly; instead, they arise concretely, in terms of specific deliberations, choices, and encounters. The result is a subdued yet engrossing investigation of the big questions.

In an early scene, we meet Walker (John Turturro) and his wife Patricia (Amy Irving). Sensing the depths of his disaffection, she asks, "What is it you want?" to which he replies, "What everyone wants. To experience life. To wake up enthused. To be happy." Walker has just been mugged and is transfixed by the apparent similarities between himself and the mugger: "It could have been me." Yet his initial fascination with chance gives way to his habitual mode of thinking of the flow of events as "irreversible," the term he writes on the board for the students in his physics class. One of the most impressive features of the film is the way it underscores complexity of character by unveiling tensions in the desires and thoughts of individuals. The film shatters any naïveté we might have about happiness, whose achievement and sustenance seem thoroughly contingent on circumstances outside of our control. The film conjoins the inevitability of the quest with skepticism about our ability even to know, let alone grasp, what would make us happy. "May you get what you want," is the grim gypsy curse running through the film.

Precisely that happens to Walker, a physics professor, after he leaves his wife and begins an affair with a fellow academic. A Milton scholar, she quotes *Paradise Lost*: "The mind is in its own place and in itself can make a hell of heaven, a heaven of hell." These are the self-deluding words of Satan in Milton's epic; for its part, the film lays bare the illusory nature of the human attempt at the autonomous construction of happiness. In a comic note lost on Walker, he begins his affair in order to add diversity and novelty to his life, but insists that their meetings occur at the same time and place each week.

Walker's own routinized self-absorption, captured in the way he treats a mediocre student with indifference, has devastating consequences. Here his penchant, emblematic of a certain strain of Enlightenment science, for cold, impersonal, objective necessity, leads him to be curt with a struggling student. In response to the student's pleas, he remains unmoved and replies "cause and effect, the third law of motion," as he sets in motion the Newton's Cradle toy on his desk. The chilling result of his indifference is driven home powerfully in a scene at the beginning of the next class when he asks about the absence of the struggling student. When his classmates say he died in a fall, one student interjects with frigid analytical detachment, that he must have jumped because of the trajectory of the fall: "Isn't that right, professor?"

In another introductory scene, a prosecutor, Troy (in a terrific performance by Matthew McConaughey) celebrates a guilty verdict during "happy hour" in a bar. He strikes up a conversation with Gene (in an even better performance by Alan Arkin), a down on his luck middle manager in an insurance company. Troy mocks Gene's pessimism, evident in his prophecy, "Show me a happy man and I'll show you a disaster waiting to happen." The apparently unflappable Troy, initiates the chants, "f--- guilt," as he rejoins his buddies in their booth. Troy will soon find himself attempting to avoid responsibility for a crime, but guilt will eat away at his soul and body in ways he could never have foreseen.

The film underscores the significance of this exchange and of the fates of the two characters by splicing it into the middle of two separate narratives. As we realize by the end of the film, one person's story is just ending while another's is just beginning. The temporal discontinuity in the presentation of events further reinforces the importance of the question concerning fate, contingency and providential design.

Leaving the bar and now driving home in his car, Troy unintentionally hits a pedestrian and flees the scene. But he cannot escape his sense of guilt, dramatically embodied in the cut from the accident that he will not let heal. In a wonderfully revealing scene, he interrogates and gazes at a criminal only to see his own reflection in a mirror. He is now compelled to identify himself with the "lowlifes" that in the past he giddily "locked up." In a ritual reminiscent of what Dostoevsky called "self-laceration," Troy repeatedly uses a razor blade to cut open his wound just as it begins to heal. Near death from blood poisoning, he writes up a will to leave everything he has to the family of his victim, only to learn that she survived. Here, the comment of another character, that "sometimes people get lucky and get a second chance" is proven true.

With a drug addict for a son, Gene is growing old in his middle manager's position. His biggest torment is the daily presence of an unflappably happy underling, known as Wade "Smiley" Bowman, whose buoyancy Gene decides to test. Here he even uses words from the book of *Job*, "The Lord giveth and the Lord taketh away." It is a credit to the film's presentation of its characters that it manages to depict Gene's malicious cynicism unsparingly, yet he never becomes a completely unsympathetic character. Conversely, Smiley's apparently naïve happiness is not without substance. Indeed, Smiley's continued good faith and positive demeanor seem even to have softened Gene a bit. After firing Smiley, he regrets his callous act, and secretly arranges another job for him. In the final scene in the bar, which picks up where the opening left off, he goes on to admit to a friend that one needs faith of some sort in this world.

Conversation's freshness is also evident in what it avoids, an exclusive focus on intellectuals or the rich or suburban angst. It draws characters from a variety of socioeconomic levels and professions (lawyers, professors, house-cleaners, and insurance claims adjustors). We are persuaded that these are real lives; the breadth of human types gives a convincing universality to the issues raised in the film. The detection of common themes in complex specificity recalls Pascal's list: "old, young, strong, weak, learned, ignorant . . . in every country, at every time, of all ages, and all conditions."

The film makes effective use of two, increasingly common, structural techniques: the chance intersection of lives and the splitting of the temporal sequence of events. The overlapping occurs at the edges of lives, where in slight but devastating ways we discern the unintended and unanticipated impact of one life on another. The rejection of linearity is less dramatic and easier to follow than in *Pulp Fiction* or *Memento*. Discerning the intersections and reconstructing the narrative sequence provide the viewer with satisfying moments of recognition and insight.

The film ultimately frames the question of happiness in terms of fate, destiny, or providence. One has the sense that these thoroughly secular characters exist on the cusp of the religious. The best they can do is to talk about fortune, which "smiles on some and laughs at others." But religious themes are never far from the surface. Gene's testing of his serene employee, for example, has strong overtones of the trial of Job.

The most overtly religious character in the film is Beatrice, Troy's victim, a working class cleaning woman whose simple faith in the miraculous makes her the antithesis of Walker. To her co-workers protest that life is not fair, she counters, "It may seem that way now, but we don't know what's up ahead. Amazing things happen all the time." As confirmation, she likes to tell a story of nearly drowning as a child. Of course, the amazing thing that happens to her is being the victim of a hit-and-run driver, the result of which is serious injuries. Yet she is pulled back from despair by the apparently chance intervention of a stranger. In a scene at Beatrice's church, where she sings in the choir, the scriptural reading comes from the *Letter of James*, chapter 5:

> Be patient, therefore, brothers, until the coming of the Lord. See how the farmer waits for the precious fruit of the earth, being patient about it, until it receives the early and the late rains. You also, be patient. Establish your hearts, for the coming of the Lord is at hand. Do not grumble against one another, brothers, so that you may not be judged; behold, the Judge is standing at the door. As an example of suffering and patience, brothers, take the prophets who spoke in the name of the Lord. Behold, we consider those blessed who remained steadfast. You have heard of the steadfastness of Job, and you have seen the purpose of the Lord, how the Lord is compassionate and merciful.

Given that the passage refers explicitly to the patient endurance of Job and reflects on the key issues of the film, it seems quite apt. Yet the filmmakers present the text merely in passing and do not dwell on it. The film's commentary on the passage makes clear how difficult it can be not only to remain "steadfast" but also to see "the purpose of the Lord." It also explains why the double gypsy curse, "may you get what you want and like it," is such a burden. Only through the testing and maturation of what is initially naïve faith can we come to glimpse purpose of any sort. But the grammatical mood appropriate to this film is not the indicative but the interrogative. It subtly points us toward the question of who or what, if anyone or anything, is orchestrating things, and whether that being, if it exists, is benevolent or malevolent. This calls to mind Pascal again: "When I consider the brief span of my life absorbed into the eternity which comes before and after . . . I am amazed to see myself here rather than there: there is no reason for me to be here rather than there, now rather than then. Who put me here? By whose command and act were this time and place allotted to me?"[12]

8

Wide Awake: M. Night Shyalmalan

Our chief interest and chief duty is to seek enlightenment . . .
And that is why, amongst, those who are not convinced, I make
an absolute distinction between those who strive with all their
might to learn and those who live without troubling themselves
or thinking about it.

I can feel nothing but compassion for those who sincerely
lament their doubt, who regard it as the ultimate misfortune, and
who, sparing no effort to escape from it make their search their
principal and most serious business.

But as for those who spend their lives without a single thought
for this final end of life and who, solely because they do not find
within themselves the light of conviction, neglect to look elsewhere . . . I view them very differently.

This negligence in a matter where they themselves, their eternity, their all are at stake, fills me more with irritation than pity;
it astounds and appalls me; it seems quite monstrous to me. I
do not say this prompted by the pious zeal of spiritual devotion.
I mean on the contrary that we ought to have this feeling from
principles of human interest and self-esteem. For that we need
only see what the least enlightened see.[1]

I T IS A UNIVERSAL HUMAN QUESTION whether we might be, individually and communally, characters in a cosmic drama. If we are at all open to an affirmative answer to that question, we may become (potential) characters in search of our author. We embark on a spiritual quest. Of course, the starting points of such a quest are as various as are human stories and lives. Diversity is characteristic not only of the questions or doubts or hopes that prompt the quest, but even the extent to which the quest is fully conscious or merely implicit, voluntary or constrained. In the passage just quoted, Pascal urges that it befits human beings to pursue the big questions, questions he takes to be intimately connected, concerning the existence of God, the existence and nature of the soul, and whether our destinies are matters of chance, fate or providence. We are feeble, rational creatures—what Pascal calls "thinking reeds." Located between paralyzing doubt and translucent certitude, between despair and presumption, human life takes on the shape of a quest.

But we increasingly lack confidence in, or even knowledge of, our history. We suffer a diminution in the repertoire of stories and myths and an impoverishment in our vocabulary of virtue and vice. We even become skeptical of the very notion of the quest, of whether there is any good to be pursued or discovered on the journey of our lives. In such a situation, what sort of quest remains for us? How varied, even inverted, the quest can become is evident in Walker Percy's novel *Lancelot*, an extended monologue from an admitted murderer, who is now in a psychiatric hospital where he is visited regularly by an old friend, a priest-psychiatrist who has himself lost his faith in God. The main character taunts the lapsed priest about the old quest for God, which he claims is "all washed up." He poses the following set of questions: "Can good come from evil? Have you ever considered the possibility that one might undertake a search not for God but for evil? You people may have been on the wrong track all these years with all that talk about God and signs of his existence. . . . But what if you could show me a *sin*? a purely evil deed, an intolerable deed for which there is no explanation? Now there's a mystery."[2]

Something like this apparently perverse quest for evil is, I think, operative in many of our best horror films. Often derided as mindless entertainment, the genre of the horror film is, in addition to providing the shocks that audiences crave, capable of raising all sorts of interesting questions about the nature of evil, about the unanticipated dangers that attend the human attempt to control and manipulate nature, about Enlightenment science, and even about the existence of God. In the face of a behaviorist account of human action, where freedom is reducible to antecedent influences, psychological or chemical, evil, understood as an act for which an individual is freely responsible, dissolves. Many modern horror films, from *The Exorcist* to *Silence of the Lambs*, presuppose a kind of behaviorism, or at least a reductionist view of evil as susceptible to medicinal or psychiatric explanation and treatment.[3] These films raise the question whether evil exists. By implication, they also raise a host of other questions concerning human freedom, moral responsibility, and the possibility of goodness and concerning theodicy and providence. Recall the opening query in the passage just quoted from *Lancelot*: "Can good come from evil?" In traditional theology, bringing good out of evil is one of the activities of divine providence. Much of contemporary film, particularly in the horror genre, narrates evil overcoming goodness or evil ceaselessly and mechanically generating evil. The quest here is undermined in advance: characters find themselves trapped in the past, by evil deeds performed or endured, that haunt them in the present and whose repetition awaits them in the future, a future dictated by past malevolence.

If it avoids even a glancing interest in these big questions, the horror genre degenerates into an obsessive competition at the level of surface aesthetics, as one director after another is forced to increase the body count and devise more complex and more revolting mechanisms of torturing and maiming victims. The gory, nihilistic bloodfest into which horror movies had sunk by the 1990s put filmmakers in a bind. The only way forward involved a competition to outdo previous films in the quantity and quality of the acts of maiming, raping, decapitating, and murdering victims. The greatest novelty to emerge in the late 1990s was the genre's degeneration into self-conscious parody in the *Scream* and *Scary Movie* films. Soft nihilism, alternately frightening and humorous, reigns.

Then came M. Night Shyamalan. With *The Sixth Sense* (1999), which appeared in the same year as *The Blair Witch Project*, Shyamalan announced a new beginning in the horror genre. Even more than *Blair Witch*, whose scares rested mostly on the gimmickry of a hand-held camera, *Sense* returns us to less overt forms of horror, predicated upon audience sympathy with the dilemmas of the characters. Shyamalan's films stand out as attempts to return horror to the big questions and to replace terror with suspense. Shyamalan self-consciously locates himself in the tradition of Hitchcock, who once said, "There is no terror in the bang, only in the anticipation of it." Like Hitchcock, Shyamalan appears in his own films. At his best, Shyamalan slowly builds the tensions and then delivers bangs, as in Cole Sear's sudden vision of ancient hangings in his modern-day Philadelphia grade school in *The Sixth Sense* or the use of crop circles and mysterious sounds emanating from cornfields in rural Pennsylvania in *Signs*. Beyond horror, Shyamalan invests other sub-genres, the such as that of the comic book superhero or of alien invasion, with subtle themes and a remarkable knack for settings and character.

Much more than Hitchcock, Shyamalan exhibits an abiding interest in questions of faith and divine providence. *The Sixth Sense* is pitched at the intersection of life and death, where souls struggle for reconciliation, for a way of putting their lives in order; *Unbreakable* is the odd quest of a physically cursed character, Elijah Price, to discover his opposite, an unbreakable superhero, whose existence would be a miracle; *Signs* is about the loss and recovery of faith, about the fundamental option between chance and providence; and *Wide Awake*,

Shyamalan's second feature film, is a straightforward quest of a young boy to speak with God. Shyamalan depicts consciously embraced quests (*Wide Awake*), quests of which the main characters are largely unaware (*The Sixth Sense*), and quests that are vigorously resisted (*Signs*). The resolution of the quest typically occurs in unanticipated ways, often when characters have abandoned their journeys. In Shyamalan's films, that is the structure of providence.

These films are also about fear: fear of loss, fear of death, fear of being trapped in the evils of the past, fear of a life without purpose or place, and fear of individual and cultural catastrophe from an unexpected malevolent intervention. Shyamalan thus prompts the question: Can we learn anything from our fears? Can we learn from fear not just about the evils that horrify us, but also about the goods for which we long and long to protect? The retreat from terror to suspense is in part motivated by a desire to provoke thought in, rather than to rein tyrannically over the imagination of, the audience. Shyamalan has a sense of the significance of the question, what is the "scariest thing," the question raised by Elijah Price in *Unbreakable.* Many characters in Shyamalan's films have lost a sense of purpose and find themselves alienated from those dearest to them. But, as *Unbreakable* makes clear, the scariest thing is not the loss of meaning or purpose but the diabolical will to achieve meaning at all cost.

THE LADY IN THE WATER & THE VILLAGE

Among current, popular, mainstream filmmakers, Shyamalan is the most consistently concerned with spiritual matters, even if his plots are often criticized as bland syncretism or shallow new age–ism. In recent years, however, Shyamalan has had less success in creating credible plots. In *The Lady in the Water*, for example, Shyamalan takes the willing suspension of disbelief, thought to be a presumption of serious engagement with fiction, and transforms it into a directorial demand of a will to believe. One of the odd things about *Lady in the Water*'s credulity is that the potential dangers accruing to naïve belief in traditional tales appeared to be a central lesson of Shyamalan's previous film, *The Village*. Even that film, which poses interesting philosophical questions in a less than gripping drama, imposes on viewers' sense of the credible. In these most recent films, Shyamalan simply bypasses what was a distinguishing feature of his early dramas—the confrontation of modern skepticism with the world of myth or the supernatural.

On this score, *Lady* begins promisingly, with an assertion of the primacy of myth and the alienation that springs from forgetfulness of ancient stories. *Lady* offers a mythic history that traces man's alienation from the natural world of water. From an original union with water, men have traveled onto land in a greedy quest for possession. The water world has not entirely despaired of men, whose world is now rent by war and void of guidance. Occasionally a creature is sent on a mission to the human world, but mankind has "forgotten how to listen."

With that introduction, we make an abrupt transition to modern Philadelphia, where Cleveland Heep (Paul Giamatti), a stuttering and down on his luck superintendent at an apartment complex, suspects that kids may be swimming in the pool at night. One night he sees someone emerge from the water, grab something off a chair, and return to the water. Heep begins to panic when the swimmer remains submerged; his efforts to find the swimmer leave him exhausted. He collapses into the pool and nearly drowns. But a young woman named Story (Bryce Dallas Howard playing the same sort of frail ethereal character that she played in Shyamalan's *The Village*, only here with sight but no clothes) saves him and takes him back to his apartment. Soon—too soon, in fact, to salvage the credibility of the plot—Heep is a true believer in Story's story about the Blue World, how she was sent to meet a writer, and how her role as a narf is threatened by a vicious animal called a scrunt, which bears a striking resemblance to the ominous creature from *The Village*.

Cleveland discovers that his Korean neighbors, Young-Soon Choi (Cindy Cheung) and her mother (June Kyoto Lu), know a good bit about the traditional tale of the narf, or at least the non-assimilated mother does. Having heard the tales as bedtime stories in her youth, Young-Soon responds to Heep's plea for information by saying, "I don't remember." There is an obvious echo here of the film's opening lesson but Shyamalan does nothing with this plot possibility. The contrast between an older eastern culture and a modern rationalistic, individualistic and skeptical western culture would seem to be a perfect foil for Shyamalan's story. But, except as a source of details for the myth, the Choi family is simply left out of the plot. Shyamalan here misses a great opportunity to play against one another two ways of approaching myth and culture.

Without such a serious and engaging human plotline, the film becomes an exercise in pious credulity. The problem is that no one exercises sufficient skepticism to meet the audience where it is. In this, *Lady* is unlike *Signs, Unbreakable, Sixth Sense*, or even his early film, *Wide Awake*. Here everybody just cannot wait to play a role in a real-life fairy tale. As one of the characters urges the others, "it's time we made a story come true." If heavy doses of dour and despairing films can drive certain viewers to reconsider God or at least to feel His absence in ways they would not otherwise, Shyamalan's latest entry could have thinking viewers longing for atheism.

Even where he fails, as he does here, Shyamalan still instructs. His struggle as a filmmaker embodies the plight of all those who long for a sense of purpose in a contemporary world that often treats grand narratives with derisive scorn. The problem with the mythic world of *Lady* is not that the fairy tale itself is incredible, but that the adult characters in the film are so desperate to believe in any story whatsoever, in any myth larger than themselves, that it all becomes matter of fact. It is a myth without a mystery.

As we noted above, *Lady* seems to fall precisely into the trap that had been investigated so thoroughly in Shyamalan's previous film, *The Village*. While it raised important questions, that film also placed viewers in the difficult situation of having to believe and care for characters whose words and actions were too often preposterous. Put slightly differently, *The Village* is much better at raising interesting philosophical questions than it is at dramatically depicting or resolving them.

The theme of fear, in this case fear of the entire, tainted modern world, is at the forefront in *The Village*, which features a late-nineteenth-century Amish-like community that has purposely isolated itself from the rest of society. In this film, Shyamalan wants to create a mood of unseen but encroaching menace, the sort of mood captured so effectively in Peter Weir's underappreciated *Picnic at Hanging Rock* (1975). In *The Village*, the menace, represented as the "ones we don't speak of," is associated with the color red, the "bad color."

A boundary demarcates village property from the woods, where the threatening creatures live and beyond which is the civilized world. The menacing creatures, blamed for the mutilation of animals on village property, make an appearance fairly early in the film, wearing red outfits that make them look like giant rats in Little Red Riding Hood costumes. Viewers will likely already have anticipated the truth about the mysterious creatures by the time it is revealed just over midway through the film. From this moment forward, the real questions concern the community's motive in removing itself from the wider world. The individuals who have sought refuge in this community once lived in the midst of modern society. A series of violent events led them to judge the modern world, pervaded as it is by greed, lust, and violence, to be incorrigible. They then constructed a community in complete isolation from that society. But keeping all the members of the community, particularly the younger generation, which lacks a potentially salutary experience of the evils of the outside world, cut off from the modern world requires a palpable fear of the area lying just beyond the boundary of the community's land. Hence, the stories and occasional destructive activities of "those we do not speak of."

One character, Alice Hunt (played by Sigourney Weaver), keeps mementos of evil things from the past stored in a chest. She explains to her now adult son, Lucius Hunt (Joaquin Phoenix), that she keeps them to fend off forgetfulness, which would in turn allow the evils to return. But there is no effective strategy to fend off the past. Escape and isolation seem futile: "You run from sorrow . . . but sorrow will find you. It can smell you." The action of the film will provide ample illustration of the truth of that statement. The story is a kind of parable about fear and evil, about the human longing to recover and protect innocence, and about the costly and futile attempt to construct a pristine and safe world. But it fails because its themes and moods are not woven into a credible plot.

WIDE AWAKE & THE SIXTH SENSE

Although Shyamalan has always been interested in surprise endings and has a proclivity for overt, providential resolution of plots, he has not always imposed upon viewers' sense of the credible from the opening scenes of his films. He has in fact been the most successful mainstream filmmaker at constructing stories of spiritual quest. The most explicit such film is probably his early film, *Wide Awake*, the tale of a young boy's quest for God in the aftermath of the death of his beloved grandfather. Joshua (Joseph Cross) is a fifth-grader at a Catholic school for boys, where he is known for asking "too many questions." In a hilarious scene in his religious class, the teacher (Rosie O'Donnell as a nun with a fondness for baseball analogies) reminds them to complete their reading assignments in their two texts, *Next Stop Salvation* and *Jesus is My Buddy*. Suddenly, Joshua interrupts the teacher's banal descriptions of a very user-friendly Jesus, to ask about the Catholic teaching that you have to be baptized to save your soul from damnation. The mere posing of that serious point of doctrine causes a disturbance in class, as young boys, one after another, start to realize how many people (family and friends) have never been baptized and insist on knowing whether those souls are destined for damnation. Instead of answering their questions directly, the teacher attempts to deflate the issue and then distract the kids. In the face of the benign, or perhaps not so benign, neglect of the big questions, Joshua's gravity is testimony to his being more rational than others in his community. For as Pascal eloquently stated, to be engaged in a quest for the truth about the big questions is not a matter of piety; it is instead a matter of simple human dignity and reason. To remain indifferent in the face of questions, on whose answer depends the destiny of our very being, is, for Pascal, monstrous. The least enlightened, including, it seems, some fifth-grade boys, have the ability to see this.

Until the death of his grandfather, Joshua divided his free time between visits with his grandfather, whose room is just down the hall from his own, and his daredevil friend, Dave, the kind of fearless kid who takes on any challenge and succeeds. From his grandfather, Joshua receives two precepts: one about football (keep both hands on the ball) and the other about God, never lose your faith.

But his grandfather's death shatters Joshua's sense of stability and trust. Recalling that his grandfather told him that he was "not going anywhere," Joshua laments, "He lied." He remains preoccupied with his absent grandfather, in whose room he still spends much time. He tries football but with little success: "Football is not the answer," he confesses sadly. That leaves God. Experiencing a painful mixture of nagging doubt and increased desire to know God, Joshua embarks on a more serious mission, one that will have his parents and teachers even more worried about his precocious seriousness. Chatting with his buddy, Dave, in the hallway at school, Joshua's mind is suddenly arrested by a flood of light pouring through the windows. He stops and, in a voiceover, comments, "It's strange when you first get an idea sometimes. You look at something that you've looked at a thousand times before" and see it for the first time. Joined by Dave, Joshua asks him whether he thinks about God, to which Dave responds, "We go to Catholic school; thinking about God is kind of our homework." To Joshua's follow-up question, "Do you think he's real?," Dave shrugs and calmly enumerates reasons for doubting God's existence. Soon Joshua decides on his mission, to talk to God. But the problem is, where? Where do you find God? How do you converse with him? Joshua thus formulates some of the central questions that have preoccupied theologians for centuries.

When he learns that a cardinal, renowned for holiness and rumored to have conversed with God, will be visiting his sister's school, Joshua's mood brightens considerably. But when he sneaks into his sister's school and finds the cardinal alone, he discovers a weak and sickly old man and decides that he does not look like the kind of man to whom God would speak. He looks, well, like someone's grandfather. Disappointed but not yet ready to quit, Joshua states, "this mission could take days."

Not wanting to close off any options, Joshua avails himself of the practices of other religions, Muslim and Jewish. He tells his teacher that he cannot meet with her on a certain day because it will be Hanukah and he has already bought candles. But Joshua is not just adding to his religious options, he is also coming to question certain childish ways of seeing the world. In a toy store with his mother, he explains that he has just had a "revelization." He used to think that the superhero section of the toy store was pure magic. Whenever he looked at the toys, he would see magical worlds. But now? "Just plastic and paint. Every year, there is less magic."

As Joshua's search drags on, Dave tells him that he needs to give up his quest, not least because he has been telling girls about it and they probably think he is a "mental patient." Dave also has philosophical doubts. He puts the issue in terms of a dilemma: Either there is no God or there is but he does not care that you are looking for him.

What this dilemma wrongly assumes is that we can be certain that we are in a good position to make a judgment about divine communication. Pascal formulates the problem thus: It is not evident that whatever is not immediately evident to me as I am now must be false or non-existent.[4] We do not assume that about complex scientific claims or about the capacity of a poem to communicate deeps truths about the human condition or about a novice's ability to judge fine wine. Underlying that assumption is another dubious presupposition, namely, that we can know exactly how God ought to behave and that we can confidently assume that God could have no good purpose in withholding an explicit revelation of his existence from us. But this is to assume that every reasonable belief in God entails the obviousness of God's existence. Pascal counters, citing the Old Testament, that "God is a hidden God." Any religion, he boldly claims, that does not proclaim the hiddenness of God is false; and any religion that does not explain why it is appropriate for God to be hidden fails to instruct. To put this point in terms of the film, Joshua exercises an admirable and brave humility in continuing his quest. He does so not just because it has yet to be fulfilled but also because he cannot be sure that he has exhausted all possible paths to the answer.

Near the point of abandoning his mission, Joshua sits with eyes closed in his grandfather's chair and begs God for a sign. After his prayer, he runs from room to room in his house, inquiring of his parents and sister, "Anything godly in nature reveal itself to you just now?" He then remembers a conversation he had with his grandfather during a walk in the snow. To Joshua's question about why his grandfather is not afraid to die, the answer is "God will take care of me." Joshua persists, "But how do you know for sure? Maybe God isn't real. Superman isn't real." When Joshua asks for proof, his grandfather cites snow as a sign of God's existence. Joshua offers a scientific account, which he learned in his earth science class, of snow as water vapor. His grandfather concurs, "you're right but there's more, much more." Emerging again from his grandfather's chair, he looks out the window to see his yard blanketed with a unexpected snow.

Thus begins a series of signs that Joshua himself, weary of his apparently empty quest, is unable to interpret. The next comes in the form of a strangely answered prayer. Dave talks Joshua into helping him sneak into a teacher's classroom to change the grade on Dave's test. After they safely enter the room and Dave begins altering his test, the teacher approaches the room. Dave and Joshua crouch under the desk and Joshua desperately prays a "Hail Mary." Although neither boy recognizes it, the prayer is answered in an impressive way. The teacher does not detect their presence and she takes the tests with her and thus removes the possibility of Dave succumbing to his temptation. Joshua's intervention on behalf of his friend becomes even more dramatic a few days later when on the way home from school he asks his mother to stop by and visit Dave who is home sick. When Joshua enters the house where Dave's mother is napping, he finds Dave alone, afflicted with a seizure. Joshua's chance visit saves Dave's life, the implications of which event are lost on Joshua but not on Dave. Joshua concedes to a recovering Dave that he was right to doubt the mission; his grandfather was in error; someone just made God up. But Dave tells him that he would be wrong to give up his mission. Dave now believes that Joshua's arrival at just that moment was a sort of miracle.

In a final scene, Shyamalan cannot resist hammering the audience with religious resolution. He all but states that Joshua has had a guardian angel with him the whole time, someone whom he could not see because his faith had not yet matured. Evidence of that maturity is present in Joshua's end of school year speech before his entire class on the topic of what fifth grade meant to him. In this scene, which would have made a much better ending to the film, Joshua speaks of the many changes that fifth grade has wrought—how before this year, girls did not exist for him and everyone he loved lived forever. He ends by saying, "It's as if I was asleep before and finally woke up. I'm wide awake now."

Being wide awake in this Shyamalan film means to have an intellect full of questions; it means to be someone willing to embark on an uncertain quest; it also involves a communal dimension, where the quest cannot be successfully undertaken in isolation from others; and, finally, in contrast to modern Enlightenment teachings that equate adult intelligence with the acceptance of atheism, agnosticism, or deism, being awake here involves receptivity to the word that speaks providentially through the otherwise inexplicable gaps in human experience, in the narrative structure of our lives. The film indirectly confirms Pascal's observation that deism and atheism, both of which remove God from the human scene, are equally distant from Christianity or from any religion that teaches the decisive and providential intervention of God into human history.

Shyamalan's next film, *The Sixth Sense*, which remains one of the top-selling movies of all time, treats the theme of the spiritual quest in quite a different manner. The two main characters, Cole (Haley Joel Osment), a young boy afflicted by ghosts, and Malcolm (Bruce Willis), an award winning child psychologist plagued with guilt over a single, devastating failure, are on spiritual quests of which they are largely unaware. The film begins on the evening of Malcolm's big award ceremony, after the ceremony in fact, as he and his wife return home still relishing the evening's events. When they enter their bedroom, they quickly realize that there is an intruder in the adjacent bathroom. The man, stripped naked, asks repeatedly whether Malcolm remembers him; it turns out that he (Vincent) was a patient very briefly in his childhood, that he was being abused by his family, and that Malcolm did not help him. After a brief conversation, he pulls a gun and shoots Malcolm, who lies on the bed awaiting the arrival of the ambulance. When next we see Malcolm, he is arriving for a scheduled meeting with Cole. Like Vincent, Cole suffers from acute anxiety, has an unusually high level of intelligence, and thinks of himself as a freak.

Malcolm is a successful child psychologist with a gift for making children feel strong. But in this film there are no heroes who stand above the fray and effortlessly intervene in human affairs to set things right. It becomes clear very quickly that Malcolm has not recovered from the encounter with Vincent and that his marriage has fallen apart. When he is not meeting with Cole or having failed attempts at meeting his wife, he listens to tapes of his interviews with Vincent. The new case concerning Cole appears to be his chance to recover his gift.

When Malcolm follows Cole into a local church, he overhears him chanting: *De profundis clamo ad te, domine.* "What's that?" he asks, to which Cole responds, "It's called Latin." Observing the way Cole takes refuge in the church, Malcolm explains, "People used to hide out in churches where they claimed sanctuary." The Latin phrase Cole chants is from the Psalms—"Out of the depths, I cry to you, Oh Lord"—is a desperate plea for assistance, a plea felt if not articulated by all the characters in *The Sixth Sense*, in a world in which individuals have already lost, or are in imminent danger of losing, what is most dear to them and in which the temptation to despair is nearly overwhelming.

Cole lives alone with his mother, who is financially strapped, still grieving over the death of her own mother, and worried about the odd phenomena that surround her son. When Cole experiences what looks to outsiders like some sort of seizure, he is taken to the doctor (played by Shyamalan) who finds nothing physically wrong with the boy but questions his mother about cuts on his body. The wrongful accusation stings and not just because it is false, but also because it preys upon her sense of guilt that she has not been able to provide a proper home for her son.

With the help of Malcolm, Cole comes to realize that his role is to answer the pleadings of the ghosts. Malcolm asks him, "What do the ghosts want?" To which Cole responds, "Help." Malcolm suggests that maybe they just need someone to listen to them. The most striking instance of this deceased need for assistance has to do with a little girl who had been slowly poisoned by her mother. Unknown to anyone in her family, the girl managed to record the poisoning on tape. Malcolm accompanies Cole to the girl's funeral and then to the house of the dead girl where family and friends have gathered to remember and to mourn. Cole delivers it to the father, saying, "she wanted you to have this." The father plays the tape and the mother's guilt is revealed to a now doubly horrified community. But Cole's assistance is not limited to the dead. He also helps his mother, consoling her at one point after she has a nightmare.

Still, Cole has resisted telling his mom the truth about his condition, because he fears that it will only confirm her suspicions that he is a freak. Toward the end of the film, as he sits in his mom's car in a traffic jam, he tells his mom that he is ready to communicate. Then he explains that there has been an accident in the cars ahead of them. He adds that a lady died in the crash. As his mom strains to see through the line of cars to see what Cole is seeing, she asks, "How do you know that? Where is she?" Cole responds, "Standing right next to my window." As his mother becomes increasingly concerned, he explains, "I see dead people. Ghosts ask me to do things for them." Her fear begins to turn to anger when he claims that grandma says hello and that she visits him occasionally. Just as it appears that the mom might begin to think Cole is cruel and manipulative for playing upon her emotional vulnerability regarding her dead mother, he provides information that could only have come from communication with the dead. He tells his mother that his grandmother wants her to know that the answer to the question that she asked at her grave is "every day." "Mom," Cole inquires, "what did you ask?" Tearfully his mother says, "Are you proud of me?"

After the opening scenes in the church, God is not explicitly invoked. Indeed, one might be tempted to think that the world of *The Sixth Sense* is one in which the natural and the supernatural, the five natural senses and the supernatural sixth sense, the living and the dead interact but where this larger human universe is cut off from the divine. As Cole's mom says to him at one point, "we're going to have to answer each other's prayers now." Cole and his mother end up doing that for one another, but only after Cole and Malcolm have answered one another's prayers.

Meanwhile, across town Malcolm is in the living room of his house, where his wife slumps in a chair and drifts in and out of sleep. He becomes perplexed when she asks softly, sadly, "Why did you leave me?" Then, as she drifts more deeply into sleep, a ring falls out of her hand and rolls on the floor. Confused fear and then the shock of recognition overcome Malcolm as he realizes that she has just dropped his ring. The only reason she would have his ring is if . . . Then his mind shifts to a conversation with Cole: "I see dead people but they don't know they're dead. They only see what they want to see." Like the ghost of Hamlet's father, unsettled souls in *The Sixth Sense* wander the earth in search of the justice that will give them rest. The difference is that King Hamlet knows he is dead, while the dead characters in the film are not cognizant of their state, at least until their desire for justice has been satisfied. In the final moments of the film, Malcolm realizes both that he has made reparation for his previous failure and that he is dead. He thus has a retrospective insight into the providential order of his mediating status between the dead and the living. If he is unaware of the precise structure and intent of his quest, its realization brings illumination, even as it underscores the communal character of the quest. Earlier we stressed the difference between the quest motifs in *Wide Awake* and *The Sixth Sense*. But, in addition to the communal dimension surfacing in each film, each film stresses the way the providential fulfillment of quest comes upon individuals in a surprising way. As much as Joshua may consciously elect to embark on a quest, its completion comes only after he has abandoned his search. So, too, Malcolm is ignorant of the constituting conditions of his own quest.

UNBREAKABLE

I have been focusing on the different types of spiritual quest in the films of M. Night Shyamalan. Another way to think about Shyamalan's films is in terms of the modern phenomenon of disenchantment. Intellectual historians of the modern world often describe the impact of modern science on our experience of the natural world in precisely these terms. We inhabit a universe void of purpose, mystery, and meaning. What is of interest in nature is what is subject to abstract quantification, not the qualitative richness of concrete experience; what is real is merely physical, not the realm of soul or spirit; and what is knowable is what can be seen, grasped or detected by experiment. According to the proponents of scientific reduction, the alternative is to retreat to a world of perpetual childhood, to believe, against all rational evidence, in a world of superstition. The question for artists and others is how to recover a sense of enchantment, of the magic of human life, whose vanishing, as Joshua laments in *Wide Awake*, seems a necessary result of adulthood. Shyamalan specializes in the depiction of various attempts to restore enchantment. *The Village* portrays a community whose leaders elect to abide by consciously constructed myth, while *Lady in the Water* examines a group of apartment dwellers eager to embrace a fairy tale.

The dialectic of enchantment, disenchantment, and re-enchantment is one of the reasons for Shyamalan's preoccupation with comic books. Recall Joshua's remarks about the way superheroes are no longer a source of magic. Of course, disenchantment, as undergone by most ordinary human beings, has less to do with modern science than with the universal experience of tragedy, loss, and despair. In *Wide Awake* and *Signs*, it is triggered by the death of a beloved family member. In *The Sixth Sense* it is the experience of humiliating failure. Shyamalan's follow-up to *Sense* is *Unbreakable*, whose entire plot is invested with the theme of the comic book superhero. It also features two characters who suffer from disenchantment, but whose sources of despair and whose recovery of enchantment are quite opposed.

The opening scene of *Unbreakable*, which reveals Shyamalan's gift for detecting the potential for horror in the most ordinary and even blessed of human events, depicts the terrifying birth of a male baby, delivered malformed with numerous broken bones because of a previously undetected disease. In later scenes as an adult, Elijah Price explains his affliction: "I have something called *Osteogenesis Imperfecta*. It's a genetic disorder. I don't make certain protein very well and it makes my bones very low in density . . . very easy to break." The disease makes him not only physically fragile, a sort of freakish spectacle of nature, but also a social misfit, ill-suited for normal life and consigned to the margins of human events.

Inspired by the comic books his mother gives him as a child to encourage him to overcome his fear, Elijah grows up to own an artsy comic book store, Limited Edition. He prefers the early era in comic books, before commercialization rendered heroes both exaggerated and superficial. In the classic, restrained, and realistic depictions of the superhero and his arch-nemesis, Elijah discerns the purest conception of the battle between good and evil. Classic comic books are, Elijah asserts, a way of "passing on history." But Elijah is much more than just a fastidious judge of comic book plots and characters. He comes to think of his entire existence in comic book terms, which always contain a wide spectrum of characters, from evil to good and from weak to strong. Conflating the fictional and the real and hoping desperately to inhabit a comic book plot come to life, he envisions himself on one end of a spectrum with an as yet to be identified superhero on the other. His life is a quest to identify that contemporary superhero and thus to understand his own apparently cursed existence in relation to his opposite.

The next scene after the birth of Elijah returns us to the present and a commuter train traveling from New York to Philadelphia. The camera focuses on David Dunn (Bruce Willis), who is returning from a job interview in New York. Estranged from his wife and distant from his adoring son, Dunn is unhappy and unsure of himself. He sees an attractive woman on the train and conceals his wedding ring, but the train derails. From the mangled wreckage emerges a lone survivor, Dunn. An examining doctor gawks at him in disbelief. When Dunn asks why he's looking at him strangely, the doctor responds that there are two reasons: "One because it seems in a few minutes you will officially be the only survivor of this train wreck, and two, because you didn't break one bone, you don't have a scratch on you."

Not long after the accident, David receives an unsigned note with a question, "When is the last time you were sick?" Intrigued but unsure of the answer, David consults his wife, "I'm going to ask you a question and it's going to sound a little weird, so just think about it. Do you ever remember me being sick?" His wife, too exhausted to think clearly, hesitates, "I, I don't know. I can't remember." David persists, "No cold? No fever? No headache? Isn't that a little weird? What do you think it means?" One of the striking features of his superhero status is how contentedly unaware he is of his own powers. He has to be prodded into the realization.

Soon he traces the letterhead to Limited Edition and Elijah. Elijah prods David: "Why did you become a security guard? You could have become so many other things . . . you could have started a chain of restaurants." Elijah's supposition and the basis of his quest is this: "If there is someone like me in the world, shouldn't there be someone at the other end of the spectrum?" While Elijah is hyper-conscious and consumed with self-discovery construed as the best avenue for self-assertion, Dunn by contrast is nearly void of self-reflection. His life is composed mostly of ordinary failures and disappointments, but he retains an unspoken sense of what it means to be a decent human being, to be a husband, a father, a reliable employee. As the action of the film proceeds, it is clear that the mismatch between his aspirations and his failures has to do with his inability to find his place in the world. He is in this respect exactly like Elijah.

Because we have an awareness of Elijah's affliction from the start, because he has a remarkably alert mind, and because he appears to be on a self-effacing quest to determine whether Dunn is a superhero, we have a certain respect even affection for him. In a scene outside a stadium where Dunn works as a security guard, Dunn singles out a man whom he thinks is carrying some sort of concealed weapon but the man departs as soon as he sees that the security guards are conducting searches. Not content to let the man wander off, Elijah, hobbling along on his cane, pursues the man. The pursuit heads down a steep set of steps where the awkward Elijah tumbles and crushes multiple bones. The scene is expertly choreographed and filmed; the camera offers only a series of tight shots, isolated images of parts of Elijah's body accompanied by a series of sounds—thuds, crunches, and groans. The impact on viewers is more chilling than anything on offer in mainstream horror films. But Shyamalan uses the scene to do even more than inspire subdued terror in his audience. Just before he collapses under the weight of unbearable pain, Elijah, with his eyes remaining stoically fixed on the fugitive, sees the gun inside his coat. Thus do we see his relentless commitment to his quest. The fugitive provides precisely the confirmation of Dunn's superhero sixth sense that Elijah craves.

Even more than Dunn, his son, Joseph, craves the same confirmation that Elijah seeks. In an interesting parallel to Elijah's quest, David's son, who is aware of Elijah's claims about his father, wants desperately to esteem his father. The son joins his father as he tests his strength by working out. When his father easily bench-presses all the weight available, the son becomes a believer. In a desperate attempt to confirm his father's superhero status, he finds a gun in his home and turns it on his father. In this scene, Shyamalan once again exhibits his gift for unveiling the terror latent in every day family life. He also deftly mixes in comedy. As the parents attempt to persuade the boy not to use the gun, Dunn warns his son that they are friends and then the parents verbally remind each other of the rule that we do not shoot friends. "That's right," the mom says, "no shooting friends, Joseph."

Eventually, Dunn learns enough about himself to confirm Elijah's suspicions and turns to him for advice: "I've never been injured. What do I do now?" Elijah advises him to go "where people are." It turns out that Dunn has a kind of sixth sense for criminality that kicks in when he has any sort of physical contact with someone bent on evil. In anticipation of his new role, Dunn dons his security guard rain poncho and pulls the hood over his head. This is one of the nicest touches in the film, as Shyamalan uses darkness and shadow and careful framing of Dunn in his poncho to make him look like a blue-collar batman figure. As he does throughout the film, here Shyamalan plays off audience awareness of the comic book genre, only to use it to his own independent ends.

Having embraced his life as a crime fighter, Dunn attends an exhibit of comic book art at Elijah's store and visits privately with him in his office. Elijah mysteriously comments, "It has begun" and then proposes that this is the time for the two men to shake hands. That physical contact with Elijah triggers a series of image of destruction in Dunn's mind: a plane wreck, a hotel fire, and then the train crash that killed everyone except Dunn. Reeling from the implication of these images, Dunn listens as Elijah espouses his thesis: "You know what the scariest thing is? Not to know your place in this world. Now that we know who you are, I know who I am—I am not a mistake. It all makes sense, in the comics you know who the arch-villain is going to be? He's the exact opposite of the hero. And most times they're friends like you and me. I should have known way back when, you know why, David? Because of the kids! They called me Mr. Glass." Ignoring his theory, Dunn comments in horror, "You killed all those people." To which Elijah confidently responds, "But I found you. So many sacrifices just to find you."

Although Dunn never counters Elijah's argument about the "scariest thing," his reaction indicates that he thinks there is something more frightening than failing to find your purpose in the grand scheme of things—the contravention of all moral standards in the face of one's own, all-powerful will to meaning. In a meeting with Dunn's wife, Elijah states, "We live in mediocre times. It's hard for many people to believe that there are extraordinary things inside themselves, as well as others." Bereft of the sense of human life as a great drama, a great quest, human life lacks grandeur and purpose. Samuel Jackson invests Elijah with enormous human depth, with a complexity of motivation alien to the arch-nemesis character in the comic tradition. As we have seen in Nietzsche, there is much talk among critics of liberal modernity of the way it is at war with excellence, the way it naturally inclines toward a homogeneous mediocrity. But there is no guarantee that the recovery of the quest for purpose and greatness will generate virtue rather than vice, that it will contribute to, rather than undermine, the common good. Elijah has a purpose-driven life.

SIGNS

By contrast with the multiple and contradictory quests in *Unbreakable*, *Signs* hearkens back to the quest in *Wide Awake*. Both films explicitly involve the issue of faith, or loss of faith, in the Christian God and both take place largely within the doctrinal and sacramental world of Christianity, in one case Catholicism and in the other Episcopalianism. In one crucial respect, the quests are quite divergent. As we noted above, *Wide Awake* involves a conscious embrace of the quest, while *The Sixth Sense* features quests of which the main characters are largely ignorant. By comparison, *Signs* involves a quest that is explicitly and consciously repudiated by the main character, Father Graham Hess, a man who has rejected his God and his role as priest and father.

Nearly all the action in *Signs* takes place in or around the large Victorian farmhouse, which is one of multiple targets across the earth as of an alien takeover of the planet. The setting, Buck's County, Pennsylvania, some forty-five miles outside Philadelphia, is reminiscent of the idyllic setting of *Field of Dreams*. But the visitors to this farm are not looking to spend eternity at the American pastime; instead the setting, the invaders, and their goals resemble more the subject matters of three other films, all of which Shyamalan cites as influences: *The Birds*, *Night of the Living Dead*, and *Invasion of the Body Snatchers*.

Mel Gibson stars as Hess, who lives with his two children on a farm. We discover he is a priest only belatedly, when someone calls him "Father." "It's not 'Father' anymore," he says. But he cannot completely eradicate his vocation. A teenage girl who waits on him in a store demands that he hear her confession before the world ends and then as he prepares his children for what may be their last night on earth, he tells each of them a story about their birth designed to impress upon them how much they are loved. Gibson's character here meets modern humanity on its own terms, as a wavering people of faith, whose initial belief and enthusiasm has been disrupted by experience and time, by the loss of a loved one or the sense of abandonment by God or just by exhaustion and distraction.

The film takes its time in revealing the source of the plot, a "war of the worlds" scenario where aliens have chosen this night to take over the earth; it also takes its time before disclosing the source of Graham's loss of faith—the death of his wife in a freak car accident. About mid-way through the film he receives a call from Ray, whose voice he can barely discern before the phone line cuts off. He hurries over to Ray's house to find him outside in his car ready to vacate his property. Before Ray tells him that there is an alien trapped in his pantry, he begs his forgiveness for having fallen asleep at the wheel thus losing control of his car, which drifted off the road at precisely the place where Graham's wife was out walking. Ray muses sadly on what a freak coincidence it was that he should have fallen asleep at that very moment and not before or after. It is almost as if it were meant to happen. As Ray apologizes, Graham's eyes fill with tears and he nods in acknowledgment of the plea for forgiveness.

Signs is replete with the suggestion of the imminent threat of the supernatural or at least the extra-terrestrial; a clandestine presence is suggested through noises on the roof, the rustling of corn, and the unprovoked motion of a child's swing. Roger Ebert commented about *Signs*, "I cannot think of a movie where silence is scarier, and inaction is more disturbing." Shyamalan expertly builds a sense of menace, suspense and dread. The crop circles, the domesticated dog that turns on its human owners, and the strange clicking sounds that show up on the baby monitor—all these mysteries provide converging conference of what might otherwise seem impossible. Shyamalan nicely uses humor to relieve the suspense, as, for example, when Bo enters her dad's room at night and states: "There's a monster outside my room.

Can I have a glass of water?" As is clear from *Wide Awake*, Shyamalan is very good at capturing the world of children, their language, their fears, their sense of humor. One of the most chilling scenes in the film is a television replay of home video of a child's birthday party, in which the children are seen fleeing in terror from a creature outside the house. As the camera pans the children scurrying for the window to get a glimpse of the alien, it moves past the kids and out the window to an alley and then across the line of vision walks an alien.

Shyamalan is best at indirection, as for example when Graham enters Ray's house to investigate Ray's claim that he has trapped one of the aliens in his pantry. Graham hears the clicking sounds and feet scampering across the floor, then as he tries to look under the door, a claw pokes its way out. When the alien finally appears at the house, he is seen reflected on a television screen that Graham is pulling through the living room of his house.

As reports of the alien invasion intensify, Hess and his family board up the house and sit down for what may be their last supper together. Just as they are about to begin eating, Hess adamantly refuses to pray: "I'm not wasting one more minute of my life on prayer." But this is just the beginning of Hess's dark night of the soul. Fending off the alien attack, in order to save his children, Hess recovers a sense of the meaning and purpose of fatherhood, in both the biological and spiritual orders. In a film that frequently overlaps with horror, an apocalyptic alien attack is the providential path through which Hess recovers his faith in God.

Apocalypse now for Shyamalan is not the "heart of darkness" war film in exotic locations nor is it a blockbuster war of the worlds drama with loud special effects and massive destruction. The only hint of such large scale destruction is given indirectly, through the use of television news broadcasts of invasions in various parts of the earth. Shyamalan's focus is on a small-scale version of the battle and even here it is less on the powerful destruction threatened by aliens than it is on the human drama of faith, doubt, despair and fatherhood. The threat signified by the crop circles is in the end subordinate to the threat of the cynicism and wrath that afflict Graham Hess after the death of his wife and mother of his children.

By contrast to its supple shaping of individual scenes, the film's multiple affirmations of divine providence at the end are far too overt. It is as if Shyamalan thinks he can make the role of providence more convincing by having Hess invoke it repeatedly, each time with greater passion. The problem with the ending has not escaped the notice of critics. In *Salon*, Andrew O'Hehir describes Shyamalan as "winding the audience up to a pitch of near hysterical suspense, and then squander[ing] it all in promiscuous geysers of sentimentality and random New Age brain fog."[5] *Signs*, he writes, "flirts with religiosity more ardently than either *The Sixth Sense* or *Unbreakable*, but finally never gets out of that pop-spirituality territory Shyamalan has made so uniquely his own. . . . we get vague, pseudo-universal nostrums: The world divides into two kinds of people, those who believe in co-incidences and those who believe in signs."

That is precisely how Graham puts it to his brother: There are, he explains, those who perceive lucky events as sign that someone is watching out for us and those who see such events as mere chance and know that they are on their own. Graham claims that he is the latter sort of person. But his anger, evident in his refusal to pray and then in the basement when he thinks his son may die of an asthma attack and curses God ("I hate you.") indicates that he has not made peace with his own atheism. Before the hyperbolic ending, the film is quite measured in its treatment of faith, doubt, and the possibility of providence. The most striking religious allusion is one that is easy to miss. It occurs early in the film as Graham walks through a room in his house; on one of the walls there is an imprint of a crucifix that has been removed.

That haunting sense of an absent or eschewed symbol of redemption that nonetheless has not been, and in fact cannot be, completely repudiated locates *Signs* among the most influential contemporary quests for a lost code of redemption. That the quest is provoked by, and occurs in the midst of, the threat of earthly apocalypse, both for the human race and for the Hess family, makes it a dark tale worthy of note. In this film, the "scariest thing," to borrow the phrase from Elijah Price, is not the threat of aliens but a father's abdication of his calling.

The reworking of the conventions of a received genre, in this case, the alien invasion film, is typical of Shyamalan's creativity as a writer and director. In contrast to mainstream horror, where scares are indistinguishable from visceral repulsion and where fear is incapable of teaching us anything about the human condition, Shyamalan has a sense of the significance of the question of what the scariest thing is. He also thinks that the dramatic probing of that question can teach us something about the human condition, a condition that Shyamalan's films often depict in terms of a quest, amid the ruins of individual lives and the disorder of contemporary culture, for a lost code of redemption.

9

Paint It Red

"**T**HERE'S SOMETHING INTRINSICALLY COOL ... something intrinsically more painful about beautiful women being abused that
way, all right?" Thus does Quentin Tarantino describe his enthusiasm for the plot of *Kill Bill, Vol. 1*. Beyond the intellectual excitement of the torturing of the bodies of pregnant women; beyond the
affirmation of female empowerment (actress Vivica A. Fox thought it
was "great" that the women "were in control of our own little world");
beyond the homage to Japanese anime, samurai movies, and spaghetti
westerns; beyond all this and through all this, there is Tarantino's giddy
obsession with blood—splattered blood, oozing blood, gushing blood.
On this subject, his enthusiasm knows no bounds: "Japanese blood is
the prettiest. It's like nice, and it has a scarlet redness about it." Chinese
blood is "like Kool-Aid almost." And American blood is "more syrupy
kind of stuff."[1]

One of the most influential filmmakers of the 1990s, Tarantino
attained fame with a trailblazing and hyper-ironic mix of humor and
violence in two films, *Reservoir Dogs* (1992) and *Pulp Fiction* (1994),
both of which deploy *noir* themes and stylistics. With *Kill Bill*, released

in two parts or volumes (2003, 2004), Tarantino, whose films have provoked numerous mediocre imitations, proves that only he can one-up himself. *Kill Bill* is a more intense and more astonishing fusion of the comedic and the violent, a cornucopia of bloody revenge, a celebration of violence not just as entertainment but as a "sacramental" feast for the jaded, perverse contemporary intellect, a "catharsis of bloodletting" that Martin Scorsese has described as a central function of film in our time. Yet it is unclear precisely what sort of catharsis contemporary film provides; it seems to incite precisely what it purports to satiate—a longing for ever more sophisticated aesthetic mechanisms of bloodletting. Filmmakers thus engage in a competition to increase both the quantity and novelty in the scenes of bloodletting.

From *Reservoir Dogs* through *Pulp Fiction* and to *Kill Bill*, Tarantino has been one of the masters of this style of filmmaking. Never predictable, Tarantino infuses explicit bloodletting with witty dialogue, memorable characters, and even more memorable aesthetic mechanisms of violence. At least in his early films, he also played off classic film *noir*, whose assumptions he often subverted even as he called them to mind.

In an odd pop culture coincidence, *Kill Bill Vol. 2* vied with *The Passion of the Christ* atop the Hollywood box office charts. The blockbuster success of a subtitled religious film saturated with violence is the most remarkable event in recent popular culture. Released between the two volumes of *Kill Bill*, *The Passion* aims to provide something more than a catharsis of bloodletting. But as the premier example of a dark religious film, it plays off the popular obsession with the aesthetics of bloodletting. Such an embrace of stylized violence is dangerous in any film but particularly in a religious film whose risky goal is to reverse the standard effect of violence on audience's; in this case, the point is to move the audience from detached irony to sympathetic identification with the victim, the most wronged man in history. The accentuation of the aesthetics of violence locates *The Passion* closer to horror than to classic film *noir*. One of the most perceptive reviews of the film came from an anonymous review on the pop horror film website, ESPLATTER: "As any horror fan knows, the story of Jesus plays a huge role in the genre, from the use of crucifixes in vampire films to frequent references to God and Jesus in any movie involving the anti-Christ. Typically, Jesus films are watered down made-for-TV affairs, basically designed for after-Sunday-school education. Not so with *The Passion of the Christ....* This is not some kiddie Christ film. This is the real deal."[2]

Still, *The Passion* nonetheless overlaps broadly with a few *noir* motifs. In *The Passion*, this world is a kind of maze, a disordered universe where those appointed to uphold justice are precisely those most inclined to subvert it. The official trials to which Christ is subject are at best farcical; none provides an accurate verdict in this, the most extreme version of the wrong-man scenario. The only true verdict is in death. To put that point more precisely, we should say that the verdict is evident in the manner in which death is embraced. *The Passion* is the story of a man whose "only companion is darkness" (*Psalm* 88, 18).

In Pascalian terms, Christ meets the contradictions of the human condition with paradoxes of his own: victory through the folly of the cross in which "strength is reconciled with lowliness." But even for those who accept this truth, the journey is not over; they must travel a dark path where questions linger concerning the disarray of this world and how we are to navigate our way within or through it. The formative memory is that of a crucified and humiliated God. Thus does *The Passion* locate the religious quest at the intersection of *noir* and horror, an overlap we have already detected in other contemporary stories.

The quest of the audience concerns a judgment about the main character, about whether he is who he says he is and whether his suffering is indeed the source of redemption. The way out of the traps of sin and death is not an "other-worldly" solution; nor is it a Gnostic answer to the dilemmas of the human condition. Instead of the human attempt at self-divinization through a knowledge that frees the hero from the limits of the human body, here God intervenes in this world and embraces the vulnerability of the human body. The Incarnation evinces what some theologians call the scandal of particularity. It is only in and through the moments of time, indeed in and through this particular human body and its bloody sacrifice, that redemption is possible. Moreover, the film establishes, in its flashback focus on the last supper, a way of memorializing this body through a communal meal. Christ's most striking commandment is that of Holy Thursday, "Do this in memory of me."

Of course, the scandal of particularity is a contributing factor in the rift between Christians and Jews over Christ. Is this man the fulfillment of the covenant between Yahweh and the Jewish people, or not? How does the claim of fulfillment alter the Jewish covenant? And how ought Jews and Christians to think about themselves and one another? *The Passion* brought these questions and others to the fore. The most serious objection raised against the film was that of anti-Semitism. Does the film deserve that label? In a very perceptive piece on the film, Dennis Prager observes that Jews and Christians are watching two different films.[3] Acknowledging that American Christians will not be inclined to blame the Jews but rather all sinners for Jesus' death, Prager points out, nonetheless, that the "Jews in the film (except, of course, for those who believe in Jesus) are cruel and often sadistic." He concludes, "For Jews to worry that a major movie made by one of the world's superstars depicts Jews as having Christ tortured and killed might arouse anti-Semitic passions is not paranoid."

With certain needed qualifications, Prager's judgment is astute. Despite the progress that has been made in Jewish-Christian relations in recent years, the tragic history of Christian anti-Semitism is undeniable. Medieval Passion Plays occasioned attacks on Jews, and Hitler was a fan of the Passion Play at Oberammergau, which he praised for its convincing portrayal of the "menace of Jewry," although it is interesting that the character Hitler found most admirable in the Passion Play was not Jesus, but Pilate. Is Gibson's version anti-Semitic? His only concession to the critics was to remove, from the English subtitles, the chant from the Jewish crowd: "Let his blood be on us and on our children." Because he left the line of the dialogue into the statements of the crowd, this move only reinforced suspicions of Gibson's intent. Such worries were exacerbated after Gibson's irrational, bigoted outburst against Jews. But what else can be said about the film?

The very Jewishness, not just of the Pharisees, but also of Jesus, Mary, and the disciples—a point underscored by Gibson's risky insistence on using the very languages Jews spoke in ancient Palestine—implies that the divide over Jesus is a divide within Judaism, not between Judaism and something utterly separate from it. The only instance in which someone is referred to derisively as a "Jew" is when a Roman soldier shouts at Simon to assist Jesus in carrying his cross. Although Prager is certainly right that the chief priests are depicted, even physically, in menacing ways, not all the non-Christ–following Jews are depicted in this way. One of those present at the hastily arranged trial proclaims, "This trial is an outrage. Who called a trial at this hour? Where are the other members of the council?" Jewish officials are thus depicted as less than fully unified in opposition to Jesus. One of those present calls the trial a "travesty."

Concerning the issue of how faithful the film is to scripture, Gibson's statements were flatly incoherent. In one interview, he declared that his passion is presented "just the way it happened. It's like traveling back in time and watching the events unfold exactly as they occurred . . . . We've done the research. I'm telling the story as the Bible tells it."[4] Yet in his preface to the book accompanying the film of The Passion, he states that the movie is "not meant as a historical documentary nor does it claim to have assembled all the facts."[5] While acknowledging the significance of these questions and the strengths and weaknesses of The Passion's ethical assumptions and theological lessons, our focus is not so much on these debates as on The Passion as an example of a dark religious quest.

LITURGIES OF BLOOD

Before turning to an extended exposition of *The Passion*, it will help
to consider the way violence figures in some notable contemporary
films. We have already cited Tarantino's work, which often turns violence into high art. In its fascination with the aesthetics of violence, its
varied soundtrack, and its rapid interspersing of brutal violence and
light comic touches, *Kill Bill* resembles *Natural Born Killers* (1994), a
film for which Tarantino originally helped write the script but from
which he removed himself entirely after a dispute with Oliver Stone.
Deprived of Tarantino's macabre playfulness, *Killers* became an incoherent combination of over-the-top violence and heavy-handed
Stone moralism about contemporary society. By contrast, *Kill Bill* is
thoroughly coherent, perfectly executed, and without a hint of morality, at least until the final segments of volume two, when the film
falls prey to Tarantino family values. Both volumes deploy stylized,
orchestrated sets, the upshot of which is to turn the entire film into a
vehicle for the aesthetics of violence. For example, Tarantino deploys
a sort of *CSI* effect, wherein bullets are shown in slow motion tearing
into bodies; he highlights the end-over-end trajectory of an axe that
comes to rest in an opponent's skull; and he is ever attentive to blood,
which appears first as oil, then as paint, and finally, in cascades, as
discolored rain water.

Tarantino thus turns unremitting violence into a sort of religious
spectacle, a perverse liturgy that appeals as much to the intellect as to
the imagination. Since the 1980s, filmmakers, especially in the horror
genre, have sought to overwhelm the imagination of viewers with a
magnification of evil. But Tarantino is doing something more than
simply competing for the title of most violent director. He is in the
business of making viewers aware of precisely how the films work on
them. Following *Kill Bill*'s art and action—from humor to excruciating vivisection back to humor—forces viewers to "turn on a dime"

and switch emotions. *Kill Bill* is so stylized and so ironic that viewers cannot help but be aware of how the film is working on them.

Now, Tarantino is to be credited with forcing on his viewers a cognitive awareness of his film's liturgy of blood. The question is whether the surface irony is sufficient to justify the willing suspension of moral judgment. The issue is not, as it is often construed in public debates about the real-world consequences of Hollywood depravity, moral judgments about the film's hypothetical causal effects on the behavior of already deranged adolescents. Rather, the issue concerns the indispensably moral element we bring to any work of art.

Similar questions can be raised about the stylistically stunning neo-*noir* film, *Sin City* (2005), based on Frank Miller's famed graphic comics. As violent and stylized as anything in the film *noir* canon, *Sin City* has been described as so electrifying that it "kisses the blood right off its own violent hands." The film does indeed have a stunning look, but not much more. This is not to say that *Sin City* has trouble filling the time or the screen. It overflows with spurting blood, decapitations, severed heads, dogs eating human bodies, cannibalism, and vomiting. It culminates in a decisive battle whose victor manages to rip the genitals off of his opponent and then smash his skull. Its sole focus is on surface aesthetics. The slender plot lines—there are three of them—are merely the occasion for what one character calls the "pure hateful bloodthirsty joy of slaughter."

In the winter of 2006, two films (*Hostel* and *Wolf Creek*), released at roughly the same time, took the "bloodthirsty joy of slaughter" in a somewhat different direction, away from artsy stylization and toward a more literal infliction of pain and maiming on human bodies. These films represent one possible response to what a perceptive studio executive suggests is a "burning-out of the sub-genres" of the horror film. Before the burn-out of the sub-genres, there was the burn-out of the horror genre's staple—at least in the 1980s and 1990s—the slasher flick. The modern genre in horror actually dates all the way back to 1960 with *Psycho* and the British classic, *Peeping Tom*. It picked up steam over the next twenty years, with *Rosemary's Baby*, *The Exorcist*, *The Omen*, and *Halloween*, all of which are well-executed horror films. Two features of these films proved most influential over the next thirty years. First, there is the motif of the serial killer who just can't seem to be brought under control or even killed. Of course, this dramatic device paves a path to endless sequels, but it also stresses a theme of the modern horror genre that evil is something primordial and incapable of being contained by civilization. Second, there are the surface aesthetics of evil, the attempt of one filmmaker after another to outdo his predecessor in the number, complexity, and offensive nature of acts of torture, dismemberment, murder, and so forth. Both of these plotting devices are subject to the law of diminishing returns. Audiences, once driven to paroxysms of fear by the artistry of *Rosemary's Baby* or *The Exorcist*, are no longer surprised by such things—or at least no longer terrified. Jaded audiences have come to expect such performances, and even find them humorous. This trajectory reaches its conclusion in the *Scream* trilogy and the *Scary Movie* films, wherein the conventions of the movie genre (never drink, never have sex, and never say "I'll be right back") are made explicit and spoofed.

As we noted in our discussion of the films of M. Night Shyamalan, the mainstream horror film, to which Shyamalan's films stand in striking contrast, seems inclined toward three possibilities: the artsy, heavily stylized treatment of the aesthetics of evil, as is evident in Tarantino's films and in *Sin City*; pure ironic camp and parody from within, as is most evident in the *Scream* trilogy; or the pursuit of ever more explicit and deliberately literal depictions of gore and physical brutality, evident in films such as *Hostel* and *Wolf Creek*. These three tendencies are not mutually exclusive. Tarantino's films also contain a great deal of irony and camp. And as I argued in the introduction, he has at least in one film (*Pulp Fiction*) depicted what it might mean to discern in a world of pure, unintelligible chance and irrepressible violence the suggestion of divine intervention and the calling to a spiritual quest.

If in the last twenty years, Hollywood has witnessed in the horror film a nihilistic celebration of violence as pure spectacle, it has also seen a return to heroism in the war film, wherein violence is exercised not for pointless entertainment but for the sake of preserving the common good. In the wake of the popularity of films such as *Braveheart* and *Gladiator*, Hollywood may be veering away from the nihilistic bent that became so prominent in the late 1980s and 1990s. Concerning the popularity of epics, screenwriter Erik Jendresen, who penned the script for *Band of Brothers*, observed in an interview with *Entertainment Weekly*: "They're about men and women of unusual vision, individuals who stand for something greater than themselves. Right now Hollywood might have detected a need for stories like that." It is instructive that, in its pursuit of stories of noble, adult characters, Hollywood typically looks to other times and other places, not to contemporary America. Add to this tendency, the popularity of religiously tinged quest films such can be had in the *Harry Potter* films, *The Lord of the Rings* trilogy, and in the prequels to the *Star Wars* industry, and some of the cultural groundwork is laid for Mel Gibson's *The Passion of the Christ*.

THE PASSION OF THE CHRIST

Still, the success of *The Passion* was both unanticipated and unprecedented. Gibson sought a revolutionary overturning of the Hollywood tradition of Jesus films. "Cheesy epics" with "corny" acting and "bad hair or really bad music" is the way Gibson describes classic Hollywood depictions of the life of Jesus. By contrast, *The Passion of the Christ*, in Aramaic and Latin with scenes of such intense violence that it received an R-rating, is unlike anything in the history of American film. It is even something of a departure from the Gospel accounts of Christ's passion, which are remarkably restrained and laconic in their depiction of the precise details of his suffering. We are told that he was scourged, mocked with a crown of thorns, forced to carry a cross, and then crucified. We derive what little artistic appreciation we have of

Christ's life from the Italian Renaissance and its idealized depictions of the passion. For example, Michelangelo's *Pieta*, which depicts Mary holding her dead son's body, provokes a sense of awe at its beauty, not the horror that makes us want to look away.

In *The Passion*'s parallel scene to the *Pieta*, Mary's face is smudged with blood. Christ's body is blood soaked and battered, with swollen eyes and gaping wounds where his flesh has been torn away. The scenes of Christ's scourging, with the Romans' making use of multiple implements of torture, and the crucifixion itself, with the blood dripping from the nails as they pierce flesh and wood, are emotionally wrenching on a scale rarely experienced even in contemporary Hollywood where bloodsport is the order of the day.

Responding to the accusation of gratuitous excess in *The Passion*'s depiction of violence, Rene Girard, the author of *Violence and the Sacred* and renowned expert on the logic and practice of religious scapegoating, wonders, "How can one exaggerate the sufferings of a man who must suffer, one after the other, the two most excruciating tortures devised by Roman cruelty?" As to the derisive dismissals of *The Passion* as a "snuff film" or as indulging in "pornography" of violence, Girard notes that the film is a rare case where there is no mixture of eroticism with violence. Instead, the violence heightens the audience's sense of urgency about the life of this man who claims to be God in the flesh. It thus fosters disorientation and confusion in the audience. The lines from the final section of T.S. Eliot's *Wasteland*, an archetypal *noir* quest poem, capture the same mood of specific loss, cosmic disorientation, and personal implication:

> After the torchlight red on sweaty faces
> After the frosty silence in the gardens
> After the agony in stony places
> The shouting and the crying
> Prison and place and reverberation
> Of thunder of spring over distant mountains

He who was living is now dead
We who were living are now dying
With a little patience

Eliot knew that indirection was necessary to revive our sense of the significance of the Gospel narratives. Gibson opts for immediate realism, immersion in which takes viewers, accustomed to regarding film as entertainment, unaware and eliminates the possibility of watching the events in detached comfort. Rene Girard suggests that one of the most powerful impulses in the development of Western realism came from the teaching of the Passion, from the desire to strengthen religious meditation. Girard expresses surprise that it took so long for cinema, "the most realistic technique that ever existed," to come round to portraying the Crucifixion "as if we were there."[6] Of course, Girard's case leaves unanswered the artistic question of whether the film would have been even more effective if it had opted at least occasionally for greater restraint and for the deployment of mechanisms of indirection. To put the question another way—could Gibson have learned something from the techniques of Shyamalan?

If Gibson's film embraces too readily or at least too exclusively the contemporary zeal for the spectacle of violence, even if for quite different ends, the film stands athwart the contemporary Hollywood tendency to treat religion with derision or at best in terms of vague sentimental inclinations toward the transcendent. As Stephen Prothero observes in *American Jesus: How the Son of God Became a National Icon*, our cultural Jesus is an "other-directed" personality type, eager to please whatever constituency will have him. Instead of the man of sorrows bearing a cross, we have the smiling, winking "Buddy Christ" who gives America a big thumbs-up in the 1999 film *Dogma*. In its style and themes, Gibson's depiction of the last twelve hours of the life of Jesus of Nazareth is a complete revolution of the genre. *The Passion* casts out the demon of sentimentality that has haunted Hollywood films about Christ.[7]

If the film *Dogma* would have us drop specific truth-claims in favor of a construal of love as toleration, *The Passion of the Christ* would have us return to the roots of dogma, in the experience of Christ of the early Church. A saying from the early church is *ordo credendi, ordo orandi,* the order of belief is predicated on the order of prayer or worship.[8] At the heart of the Church's life of prayer is the commemoration of the Last Supper, Christ's offering of himself to the Father.

Gibson clearly knows Hollywood's penchant for violent spectacle. He also knows that there is a voracious appetite in the viewing public for such spectacle. If there is a marketing genius to *The Passion*, which subordinates the spectacle of violence to a vision of self-sacrificing love, it consists in the bringing together of the contemporary scripting of explicit violence with a very traditional approach to Christ's passion. *The Passion* avoids wallowing in violence by hearkening back to another tradition of engaging the Gospels, one that attempts to provide a sense of what it was like to be with Christ on the way of the cross (*via dolorosa*). The tradition of meditation on Christ's passion and death crystallizes in St. Ignatius of Loyola's sixteenth-century manual, *The Spiritual Exercises*. Founder of the Jesuit order, Ignatius counsels the use of the imagination to place oneself in the setting of the Gospel stories, to see and hear the events and voices, and to be moved in appropriate ways. "In the Passion," he writes, "the proper thing to ask for is grief with Christ suffering, a broken heart with Christ heartbroken, tears and deep suffering because of the great suffering that Christ endured for me."[9]

The success of the film hinges upon its ability to move us beyond revulsion to ponder who this man is who endures suffering in this way. We are invited to ask, in quite a different spirit, a version of the question a tempting Satan puts to Jesus in the opening of the film, "Who is your Father? Who are you?" In an attempt to deepen our appreciation of the mystery of this itinerant Jewish teacher, the film makes uses of flashbacks. Particularly moving is one of Mary's flashbacks; as she witnesses Jesus collapse with a thud under the weight of the cross, she recalls a moment when she anxiously rushed to comfort the child Jesus after a fall. Indeed, Gibson manages to curtail and humanize our torment over Jesus's afflictions by repeatedly turning our attention to Mary's love and grief. Maia Morgenstern's performance as Mary is sure and deft. Mary is not just the human vehicle through whom we touch the holiness of God, she is also an active participant in the sufferings of her son, our model for mourning and sorrow. In its depiction of Mary, *The Passion* rivals the poetic rendering of Our Lady in T.S. Eliot's "Ash Wednesday":

> Lady of silences
> Calm and distressed
> Torn and most whole
> Rose of memory
> Rose of forgetfulness
> Exhausted and life-giving
> Worried reposeful

Mary's following of the path of Jesus parallels that of the demon; or, more precisely, rather the demon mimics and seeks to subvert Mary's devoted hope. Where there is a demonic attempt to sow seeds of doubt, Mary offers confident fidelity; where there is detached demonic exultation at the apparent defeat of goodness, Mary shares in the sufferings of her son and mourns both the innocent and the guilty. Gibson makes the parallelism explicit in a number of scenes. Other than Jesus, Mary is the only person who sees the demon as it drifts through the crowd.[10]

Gibson's *Passion* has been called the anti-*Last Temptation of Christ*, an equally controversial film, whose portrait of Jesus is in many respects closer to that found in *The Da Vinci Code*. Gibson is not interested in speculation about whether Christ fantasized about an alternative life, one in which he might wed Mary Magdalene and so forth. But Gibson does not give us an other-worldly Jesus either. As Jesus, Jim Caviezel is a human Christ, whose divinity, except in a couple notable scenes, remains veiled behind the suffering humanity. In his depiction of the sorrowful Christ of the cross, Gibson's portrayal calls to mind Pascal's marveling at the Gospel descriptions of Christ: "Why do they make him weak in his agony? The same St. Luke describes the death of St. Stephen more heroically than that of Jesus. They make him capable of fear before death had become inevitable and then absolutely steadfast. But when he is so distressed it is when he distresses himself; when men distress him he is steadfast."[11] Christ is not just a victim, a passive, pliable soul.

In the opening scene in the Garden of Gethsemane, Christ is already weary, by turns despondent and frenetic with fear, isolated from his disciples who are overcome by the heaviness of sleep. The setting is a wooded area, at night, with moonlight obscured by clouds and heavy fog. As he prays, "Father, rise up and save me from the traps they have set for me," a hooded figure, with a feminine face and a deep, guttural voice appears. Taunting him, the androgynous demon insists that "no one man can bear" the sins of mankind. "Saving souls is too costly. No one, never." As the demon queries skeptically, "Who is your father? Who are you?," a snake slithers toward Jesus and begins to wrap itself around him. A silent stillness on the screen is shattered by the sound of a loud thump, as Jesus stomps on the snake. Fully conscious of his mission, Jesus is at once afflicted and resolved. Christ is the archetype of the wrongly accused man who is in fact the right man, the one selected to bear the burden of irrational and unjust incrimination. The gap between appearance and reality, between opinion and truth, here will be pushed to the limits. Perhaps the best scene depicting this gap is the crowning with thorns where Roman soldiers bow before Christ in mock worship.

Just as the demon disappears, the torch-bearing soldiers arrive to arrest Jesus. Filmed in slow motion to underscore the deliberate, ominous way in which the soldiers surround Christ and take him into custody. This only increases the sense that things could not have been otherwise; the film plays upon the theme of a determinism that nonetheless must be freely embraced. When Mary first hears word of his arrest and encounters him in chains, she states, "It has begun, Lord. So be it." In this, she echoes the words of Christ in the Garden, where he had asked the Father to free him but then relinquishes himself to the will of the Father. Caught up in a bloodthirsty frenzy, the Jewish leaders hold a secret trial, the crowd gathers before Pilate to demand his life, and the Roman guards take perverse delight in beatings of Christ. All partake in powerful forces greater than any individual, forces that dictate Christ's execution. Christ speaks few words before the Roman guards, before the Jewish leaders, or before Pilate. What he does say reveals his integrity, his unwillingness to deny who he is; his words sharpen the reasons for the attacks upon him. In each case, Christ ultimately adopts a position of silence, an admission of the gap in intelligibility between divine justice and worldly power.

In a *Newsweek* cover story on the film, Jon Meacham notices the many ways in which Gibson departs from, or adds to, the details of the Gospels.[12] But Meacham does no more than point out that what is most obvious about the narrative in the film. Whether he is aware of it or not, what Gibson typically does is to relocate certain words from elsewhere in the Gospels into the Passion narrative. In so doing, Gibson sharpens, rather than dulls, the theological issues. For example, in the late night trial before Jewish officials, one of the charges brought against Jesus is the claim, "if we don't eat his flesh and drink his blood, we won't inherit eternal life." Here Gibson hearkens back to the *Gospel of John*, chapter 6, where Jesus's insistence on the connection between eternal life and eating his flesh offends many and causes the first serious rupture among his followers. The allusion provides a dramatic foreshadowing of the film's later focus on the Last Supper.

In contrast to the reverence expressed toward Christ's body in the sacramental ritual, the Romans assigned to torture Christ take malevolent delight in the intricacies of their brutal craft of torture. Their detached, cynical laughter reveals the depths of their evil. For them, bloodletting has become a kind of sport, a sign of their singular superiority to other races. They treat the Jewish people, especially Jesus, as if they were members of a sub-human species, void of any dignity or humanity. The thrones and dominations of this world, for which the Roman empire remains paradigmatic even in modernity, adopt a politics of spectacle that stupefies through a technology of torture exercised on the bodies of those mercilessly subject to it. The film's dramatic opposition of the order of politics to the order of the creator renders inconceivable the deployment of this story as an instrument in a national culture war, however much that point may have been missed by both the right and the left in the controversy surrounding its release. Indeed, the scenes of the Roman soldiers cackling with glee as they scourge Christ and rip hunks of skin from his body is most reminiscent of the depiction of the Nazi soldiers in *Schindler's List*.

This message is precisely what underlies Gibson's seemingly inordinate fascination with blood. There is blood everywhere, covering Christ's face, dripping from his body, splattering those who torture him, smeared on Mary's face, and dripping from the nail as it pierces the wood of the cross. The entire film is an expanded version of the line from St. Ignatius's famous "Anima Christi" prayer: "Blood of Christ, inebriate me." The places where the violence of blood seems excessive are also scenes in which Gibson finds ways to personalize and humanize the suffering. In the scourging of Christ, where we see him beaten to the ground and the camera then focuses solely on his trembling hands as the beatings continue. At this point, just before the Roman guard in control asserts, *satis* ("enough"), Jesus stares into Mary's loving and pained eyes.

In its unwavering focus on how Christ embraces his sacrifice, the film is a story not of doubt but of unwavering fidelity. His humanity is particularly evident in the powerful way Jesus's eyes meet those of other human beings, especially Mary. An even more dramatic example occurs on the path of the cross, just as Christ is being worn down by the weight of the cross, his own physical deprivation, and the continued beatings and mockery of the guards. As he falls to the ground and

Mary rushes toward him, she has a touching flashback to a moment from his youth when he had a hard fall and she anxiously ran to him in fear. Here he hits the ground with a thud, and, before rising, pauses for a moment with Mary. As she stares into his bruised and battered face, he says quietly but confidently, "Behold, I make all things new." Here the proclamation of divinity shines through a humiliated and tortured humanity.

The Passion transcends the celebration of the spectacle of violence in its depiction of Jesus's response to his persecutors. Jesus's humanity and then, as is increasingly suggested, his divinity manifest through his humanity are the film's response to the American obsession with violence, to what Scorsese calls the "catharsis of bloodletting." In this way, Gibson inscribes our contemporary fascination with the orgy of blood within a scriptural account of sacrifice, according to which Christ's crucifixion is the truly efficacious sacrifice. As Eliot writes in "Four Quartets":

> The dripping blood our only drink,
> The bloody flesh our only food:
> In spite of which we like to think
> That we are sound, substantial flesh and blood—
> Again, in spite of that, we call this Friday good.

Brutality, disorientation, and human sacrifice are repeatedly inscribed within shared redemptive suffering. An important instance of this occurs just before Simon is pressed into service to assist Christ in carrying the cross. Christ loses his balance and swings helplessly around the still standing cross. As he and the cross collapses in a swirl, the camera follows his line of sight and thus requires that the viewer participate in his humiliation, disorientation, and loss of control. At this point, the Romans force Simon to assist in carrying the cross. Christ's vision meets his and they head off with arms entwined bearing the burden of the cross together.

Throughout the retelling of the Passion, the film intersperses flash-backs to events in Jesus' life. The most sustained series of flashbacks commences just as the Crucifixion begins. Gibson repeatedly returns us to the Last Supper and thus foreshadows the sacrifice of the Mass; at the climactic moment of the film, Gibson underscores the link between the bloody sacrifice of Calvary and unbloody sacrifice of the Mass. In this way, a story that unveils the injustice at the heart of the greatest empire in human history and the corruption to which the human heart is susceptible provides the basis for the foundation and continual re-newal of a different sort of community, a community founded on the blood of the unblemished lamb whose sacrifice is eternally pleasing to the Father. Gibson thus highlights the most memorable commandment issued by Christ: "Do this in memory of me."

THE INTERSECTION OF HORROR AND *NOIR*

On the prominence of the sacred blood, there is some continuity be-tween *The Passion* and classic American films about Christ. *The Robe* (1953) stars Richard Burton as the Roman centurion Marcellus Gallio, who wins Christ's robe in a gambling context at the foot the cross. Marcellus is torn between his fidelity to Rome and his love for Diana (Jean Simmons) who has become a follower of Christ. But the torment in his soul involves forces more powerful than the ones that ensnared Antony in his love for Cleopatra and tempted him to abandon his duties to Rome. As he stands beneath the dying Christ on the cross, Marcellus leans against the wood of the cross and blood drips onto his hand. The blood has a lasting and haunting affect on him, as does the robe whose very touch he now finds abhorrent. Before his conver-sion and martyrdom, Marcellus nearly slips into madness. Another famous film from the classical period, *Ben-Hur: A Tale of the Christ* (1959), which won Oscars for best picture and actor (Charlton Heston), features Judah Ben-Hur, a Jewish nobleman whose rivalry with Mes-sala, a Roman soldier, sends him into slavery. In the film's culminating scenes, Ben-Hur encounters Christ on the way of the Cross. As the blood pours from his wounds, a heavy rain falls; the water mixes with the blood and spreads it through the land. Its miraculous powers cure Ben-Hur's mother and sister of their leprosy. In both of these films, Christ makes only occasional appearances, the brutality of his scourging and crucifixion, are hinted at, rather than shown directly.

But classical Hollywood may be more out of step with the Christian tradition than is Gibson's shockingly realistic film. Any attempt to relocate the audience to first-century Palestine requires that the audience first be transported out of its contemporary surroundings. We must experience the otherness of that world. This is precisely the motive for Gibson's use of Aramaic and Latin and for his explicit depiction of the common practices of public torture in that world. Although focused more broadly on the whole of Jesus's life, Pier Paolo Pasolini's *The Gospel According to Saint Matthew* (1964) is more effective than any Hollywood film at inducing an appreciation of the otherness of Jesus's time, place, and mission.

Filmed in a minimalist style and against the background of rocky, southern Italy, Pasolini's *Gospel* is the antithesis of the Hollywood blockbusters of that era, such as *King of Kings* (1961) or *The Greatest Story Ever Told* (1964). In its penchant for odd angles and its repeated use of tight shots of Jesus' face, the cinematography is startling. It has the effect of putting the viewer off-balance and of isolating Jesus from everyone else in the community. Equally unsettling for the viewer is the way the film alternates rapidly between light and darkness and the bizarre framing of Jesus against barren backgrounds. There are scenes that approach the feeling of horror: for example, the filming of Herod's slaughter of the first-born males of the Jews, which shows babies being tossed into the air and run through with swords. Another scene depicts Jesus as a nondescript, dark, hooded figure, shot against blistering sunlight, walking on the water to the befuddlement and fear of the disciples. Unlike Hollywood films such as *Ben-Hur*, which hid from our eyes the deformed skin of lepers, Pasolini presents the healing of a man with a hideously deformed face by holding the camera shot of the abnormality and then depicting the miraculously restored face.[13]

Jesus himself is severe and distant; for a religious film, Pasolini's *Gospel* has the feel of absence and loss characteristic of Bergmann's great films of doubt, rather than the proclamation of good news. In the culminating scenes, the film traverses familiar scriptural territory with Jesus being accused of blasphemy, Judas's betrayal and brutal suicide, the moderate Pilate distancing himself from the entire affair and the Jews plaintively demanding that Jesus's blood be on them and their children. In fact, Pasolini goes further than most treatments of the Gospel in casting doubt on the audience's ability to make sense of, or profit from, the crucifixion and resurrection. While Jesus is on the cross, the narrator speaks words from elsewhere in the Gospels, about those who have eyes but see not, ears but hear not, lest they believe and be converted. The suggestion here is that the life, teaching, and sacrifice of Christ is so distant from our disordered world, so contrary to what we consider normal, that audiences will not accept, or even recognize, it. But Pasolini's artistry forces the attentive viewer to come to terms with the gap between our world and the life of Christ.

Pasolini's Marxist-inspired life of Christ may have more in common with Gibson's effort than do any of the Hollywood Jesus films. Not as despairing as Pasolini's ending, Gibson's finale with Mary embracing the bloody, perforated body of her son and staring directly at the audience, poses a similar sort of challenge to the audience. We realize that the film that we have been watching with various degrees of empathy, horror, and inquisitiveness is now looking back at us and asking of us, "Who do you say that he is?"

Many of the devices Gibson deploys are designed precisely to engage the audience directly, to make it impossible for the audience to adopt a standpoint of detached irony. The film may have profited from greater restraint and indirection, of the sort operative not just in the films of Shyamalan but also in the fiction of Flannery O'Connor. Nonetheless, its exaggerated stylistic elements exhibit an affinity with *noir*, with Paul Schrader's description of *noir* as embodying a "nightmarish world of American mannerism."

Mannerist nightmare is an apt description of the stylistic vehicle Gibson uses to capture Judas' betrayal, despair, and suicide. Immediately after he hands Jesus over to the Romans, in scenes reminiscent of *Macbeth*, Judas is beset with apparitions of gruesome demons. Regretting his deal, he tries to return the money to the Jewish leaders but they only taunt him. In despair, he slumps down in a public street where children are playing. Discovering him, the children make sport of him. He chides them: "You little Satans." Projections of his inner demons, the children are suddenly transformed into demonic figures who chase him as he becomes completely unhinged. Suddenly there is silence and the children are gone. The camera then offers a series of gruesome images of flies, maggots, and a dead, rotting animal, after which we see Judas hanging from a tree. The camera angle here is a bit askew and from nearly directly ground level; it thus gives the impression that Judas is hovering over an abyss.

The ESPLATTER reviewer's assertion that *The Passion* provides the "iconography" of the horror genre and that it is the foundational "prequel" behind every seriously religious horror film is quite perceptive. Especially noteworthy is the connection between *The Passion* and *The Exorcist*, concerning which there are a number of interesting parallels and points of convergence. In their production phases, both films were viewed as artsy religious films with plans for limited release in select markets. Both were R-rated and neither was seen as a family film. Both films quickly reached wider audience than anticipated; the films also induced experiences in viewers unparalleled in films of their time. Despite their artistic complexity and their remarkably credible depictions of the reality of a cosmic battle between good and evil, both films quickly became notorious for an alleged obsession with the aesthetics of evil or violence. In one case, it was head-twisting, projectile vomiting, and the desecration of female images of innocence; in the other, it is the camera's lingering over the bloody wounds of Christ, over the various implements of torture of his body, and over a *CSI*-like fascination with the points of entry of the nails of crucifixion.

Both films locate the cosmic battle in a contest between a demon and a human servant of God. In both cases, the devil attempts to induce doubt, despair, and feelings of degradation. In an exchange from the book version of *The Exorcist*, the two priests assigned to perform the rite of exorcism, discuss the point of demonic possession:

> "Then what would be the purpose of possession?" Karras said, frowning, "What's the point?"
>
> "Who can know?" answered Merrin. "Who can really hope to know?" He thought for a moment. And then probingly continued: "Yet I think the demon's target is not the possessed. It's us . . .the observers . . . every person in this house. And I think—I think the point is to make us despair; to reject our own humanity . . . to see ourselves as ultimately bestial; as ultimately vile and putrescent; without dignity' ugly, unworthy."

In the extra-biblical source for *The Passion*, Anne Catherine Emmerich's *Dolorous Passion*, Satan is said to have "brought forward innumerable temptations, as he had formerly done in the desert, even daring to adduce various accusations against him . . . in words such as these, 'Takest thou even this upon thyself? Art thou willing to bear its penalty? Art thou prepared to satisfy for all these sins?'" Gibson himself comments that evil "takes on the form of beauty. It is almost beautiful. It is the great aper [sic] of God. But the mask is askew; there is always something wrong. Evil masquerades." This could be an apt description of the demon in *The Exorcist* as well, a character who creates nothing but instead operates by inverting and perverting the order established by nature and God. So the demon engages in a sort of black Mass, crudely defiling the symbolic and sacramental vehicles of holiness, as in the desecration of the Jesuit church at Georgetown University. William Peter Blatty, the author of *The Exorcist*, called *The Passion* a "tremendous depiction of evil." This is high praise from the author whose preoccupation in writing *The Exorcist* was to convince jaded moderns of the reality of evil.

In *The Passion*, the demon walks through the crowd and looks approvingly over the activities of the Roman soldiers. Of course, what the demon hopes is that Christ will not follow through on his mission, that he will quit and despair over his Father. It might seem that this will happen when Christ utters the Old Testament words from the psalms, "My God, My God, why have you forsaken me?" But these words are the beginning of a psalm that ends with praise and thanksgiving for divine deliverance. Christ faithfully delivers himself unto the Father when he adds the final words, "It is finished." The demon screeches in defeat at the moment of his death.

What these films share is Flannery O'Connor's sense that "the devil teaches most of the lessons of self-knowledge." Attention to the struggle with evil, at the center of so many dramatic plots, increases our appreciation of "the moment when grace is offered and accepted." O'Connor defended her own preoccupation with violently nasty characters as thoroughly orthodox. She was fond of the passage from St. Cyril of Jerusalem: "The dragon is by the side of the road, watching those who pass. Beware lest he devour you. We go to the father of souls but it is necessary to pass by the dragon."[14] The tendency in modern religious films has been to ignore the dragon completely. At the intersection of *noir* and horror, *The Passion* aims to restore our sense of the dragon, not the dragon of children's tales, but the dragon that infects the hearts of human beings and makes them capable of deicide.[15]

The response to evil in *The Exorcist* and *The Passion* is not so much Enlightenment science or even human virtue, but religious sacrifice, a willingness to cooperate with the mysterious grace of God and to offer oneself on behalf of others. The sacramental remedy for evil exalts lowly and weak bodily realities as signs of divine love and mercy. *The Exorcist* mirrors the divine logic of the passion narrative; from the needs of a fallen humanity unable to comprehend or rectify its own state of alienation (recall the plea that appears in blood on

Regan's stomach: "Help me") to the sacrificial offering to take the place and suffering of another (recall Karras's pugilistic encounter with the demon culminating in his challenge: "Take me!").

To be glimpsed through Karras's sacrifice is an account of the human condition deeply at odds with some of the founding assumptions of Enlightenment modernity. Blatty's script nicely juxtaposes in its opening scenes the archaic and purportedly superstitious world of the Middle East and the sophisticated, secular world of Georgetown in Washington, D.C. The mystery of evil that soon invades Regan and her family puts the adequacy of the modern world's self-understanding on trial. Blatty's narrative takes its point of departure from the unquestioned assumptions of modern audiences, that is, from our skeptical and rationalist convictions. Even the Jesuit priest, Fr. Karras, is a man of science, a psychiatrist educated at Harvard, a priest who wonders aloud whether he has lost his faith. In her attempt to find a cure for her daughter's bizarre and horrifying affliction, Regan's mother exhausts the somatic and psychological possibilities before even considering a religious intervention. When she does confront Fr. Karras to ask him how one goes about getting an exorcism, he is shocked and tells her that the first thing she would have to do is travel in a "time machine back to the sixteenth century." Yet modern science is unable to reckon with the mystery of iniquity in its midst and both secular Hollywood star and doubting priest must engage in a quest for a lost code of redemption.[16]

Like many contemporary works of art, *The Passion* invites its audience, an audience engulfed in meaningless violence and nihilistic visions of human life, on a quest to recover a lost code of virtue and vice, a lost code of redemption. As many similarities as it may have to other contemporary dramas, *The Passion* is distinctive in two respects. In addition to supplying the primordial iconography of the horror genre, it also attempts to recover the most audacious and most influential code of redemption ever articulated. Furthermore, its mode of recovery is not content with reviving useful moral myths or dramatically fertile symbols. It places before us an unavoidable question about the truth of the life of Christ, who identifies himself as "the way, the truth, and the life."

In the *pieta* scene at the end, when Mary's wounded eyes look from the murdered body of her son and into ours, she asks us to confront the "scariest thing" in human history, the brutal murder of a humiliated God, by each of us. In this case, the curse is potentially a blessing for each of us. The dark quest of *The Passion* addresses the connection, a staple in *noir*, among vice, violence, and fear. But it locates that connection on a different plane and thus suggests an intelligibility typically absent from mainstream *noir*. It proffers a specific and detailed code of redemption.

PASCAL AND THE PASSION

In this as in other ways, Gibson's mannerist style calls to mind in another way the dialectic of Pascal's apology for the Christian faith. I have noted a number of times that the part of Pascal, the part on which otherwise astute interpreters such as Goldmann have exclusively focused, offers an incomplete picture of Pascal's vision. The part on which Goldmann focuses, and which I have found to be so helpful for articulating the *noir* universe, captures the tragedy of the unbelieving individual trapped in a silent cosmos, a mazelike structure where the evidence points in contradictory directions. Still, the individual is so made that, as much as he might like to do so, he cannot give up on the quest. He is doomed to seek with groans. Of course, Pascal's goal is to exhibit the fit between that dark conception of the human condition and the Christian doctrine of redemption. But even here, in the manifestation of God in the flesh, the divine presence remains veiled. The insistence on divine hiddenness, on God as at once present and absent, has a precise pedagogical and medicinal function in divine providence.[17] The truths of Christianity are not propositions that can be detached from a way of life, a way of life that takes its bearings from the comprehensive narrative of creation, fall, and redemption. The chief authority in theological matters, according to Pascal, is memory. He writes, "It was not right that Christ should appear in a manner manifestly divine and absolutely capable of convincing all men, but neither was it right that his coming should be so hidden that he could not be recognized by those who sincerely sought him."[18] The proper recognition of God as mediator presupposes certain dispositions on the part of the agent, a precedent acknowledgment of one's own wretchedness and need for grace.[19] In our fallen state, we vacillate between pride and despair. Knowing God merely as God and not as redeemer only exacerbates this condition, as it engenders the proud assumption that we have attained God by our own powers. True knowledge of God is inseparable from self-knowledge, a recognition of our own wretchedness. Yet true knowledge must not leave us in despair over our condition; it must offer the hope of a cure for wretchedness makes for pride: "Knowing our own wretchedness without knowing God makes for despair. Knowing Christ strikes the balance because he show us both God and our own wretchedness."[20] The religion of a humiliated, crucified God—inconceivable to natural reason—accounts for the paradoxes of human nature. As Pascal writes of figurative statements in the Old Testament, a "figure includes absence and presence," but "once the secret" to the deciphering of the figure is revealed, "it is impossible not to see it."[21]

Still, it is wrong to suppose, as so many critics do, that Pascal repudiates the intelligibility of nature or denies that nature points in any direction. Instead, he offers an alternative account of the intelligibility of nature, one that locates the intelligibility of nature within the order of divine providence. As Pascal puts it, "nature . . . points at every turn to a God who has been lost, both within man and without."[22] He expands: "If the world existed in order to teach man about God, his divinity would shine . . . in a way that could not be gainsaid: but as it exists through Christ, for Christ, and to teach men about their corruption and redemption, everything in it blazes with proofs of these two truths."[23] There is, then, a path from nature to God in Pascal, but it is not the direct path of the natural theology that was becoming dominant in Pascal's day. Instead, Pascal offers what Hans Urs von Balthasar calls an "*anthropologia ancilla theologiae christianae.*"[24] His description of man as "*monstre, chimere, chaos, prodige*" underscores not the "depravity of man but his indecipherability."[25] His question is this: "From what perspective must man be seen so that the deformed is integrated into a true form, the disproportionate into a true proportion?"[26]

Seeing that the paradoxes are anything more than an interesting puzzle is impossible without the vision supplied by charity. Pascal famously speaks of the three orders: body, mind, and charity. The lower know nothing of the higher and provide for no access to what is above. "The greatness of intellectual people is not visible to kings, rich men, captains, who are all great in a carnal sense. The greatness of wisdom, which is nothing if it does not come from God, is not visible to carnal or intellectual people."

Pascal underscores the incommensurability of the orders in unrestrained hyperbole: "The infinite distance between body and mind symbolizes the infinitely more infinite distance between mind and charity, for charity is supernatural." Pascal does work out a sort of analogy: As the order of mind is to the level of the body, so is the order of sanctity to the level of the mind: "Philosophers: they surprise the ordinary run of men. Christians: they surprise the philosophers." Here there emerges a hierarchy of wonder or bafflement, of wisdom mistaken for folly. The rational satisfaction of the inquiry into the truth about man can be seen only from above and in retrospect; there is no possibility of a smooth transition or ascent from body to mind or from either of these to charity.[27] There is no dichotomy between knowing and loving, no gap between intellect and will, or between inclination and apprehension. Pascal speaks of the "impulse" of charity and accentuates the role of the will and love at the third level; yet the teaching on the heart governs here especially. Charity "opens eyes so that the mark of truth is everywhere apparent." Or again, "faith is God apprehended by the heart." For Pascal as for *The Passion of the Christ*, faith apprehends God in the humiliated man of sorrows who "destroys death through death."[28]

The bloody path of Christ's passion marks a passage through the ultimate labyrinth, death itself. But this is not the Enlightenment project of conquering death through technological power; much less is it the avoidance of death through the grand economic project of diversion. Whatever its flaws, *The Passion* explodes the sentimental myth that Christian redemption eliminates suffering and sacrifice. In keeping with *The Passion*'s dark, penitential path, salvation is a matter of following him whose only "companion is darkness."

10

The Children of Men

Thou turnest men to destruction:
again thou sayest, Come again, ye children of men.

Psalm 90

I N THE PRECEDING CHAPTERS, we have traced a little recognized convergence between the anti-Enlightenment themes characteristic of film noir and complex narratives of religious quest. From early films such as Greene's *The Third Man* and Hitchcock's *I Confess* through contemporary television series such as *Buffy the Vampire Slayer*, the films of Shyamalan and Gibson's *Passion*, dark tales of religious quest have proven surprisingly popular and enduring. We have also suggested that the thought of Pascal—on our alienated condition and on the nature of the quest—provides a previously unnoticed resource for articulating the *noir* universe, particularly that part of the *noir* universe that sustains the nobility of the quest. The combined sense of the tenuous quest with a tempered hope is evident in the passage, quoted above, from Psalm 90, a passage that provides the title for P.D. James's book, *The Children of Men*, that in turns is the basis of a recent film, a sort of science fiction film, with feminist themes, that dramatically illustrates the paradoxes of Enlightenment science and politics. Those issues are less prominent in the film than in the book, which features a main character who embarks on a reluctant quest, an uncertain and finally unresolved quest that nonetheless illustrates in a Pascalian manner the resources of the Christian narrative both to embrace the noir universe and to suggest a path toward the transcendence of its maze. An analysis of the book will enable us to see more clearly what is at stake in Pascal's comprehensive and explicitly religious account of the human condition, the broad contours of which we have yet to appreciate fully. Before turning to these matters, it will help to have before us a brief consideration of some influential contemporary conceptions of film, religion, and the human condition.

CINEMA: RELIGIOUS OR DECADENT?

Going beyond the claim that there is an occasional link between film and religious themes, some film critics argue that film itself is a religious medium. In *Film as Religion: Myths, Morals, and Rituals*, John Lyden argues that films, like religions, supply a mythic structure which "conveys a worldview" or a "general conception of reality," promotes a set of values concerning "how the world should be," and prescribes a ritual expression that links the first two.[1] There is much to be said for the thesis that films have a religious dimension, despite our tendency to treat them as mere entertainment. Filmmakers from Capra to Scorsese and Lucas have underscored their own quasi-religious intentions in the making of film. There is also the practice of watching films in the theater, of gathering in the dark, to sit in silence in the hope of experiencing—what? Mere entertainment? Or what another critic calls the "stealthy rapture of film"?

In his approach to film and religion, Lyden adopts what he calls "inclusivist pluralism." After having proclaimed the rich variety of particular religions, Lyden ends up with a bland syncretism. So capacious is his understanding that atheism itself counts as a religion and secularization is simply the "evolution of more religious alternatives," the advent of a "greater pluralism."[2] Instead of confronting and enhancing our appreciation of pluralism, Lyden simply avoids it.[3] Some years ago, in his influential book, *We Hold These Truths*, John Courtney Murray, argued that one of the chief intellectual tasks facing our society was to come to terms with religious pluralism, with the sheer variety of religions practiced in America.[4] The goal, Murray urged, was not to reduce pluralism to unity, but to reduce it to intelligibility. The problem is that in practice pluralism often ends up as a plurality of individual beliefs, with the doctrines and practices of traditional religions being seen either as threats to individual preference or as containing an underlying sameness that renders differences superficial. One of the consequences of this, as the philosopher Alasdair MacIntyre has quipped, is that religions give atheists less and less to disbelieve.[5]

There is of course something to a less exuberant thesis than the one Lyden posits. We have witnessed the pluralism of quests and the syncretism of religious paths in a variety of films and in at least one television drama. These stores deploy a diverse set of symbols in their attempt to articulate a lost code of redemption. With the exception of *The Passion*, these dramas rarely do more than hint at the symbolic key or the narrative path of redemption. As we have seen in Andrew O'Hehir criticisms of Shyamalan's tendency toward a vague pluralism, lacking a "specifically Christian or Hindu or Muslim . . . point of view," pluralism can render symbols vacuous.[6]

Empty pluralism is easily manipulated. One of the dangers for film in our time is that it might become one more branch of the advertising industry, as observers as divergent as Theodor Adorno and Flannery O'Connor have warned. What is little noticed in this regard is the way a soft version of academic postmodernism accords rather nicely with capitalist consumerism. As David Brooks notes, the indeterminacy of truth, the sense of discourse itself as an endless series of provisional constructs is "perfectly suited to the ethos of the achievement-oriented capitalist. After all, why should the achiever want to make enemies or waste time in angry conflict? Why should the time-maximizer struggle to find that thing called Absolute Truth when it is more efficient to settle for perception? Why should one get involved in the problematic rigor of judging? Easygoing tolerance is energy-efficient."[7]

A different sort of problem for any association of religion with contemporary film concerns idolatry. In his remarkable new book on Hollywood, *The Whole Equation*, celebrated film critic David Thomson focuses squarely on the problematic ethics of the moving, visual image and implicitly raises the issue of idolatry. Thomson is at once immersed in, fascinated with, and horrified by Hollywood. Unlike most contemporary critics of Hollywood, Thomson locates Hollywood's questionable influence on the culture, not in the late twentieth century and the rise in explicit violence and sexuality, but in its glory days. What is unusual and highly instructive in Thomson's way of construing the moral question is his focus on the very nature of film and its impact on audiences, on the mode of its presentation and reception. He focuses on the "enormous . . . tidal pull toward new dreams" and the consequent and far-reaching "romantic transformation," according to which the new ideal for humanity becomes the "actor, with his infinite variety."[8]

As viewers, he asks, are we "watching heightened things—great danger, great desirability, intense loveliness—without being tied by the responsibilities that attach to real onlookers?" "We are," he suggests, "like voyeurs, spies, or peeping toms." In contrast to literature, which actively engages the imagination to probe the "meaning behind events," film involves the "fetishization of appearance." Film is less about glimpsing hidden meaning than about "what happens or appears next." It thus suffers from "the crushing restriction of visibility."[9] The deadly combination for the soul is a purely capitalist conception of the person as producer-consumer with the Hollywood inspired vision of the individual as spectator.

Form here reflects or produces (it is unclear which way Thomson thinks the causal line runs) a corresponding ethical content. He compares the nineteenth-century novel—which offered an education of the passions and tried to help individuals discern whom to marry and what virtues assist in the maintenance of marriage—with twentieth-century film, with its gratification of fantasy through a "parade of dreams." Now, one might object to numerous features of Thomson's argument. He overstates the contrast between films and novels. It was, after all, in nineteenth-century novels such as Flaubert's *Madame Bovary* that the demise of marriage and the celebration of fantasy first occurred. But even if he overstates his case in certain respects, what he has to say about the differences in the form of presentation and the mode of reception of novel and film is astute.

Thomson puts his finger on the crucial ethical question regarding Hollywood, indeed regarding film itself as a cultural artifact. Hollywood film, "the professional craft of pretending," comes to the fore just as our sense of identity becomes "destabilized by the slippage of religious belief." Hollywood offers its own "images to worship," as it reveals "rather ghastly fake gods."[10] The new model for humanity becomes the actor, with his infinite variety. If in its infancy Hollywood offered certain dangerous temptations to American citizens, the situation seems hardly to have improved in recent years.

What is the stealthy rapture of film? It is the sense that a new world is opening up before our eyes, that, however much we might not directly articulate it, that we are participants in an adventure, that we are invested in the characters on the screen, and that we might discover some truth about ourselves. In Walker Percy's *The Moviegoer*, the main character, Binx Bolling, a stockbroker and film fan, who enjoys coastal drives in his MG and seducing his secretaries, has the intermittent sense that there is something more to life. When this happens, he embarks, however briefly, on a quest:

> What is the nature of the search? You ask. Really it is very simple,
> at least for a fellow like me it's so simple that it is easily over-

looked. The search is what anyone would undertake if he were not sunk in the everydayness of his own life. This morning, for example, I felt as if I had come to myself on a strange island. And what does such a castaway do? Why, he pokes around the neighborhood and he doesn't miss a trick. To become aware of the possibility of the search is to be onto something. Not to be onto something is to be in despair.

Movies are onto the search, but they screw it up. Their search always ends in despair. They like to show a fellow coming to himself in a strange place—but what does he do? He takes up with the local librarian, sets about proving to the local children what a nice fellow he is, and settles down with a vengeance.[11]

Partly inspired by his habit of moviegoing, Binx has a glimmer of the quest. He is not in complete despair, since, as Kierkegaard defines it in the epigraph to this novel, "the precise character of despair is this: it is unaware of being despair." According to Thomson's way of thinking, contemporary film is even less likely to produce and inspire viewers like Binx. The mysteries present in great filmmaking have migrated further to the margins of the industry, which itself has moved steadily in the direction of attracting a young audience for whom camp, irony, endless motion, novelty, and spectacle are the real draws. Audiences now seem enraptured by the "capacity of the visible to exceed reality," rather than illumine it. As Thomson notes, television has all but replaced film as the source of shared cultural stories. The television world proclaims that there are all sorts of things happening to which you do not have "to pay attention" and in which you have no responsibility to "take part." On this issue, Thomson leaves us with a pressing pedagogical question. How many of us have had any "education in the nature of moving imagery, its grammar, its laws or lawlessness"? Without such training, how can we be "expected to distinguish news from fantasy, art from deception?"[12]

According to an influential strain of twentieth-century European philosophy, the culture industry precludes the possibility of citizen-consumers of culture exercising any critical judgment whatsoever. A seminal document of the Frankfurt school, Horkheimer and Adorno's *Dialectic of Enlightenment* is a book laden with impenetrable jargon whose conclusions are nearly always overdrawn. Yet its focus on the way the excessive rhetoric of Enlightenment undermines its original aspiration is, I have argued, an abiding, if typically implicit, preoccupation of film *noir*. The Enlightenment exaltation of instrumental, calculative reason and its project of domination over a disenchanted natural world effectively evacuate purpose and dignity from the human world. Radical enlightenment fosters blindness to ends and a fascination with amoral managerial expertise. Horkheimer and Adorno think that bureaucratic management, combined with the "culture industry," eliminates the possibility of human freedom. Fascism lurks precisely where it is least remarked, in the banal choices offered to individuals by the advertising industry of a market economy. Without hope of world revolution, Horkheimer and Adorno offer a despairing communist apocalypse.

The contradictions of Enlightenment politics are evident not only to leftist intellectuals but also to thinkers such as Alexis de Tocqueville, who speaks of the potential for a new physiognomy of servitude, a slavery willingly embraced by those who prefer equality and physical comfort to the exacting costs of liberty. For Tocqueville, America itself provides on a grand scale a dramatic example of the restlessness, inconstancy, and anxiety that Pascal detects at the heart of the human condition.[13] Tocqueville observes, "Among democratic nations, men easily attain a certain equality of condition, but they can never attain as much as they desire. It perpetually retires before them, yet without hiding itself from their sight, and in retiring draws them on. At every moment they think they are about to grasp it; it escapes at every moment from their hold. They are near enough to see its charms, but too far off to enjoy them; and before they have fully tasted its delights, they die. That is the reason for the strange melancholy that haunts inhabitants of democratic countries in the midst of abundance."

Here Tocqueville offers a specific application of Pascal's general observation. The pursuit of happiness is a *noir* trap: "We never keep to the present. . . . We are so unwise that we wander about in times that do not belong to us, and do not think of the only one that does; so vain that we dream of times that are not and blindly flee the only one that is. . . . The present is never our end. The past and the present are our means, the future alone our end. Thus we never live, but hope to live, and since we are always planning how to be happy, it is inevitable that we should never be so."[14] Our fugitive existence renders our quest for happiness futile; yet, we are not utterly bereft of self-knowledge, since we have at least the ability to recognize the disorder of our condition.

THE CHILDEN OF MEN

Such a vision of our fugitive existence is on display in the film *The Children of Men*. Assisted by the splendid cinematography of Emmanuel Lubezki, a superb performance by Clive Owen as Theodore Faron, and a lean script that throws us immediately into the midst of revolutionary activism against an oppressive political order, Alfonso Cuaron's film version of P.D. James's novel *The Children of Men* is not so much a futuristic sci-fi film as a gripping meditation on what we already are. The stunning visual quality of the film provides access to a world much darker, but not completely other, than ours—a world in which humans have been rendered rapidly and bafflingly infertile and hence face the imminent extinction of their own species, members of whose last generation are known as the Omegas. Cuaron, who has directed such solid films as *A Little Princess* and *Harry Potter and the Prisoner of Azkaban*, takes one of the many symptoms of malaise from the book—xenophobia about immigrants—and makes it the central issue of the film. For this streamlined film, the issue of immigration works as a dramatic framing device. But it also severely truncates, and in crucial ways inverts, the intellectual and political content of the story, so much so that the political and ethical implications of the novel are completely absent from the film. One must return to James' book to see the ways in which *The Children of Men* embodies a dark and reluctant quest to recover a lost code of redemption; as in the case of *The Passion*, here too the lost code is the Gospel, but unlike *The Passion*, *The Children of Men* works by way of indirection and tentative suggestion rather than direct proclamation. It is thus more in keeping with the dominant narrative structure of *noir*.

In James's novel, infertility operates as a symbol of mankind's despair, of the nihilism that lurks just beneath the surface of modern life. The questions made explicit in the infertile world are: For what are we living? Why do we have children? What do we want to hand on to them? But as is so often the case in science fiction, disaster and despair arise out of our greatest boasts, our technological and scientific mastery of nature. As Theo Faren, the main character in the book puts it, "we are humiliated at the very heart of our faith in ourselves. For all our knowledge, for all our intelligence, our power, we can no longer do what the animals do without thought."[15] Such universal failure produces despair and even a reversion to a sense of cosmic vengeance. As Faron observes, "The discovery in July 1994 that even frozen sperm stored for experiment and artificial insemination had lost its potency was a peculiar horror casting over Omega the pall of superstitious awe, of witchcraft, of divine intervention. The old gods reappeared, terrible in their power."[16]

Cuaron's hope lies in a revolutionary unrest for something new, but that is not, in the novel, a feasible way out, since human desire has been sapped of energy and focus. Indeed, governance in the novel is precisely what Tocqueville described as the new physiognomy of servitude, a world in which citizens willingly subject themselves to the complete control of a bureaucratic apparatus, here concretized in the leadership of one man. The book makes wonderfully clear that democracy is no threat to the new tyrant; instead, it is an abiding assumption of the new form of tyranny. Because he gives the people protection, comfort, and pleasure, Britain's leader would win any election in a landslide. As Tocqueville astutely saw, libertarianism and centralization—mirror images of one another—are not so much enemies as allies in the vanishing of a spirited public life and in the diminution of humanity. The observations from the novel about the Omegas apply to the entire society of Britain: "Perhaps we have made our Omegas what they are by our own folly; a regime that combines perpetual surveillance with total indulgence is hardly conducive to healthy development. If from infancy you treat children as gods they are liable in adulthood to act as devils."[17] Surveillance and indulgence combine to sap humanity of longing and activity.

For all of its promise of protection and pleasure, the new regime seems only to exacerbate the strange mixture of fear and longing for death, even as it serves to remove pleasure from our grasp. Officially sponsored group suicide, called the Quietus, allegedly allows individuals to choose when they die; yet the book makes clear that this is subject to abuse, as the government forces death upon those who have second thoughts and offers incentives to families to ease the elderly out of this life. Cuaron's film turns this critique inside out and deprives the Quietus of any problematic status; the film's only use of the Quietus is as a private and legitimate act of euthanasia. For the increasingly tepid pleasures experienced in this world of complete sexual freedom, there is government-sponsored pornography. As P.D. James puts it in the book, one might suppose that with the "fear of pregnancy permanently removed . . . sex would be freed for new and imaginative delights." But that is not the case: "Sex totally divorced from procreation has become almost meaninglessly acrobatic," characterized by "painful orgasms, spasms without pleasure."[18] The book dwells in compelling detail, not just on xenophobia, but also on the disorders of modern sexuality, the stultifying of human passion and feeling, the flourishing of the desire for death, and the narcissistic attitudes toward children. James describes a world in which dolls (artificial children) and pets (child substitutes) have become objects of fawning desire, christened in birth celebrations and buried in consecrated ground to satisfy "frustrated maternal desire."

Cuaron reduces James's supple account of the human condition and the great political dangers of modernity to narrow ideological politics. That leaves Cuaron with nothing more to offer his audience than naïve, romantic-sounding, 1960s slogans about the younger generation. Cuaron has said, "I have a grim view not of the future but of the present. I believe evolution is happening and human understanding is occurring and that the young generation is the one that is getting some new perspective of reality of what's going on in the world. The new generation will prove that the Earth is going around the sun, not the sun going around the Earth." Cuaron fails to see that this adulation of children is one of the greatest disorders in the world of the novel. James's book treats of this issue with great clarity, in the case of the Omegas, the last generation to be born. Both book and film begin with the fawning global media attention heaped on the death of the last person to be born, the youngest individual on earth. James astutely observes, "It was a generation programmed for failure, the ultimate disappointment to the parents who had bred them and the race which had invested in them so much careful nurturing and so much hope."[19] Cuaron realizes that for this film to have more than a superficial resonance, it must draw upon symbolic resources. In fact, in a recent interview, he argues that "our culture is over-narratized" and that "we are missing one of the biggest, probably something more powerful than narrative [to] humans—that is symbols. The ability to interpret symbols." Gleaned as they are from the popular press, Cuaron's symbols—prejudice toward immigrants and threats to homeland security—have a limited power.

The "co-reference of things," as Cuaron calls it, is precisely what makes P.D. James's novel so powerful. In fact, what James offers is a set of symbolic clues to aid us in detecting the causes of our loss of a coherent symbology. In the book, there is much speculation about the source of infertility, the story's central symbol. Scientists are hard at work trying to find the cause and a cure, even as statistical paleontologists face the end with a shrug; extinction is the rule rather than the exception for life on earth. And of course there are apocalyptic preachers ranting about God's judgment on sinful humanity. Cuaron includes the latter in one scene; they seem in the film as in the book to be yet another freaky sideshow in a world gone mad. But Cuaron fails to see that James includes the apocalyptic preachers as a warning against the modern, falsely sophisticated temptation to think that religion offers nothing more than an extremist freak show. Cuaron, it seems, took the bait.[20] In a more serious reflection on religion's near eclipse in modernity, the main character in the book, the skeptic Theodore Faron, observes that the "cross . . . has never been a comfortable symbol."[21] Theo is a wonderful embodiment of the reluctant seeker, someone who at the beginning of the book is a reflective but indifferent observer of the contemporary loss of meaning. He admits, "I don't want anyone to look to me, not for protection, not for happiness, not for love, not for anything."

Amid P. D. James's long list of mystery novels, *The Children of Men* is peculiar. Its scope is much broader than that of what we called earlier the traditional detective story; it addresses the mystery of our alienated condition, an alienation that modernity seems to exacerbate in ways that render us incapable of recognizing that condition for what it is. The quandary of infertility opens onto a set of problems concerning the human condition itself, problems that resist articulation, let alone resolution. As Ralph Wood comments, "Among the many mysteries James explores in this novel, perhaps the deepest is the mystery of conversion: How can we be transformed from self-regarding into self-surrendering people? How, more strangely still, can we find the faith to resist overwhelming evil, especially in a world without a future?"[22] Indeed, the great mystery is the transformation, however partial, of

Theo Faren himself, from detached cultivator of creature comforts into someone willing to risk his life for the sake of new life. From initial indifference, he comes close to embody the sentiment of another character: "The world is changed not by the self-regarding but by men and women prepared to make fools of themselves."

The title itself, *The Children of Men*, is a direct quotation from Psalm 90, a prayer in Anglican the burial service for the dead: "Thou turnest men to destruction: again thou sayest, Come again, ye children of men."[23] The language of the Psalm captures, in sequence, the sense of the *noir* trap as a kind of divine curse and the possibility of emergence from the maze through cooperation with the signs of divine grace. And that complex account of the human condition—alienation and the prospect of a remedy—nicely encapsulates the Pascalian vision.

THE *NOIR* TRAP

To account for the paradoxes of the human condition, Pascal turns to the revealed teaching about original sin, a doctrine that Pascal admits is an affront to our customary sense of justice. But Pascal's position has itself come under fire. Sara Melzer argues that Pascal's account of the Fall reduces to an irresolvable *aporia*. How so? There is, on the one hand, the "lost truth" as "the origin and goal of our desire. The story of the Fall and Redemption implies that its narrator has transcended language to acquire, through faith, the object of his desire: the certainty of a transcendent truth, of God." But paradoxically, the historical Fall puts us in a state of uncertainty, so that we are unable to say whether a Fall, in fact, even occurred: "Trapped as we are in signs, we cannot escape the hermeneutic circle to gain knowledge of an origin from which we have fallen. Within the hermeneutic circle, all that humans can experience is a fall from the illusion of truth."[24] Thus, Pascal's own text remains within a *noir* world, with no possibility of deciding between the doctrinal truth of the Fall and the Fall as mere myth, indicating nothing more than our perpetual alienation from truth. She makes the point more tersely toward the end of the book: "As the language in which we are trapped is a fallen language, the meta-language with which we represent to ourselves our attempts to transcend language is also fallen. Language can produce only incompatible stories about where our interpretations of figures lead."[25]

Melzer's deconstruction of Pascal's text restates in a particularly concise form, objections to Pascal raised by philosophers such as Nietzsche and J.L. Mackie.[26] In fact, her interpretation accords rather nicely with Lucien Goldmann's interpretation of Pascal as a thinker who never overcomes the dialectic that gives rise to tragedy. Pervading Pascal's discussion of nature and instinct is the doctrine of original sin. Some of his statements about the fall are striking and severe. Man, he writes, "is nothing but a subject full of error, natural and ineffaceable without grace."[27] Pascal also suggests that we are unable to distinguish nature from habit: "nature itself is nothing other than first custom and custom is but second nature."[28] It seems that reason can be bent in any direction and thus cannot be a trustworthy guide in any sense. The fideist interpretation of Pascal seizes on this strain of this thought. If nature is utterly depraved, then an account of the movement from what human nature is to what it might become under the influence of grace seems undercut at the outset.

Precisely at this point does the charge of incoherence arise. The assumption of a corrupt human nature threatens to undermine Pascal's project, as it renders human beings incapable of seeing any truth, apart from grace. How could the proofs be instruments of grace? To what could Pascal be appealing in his audience? What use would the giving of reasons be? Some critics have asserted that the passages on the depravity of nature belie Pascal's positive appraisal of reason and conceal his actual intent, which is to undercut reason and to force the unbeliever into a situation where fear engenders an irrational leap of faith. J.L. Mackie, for example, has argued that the Pascal's wager demands the denial of reason, while Nietzsche excoriated Pascal's faith as a continual sacrifice of reason. If these passages are taken as Pascal's peremptory statement on human nature, then he risks reducing religion to terror, conflating it with superstition, and undermining his own project. On this view, Pascal's project is tyrannical and vulnerable to an ethical critique. All that would remain of Pascal's apology is the crass appeal to self-interest.

In the course of his defense of Pascal's wager, Nicholas Rescher compares Pascal's approach to Hobbes's appeal to "personal advantage."[29] There are indeed similarities between the two, but the differences are deeper than Rescher notes. To appreciate the rhetorical danger involved in the doctrine of the total depravity of nature, it helps to consider Hobbes's account of the origin of religious belief, a position that renders religion nearly indistinguishable from superstition. In *Leviathan*, Hobbes denies that there is any natural end to human life; instead, the "general inclination of mankind" is a "perpetual and restless desire of power after power, that ceaseth only in death."[30] Pascal nearly concurs when he writes, "our nature consists in movement; absolute rest is death."[31] For Hobbes, nature is mute concerning good and evil. Hobbes traces the origin of religious belief to two features of the human condition: "ignorance of causes," which "disposes or constrains men to rely on the advice and authority of others," and anxiety or fear over the future, which dispose human beings to posit, and then seek to appease, invisible causes controlling the future." As he puts it, "The perpetual fear, always accompanying mankind in the ignorance of causes, as it were in the dark, must needs have for object something."[32] How does this compare with Pascal's approach to religion?

One of the obstacles to answering this question is that, for all his preoccupation with method, Pascal is not a systematic thinker. His thought is mobile, discursive, and dialectical, with initial formulations being open to refinement or alteration in light of further evidence and additional reflections.[33] Moreover, Pascal's aim is not simply to lay out a position in a linear, deductive fashion, but to induce self-knowledge, a self-knowledge to which he thinks we are especially averse. He thus deploys hyperbole to shock his audience into a knowing recognition of themselves and their condition. Pascal's goal is precisely the one that has been ascribed to film *noir*: to induce a specific alienation. This much is clear. The complete denigration of reason would lead human beings to despair, which is one of two great evils of human life. The other, opposed evil is presumption. As Pascal writes, "Man must not be allowed to believe that he is equal either to animals or to angels, nor to be unaware of either, but he must know both."[34] Human nature is neither totally depraved, nor capable of achieving the good by its own powers. The largest section of the study of nature has to do with the wretchedness or corruption of human nature. Pascal adduces a plethora of examples of our wretchedness, three of which will help illustrate the intrinsic connection between wretchedness and greatness, and the way an apprehension of wretchedness entails a precedent grasp of what it means for human beings to possess integrity and health.

First, Pascal observes that we rarely live in the present; in fact, we find the present painful. We spend most of our time relishing or regretting the past and fearing or anticipating the future. And yet we incessantly and indefatigably pursue happiness as if it were somehow within our reach, as if it were inexplicable that we should not possess it. Thus, we never live but only hope to live and our inveterate tendency to plot ways to achieve happiness is the surest sign that we will never attain it.[35] Second, unable to live in the present and averse to self-knowledge, we have given our lives over to diversion. Our inconstancy reflects the need to be diverted from the present, from ourselves. The cause of the state of "inconstancy, boredom, and anxiety" is the "realization that present pleasures are false, together with the failure to realize that absent pleasures are vain."[36] Third, what typifies our condition is the apparently systematic subversion of higher, properly human capacities by lower, sub-human powers and drives. Imagination overpowers reason, truth and virtue are no match for charm and novelty, and concupiscence renders human freedom otiose.

For Pascal, all these features of the human condition are signs of the wretchedness of human nature. But does not our ability to apprehend the various sorts of disorder in ourselves presuppose some apprehension of what is natural, normative, and good? In the course of discussing the obvious injustice of homicide, Pascal states explicitly that "we know very well what is evil and false."[37] In order to lament our inconstancy and inability to live in the present, must we not recognize, at least dimly, that our natural end is happiness? Our indomitable longing for happiness, even in the face of repeated failure, is a sign that we think happiness is proper to us. The very fact that we deem our condition wretched indicates that we think some better condition would be more appropriate to our nature. Similarly, in order to appreciate the subversion of higher by lower, must we not have some grasp of the natural, proper ordering and functioning of human capacities? Does not Pascal concede all this when he states that our greatness consists in our ability to understand our wretchedness? To make depravity the whole picture is to grasp only one part of our duality, to exaggerate our wretchedness and to neglect entirely our greatness. Without a residue of greatness, we would not recognize our condition as wretched.

Indeed, even apart from revelation, Pascal is not the thoroughgoing skeptic he is often depicted as being. For, he wants to insist not just on the limits to reason and the corruption of the passions but on a more complicated account of our access to truth than what is allowed in the nascent rationalism of early modern philosophy: "We know the truth not only through our reason but also through our heart. It is through the latter that we know first principles." About the apparently inconclusive arguments over whether we can determine with certainty that we are not dreaming, Pascal concludes, "We know that we are not dreaming. . . . However unable we may be to prove it rationally, our inability proves nothing but the weakness of reason, and not the uncertainty of all our knowledge. For knowledge of first principles . . . is as solid as any derived through reason, and it is on such knowledge, coming from the heart and instinct, that reason has to depend and base all its argument."[38]

One of the difficulties with interpreting Pascal's account of the heart has to do with the misleading way in which the term is rendered in English as "feeling or instinct." But *sentiment* or *sent* has in French as in the Latin roots, cognitive dimensions as well as emotional elements. The Latin *sentire*, for example, means "sense" or "perceive." Pascal is to be taken seriously when he states the "heart has its reasons"; the heart is a faculty of perception, of awareness, and thus a vehicle of knowledge about the world. Both reason and the heart are cognitive. Thus Pascal describes those who have received the gift of faith as "judging by their heart."[39] *Coeur* is, as Hans Urs von Balthasar observes, "the sensorium of the whole."[40] The heart involves an immediate apprehension of complex wholes, rather than a discursive movement from one principle or assumption to others and through these to conclusions. By contrast to reason, the heart is receptive rather than active. Pascal insists that reason is dependent on the heart precisely because reason must assume its starting points, must be given the materials upon which it works, to reject, to doubt, or to affirm.

Pascal writes: "Man does not know the place he should occupy. He has obviously gone astray; he has fallen from his true place and cannot find it again. He searches everywhere, anxiously but in vain, in the midst of impenetrable darkness."[41] On this side of grace, we are bereft of any clear bearings. And yet all is not lost. We never quite succumb to the psychic and epistemological vertigo Pascal so dramatically describes. Pascal admits as much when he states that we are "incapable of certain knowledge or absolute ignorance." The lesson of course has more to do with an awareness of our tragic existential situation than with answers to epistemological quibbles about what we can know with certainty.

Pascal's moderate skepticism leads him to be skeptical of skepticism, at least in its extreme, paralyzing forms. Just as we do not know enough to proclaim success, so too despair reposes upon a false certainty about our condition and our dismal prospects for happiness, communication, and truth: "Just as I do not know whence I come, so I do not know whither I am going."[42] What we do know is that human life has the shape of a quest, that what it means to be human is to be engaged with thoughts about our destiny, about who we are in relation to others. Unlike the ancient pagan philosophers, who conceived of at least some human beings as easily inclined toward such a quest, Pascal envisions the entire human condition as fallen, unnatural, perversely twisted against its own good. We witness the systematic subversion of the higher by the lower and a fanatical devotion to diversion. Although Pascal is motivated by piety, he denies that we need spiritual devotion to see how monstrous our indifference is; instead, "we need only see what the least enlightened see."[43] Here Pascal anticipates the democratic ethos of *noir*. But he also thinks that we typically come to engage in a quest, not through the easy prompting of our current inclinations, but only through negation, frustration, defeat, and weariness.

The paradoxes of human nature perdure and cry out for an explanation that can be had, according to Pascal, only from the vantage point of faith. Pascal makes this point explicitly: "all these examples of wretchedness prove his greatness. It is the wretchedness of a dispossessed king."[44] Pascal does not think that the duality of human nature demonstrates the doctrine of original sin. Rather, his intent is to engender respect for religion by showing that it presents a more coherent account of human nature better than any other hypothesis. Might it be the case that we retain some memory of a happiness that once was ours? "All men seek happiness" as if it were something achievable by them and as if they knew what they were looking for. Pascal finds a sophisticated account of the multiple paradoxes of the human condition in the doctrine of original sin. Far from undermining the possibility of intelligibility, original sin is the key to the intelligibility of the human condition.

Melzer herself notes that Pascal does not leave the reader of his text with a set of irreconcilable hermeneutic possibilities. Instead, he offers a "new model of reading, one that . . . focuses on the subjective process of reading and writing oneself." The crucial move here "involves the realization that we are always being written by someone else." The activity of reading and interpreting is conditioned by what exceeds its grasp. Melzer writes, "Through the heart, the hidden Author, God, can rewrite the readers' conventional sign systems and read through them, projecting his light onto them through Jesus Christ."[45]

Far from marking an insuperable impasse in the human progress toward the divine, the insistence on divine hiddenness, on God as at once present and absent, has a precise pedagogical and medicinal function in divine providence.[46] Obscurity, combined with a complex ethical pedagogy, ill suits the deist conception of God, but it befits the Christian account, according to which nature is corrupt and in need of a redeemer.[47] The recovery of the truth of the hiddenness of God is one reason for the surprising alliance between tales of religious quest and the world of *noir*.

SEEKING WITH GROANS

For all of the attempts in numerous contemporary authors to align Pascal with a thoroughly postmodern conception of discourse, he cannot finally be subsumed within that limited horizon.[48] As much as he may anticipate some of their theses, Pascal would not entirely concur with Horkheimer and Adorno. As capacious and malleable as he deems human nature to be under the influence of habit, he thinks that, so long as humanity endures at all, there is complexity and internal conflict and hence the possibility of self-awareness. Horkheimer and Adorno's hasty dismissal of what they derisively call the "culture industry" accords with certain early reactions to film *noir*. Usually considered as mere entertainment, films typically function as distractions from our lives. In its emphasis on dreams—often enough in the form of indirect commentary on film itself as a type of dream—*noir* would seem to affirm this cultural supposition. But in fact *noir* uses dreams to jar us into realizations about how disordered our condition is; it brings us face to face with ourselves and with our wretched alienation. The audience participates in the disorientation of the *noir* protagonist, who is, as Pascal puts it, "like a man transported in his sleep to some terrifying desert island, who wakes up quite lost and with no means of escape." The result is a condition of "a*maze*ment." *Noir* illustrates an odd fact about our condition, namely, that we are "so sensitive to minor things and so strangely insensitive to the greatest."

Noir's disturbing vision awakens us from our dogmatic slumbers, from our comfortable sense that all is as it should be. By resisting the return to everydayness, *noir* avoids Hollywood sentimentality and fends off malaise. The risk for *noir* is that recovery, return, or even going forward becomes impossible. All would be lost. This would constitute a sort of knowing despair, not yet full-blown despair that does not know itself. Yet, we have seen that a certain strain in American *noir*, a strain concerned to revive a notion of human life as a quest for redemption, suggests a way of moving forward.

As scholars of *noir* have noted, there are some direct lines of influence from Marx, Freud, and existentialists. One cannot trace any direct line of influence from Pascal. But there may well be an indirect one, through the poetry of T.S. Eliot, who read Pascal with profit and penetration. Eliot penned a thoughtful introduction to an edition of the *Pensées,* in which he commends Pascal to those "who doubt, but who have the mind to conceive, and the sensibility to feel, the disorder, the futility, the meaninglessness, the mystery of life and suffering, and who can only find peace through a satisfaction of the whole being."[49] And Eliot's impact on noir extends from its inception to its neo-*noir* resurgence. The great noir novelist, Dashiell Hammett, was fascinated with *The Waste Land*. Paul Schrader described the spiritual and psychological crisis he endured while writing the script for *Taxi Driver* as akin to the crisis portrayed in *The Waste Land*. Eliot's great poem contains many noir themes: with its cities cut off from nature, facing an inexplicable apocalypse, its sterile and mechanical sexuality, its protagonist and narrator, haunted by the past yet unable to piece the fragments of memory together, whose quest seems doomed, but who is under some sort of compulsion to continue, to tell the tale of contemporary dislocation and alienation, to pursue the veiled clues buried amid the ruins of western civilization. Conversely, just as in *The Waste Land*, so too in Pascal's *Pensées*, the text embodies a number of voices whose varied degrees of distance from, or affirmation of, faith give the book a striking universality.

The problem with many modern philosophers, including Hobbes and Freud, is that they systematically reduce the higher to the lower, the immaterial to the material, freedom to physical necessity, right to might, and the desire for love and beauty to the subconscious, infantile drives of the ego. They thus undercut the possibility of the quest; the effect, intended or not is to transform human beings into tame, herdlike animals. Now, Pascal is no naïve realist when it comes to our desires and purported ideals. He observes tartly that justice is as much a matter of fashion as charm is. He suggests that the massive projects of modernity to build a civilization spanning the globe is rooted in our cupidity and that many of our most noble pursuits are but species of diversion. The restless motion, apparently signaling that we are but automatons, mobile machines, as Hobbes would have it, is just one part of the picture, however. Pascal concedes something to Hobbes's description of our present state. On account of our failure to realize "the insatiable nature of cupidity," we think we "genuinely want rest when all we really want is activity." But for Pascal, the evidence is more complex than Hobbes allows. He observes of human beings, "They have

a secret instinct driving them to seek external diversion and occupa-
tion, and this is a result of their constant sense of wretchedness. They
have another secret instinct, left over from the greatness of our original
nature, telling them that their only true happiness lies in rest and not
in excitement." Once again, and here in direct contrast with Hobbes,
Pascal highlights the duality of the human condition. Hobbes refuses to
make any judgment on the state of nature; he calls it "inconvenient" and
yet "natural" and this evinces his distance from Pascal, who perceives
that something is deeply awry in the human condition, something for
which there is no adequate natural explanation or remedy.

Pascal does not think that we can prove, beyond doubt, that we
know the external world or that we are not simply bodily. But we cannot
prove that we are purely material either. The mechanical materialism
that haunts the characters in classic *noir* and that becomes the central
issue in sci-fi neo-*noir* is an abiding concern of Pascal. He observes, for
example, that our "passions automatically make our decisions" for us.
His assertion that we are as much "automaton as mind" nicely captures
his open-ended approach to human nature. There are numerous signs
that man is more than mere matter in motion: in the openness to the
infinite, in the insatiable desire for a happiness distinct from physical
pleasure, in our capacity for thought, self-reflection, self-appropriation,
and self-direction. "Instinct and reason," he writes, are "signs of two
natures."[50] The relationship of soul to body, mind to matter, is a deep
mystery that we shall never resolve. Against dogmatisms of materialism and dualism, Pascal wants to maintain the mystery, to embrace
the paradoxical structure of human existence.

The godless universe that Pascal describes, or to be more precise,
the universe as seen by the godless, is quite close to what Paul Schrader
calls the "nightmarish [*noir*] world of American mannerism."[51] But, at
least according to some commentators, that world need not be utterly
amoral. If not, then what precisely is its moral vision? Telotte proposes
that the moral core of *noir* style is its emphasis on narration: "The effort

to speak, as well as the ethics prompting it, is central to the film *noir*; for it points to a persistent, driving, and finally human force that qualifies the form's otherwise fatalistic bent, and that can help us understand why such a dark form would have proved so popular."[52]

"The pattern of desire," Telotte suggests, is "for a kind of communication—or to be more accurate, for a way of formulating our place in the cultural landscape and articulating that formulation for others."[53] Consider, for example, the voiceover and flashback techniques, central to so many *noir* films. Even though the voiceover often expresses a frenetic, nearly maddening obsession with the details of the story and a compulsive penchant to rehearse the past, it also bespeaks an effort at understanding and communication. The voiceover exhibits a degree and type of awareness, or at least a desire for awareness, that is often absent in the first order story. As we noted previously, it is often the failure to get what was wanted or expected in the first-order story that provokes this crisis of understanding and engenders the quest in time and memory. The voiceover thus typically represents a partial transcendence of the mechanical necessity that seems to dominate the action.

As Pascal observes: "Man's greatness comes from knowing he is wretched." For Pascal, this does not make the picture rosy or optimistic, as he immediately adds, "it is wretched to know that one is wretched but there is greatness" in this knowledge.[54] Although the awareness of wretchedness constitutes a transcendence of the realm of brute necessity, it does not provide rest or exultation for human beings. Rest comes, Pascal thinks, only at the cost of sacrificing one side of the duality of our condition; thus do we lapse into presumption or despair. Pascal wants us to avoid both: "If he humbles himself, I exalt him. If he exalts himself, I humble him. I go on contradicting him until he realizes that he is a monster that passes all understanding." In *noir* fashion, Pascal plays off against one another two convictions about the human condition.[55] The human being is a monstrous paradox.

Abandoning the task of communication, many neo-*noir* films are simply decadent, conveying the aristocratic nihilism of the amoral superhero or wallowing in a surrealist dream world. As we have seen, the transcendence of the purportedly petty and arbitrary moral conventions involves at once a radicalization and trivialization of the distinctively modern project of autonomy. Pascal would object that this is but another example of diversion from the limits of the human condition; in this case diversion takes the form of self-deceiving fantasy. Man is neither to be praised nor condemned for what he currently is; nor is he to be encouraged in his addiction to diversion. Instead, he should be encouraged to "seek with groans."[56] What better way to describe the quest of the noir protagonist?

Notes

Preface

1 *The Road* (New York: Knopf, 2006).

2 *Voices in the Dark: Narrative Patterns in Film Noir* (Urbana, IL: University of Illinois Press, 1989), p. 221.

3 Pascal, *Pensées*, #449. All quotations from Pascal are from the A.J. Krailsheimer translation (New York: Penguin Classics, 1966). All references are to the numbered sections in that edition.

4 *Pensées*, #198.

5 R. Barton Palmer, "Moral Man in the Dark City," in *The Philosophy of Film Noir*, edited by Mark Conard with a forward by Robert Porfirio (Lexington: University of Kentucky Press, 2006), p. 191.

1 Arts of Darkness

1 Flannery O'Connor, "The Fiction Writer and His Country," in *Collected Works* (New York: Library of America Classics, 1988), p. 806.

2 In this context, another author who comes most dramatically to mind, especially with all the attention afforded him in 2004, the centenary of his birth, is the British novelist, Graham Greene, whose biography, *The Life of Graham Greene*, volumes 1-3, has recently been completed by Norman Sherry (New York: Viking, 1989-2004).

3 The phrase "American *noir*," as we shall see in detail as we proceed in this study, signifies a hybrid of the European and the American.

4 The influence of religious themes in Greene's fiction is palpable, while Hitchcock's interest in theological issues is little noticed, even by Hitchcock himself. Unlike most American critics of Hitchcock's films, French commentators have persistently made reference to underlying religious preoccupations in his films. See, for example, the exchanges between Hitchcock and Truffaut in Francois Truffaut, *Hitchcock* (New York: Simon and Schuster, 1983).

5   R. Barton Palmer, "Moral Man in the Dark City," in *The Philosophy of Film Noir*, edited by Mark Conard with a forward by Robert Porfirio (Lexington: University of Kentucky Press, 2006), p. 191. Palmer identifies a list of films that fit this sub-genre and claims that something in the range of 30 percent of all *noir* films are films of redemption (p. 204, note 9). Palmer may well overstate the percentages here and nothing in my study presupposes that redemptive strategies pervade *noir*, but it would be pleasant to think that this study might illumine a neglected strain of *noir* film as well. A number of classic *noir* films, released via Warner Home Video in a series of *Film Noir Classic Collections*, contain more or less explicit happy endings or at least show that it is possible, under certain circumstances, for defeat to count as victory. These films include *Narrow Margin*, *The Set-Up*, and *On Dangerous Ground*.

6   Pascal, *Pensées*, #198.

7   *Voices in the Dark: Narrative Patterns in Film Noir*, p. 221. Telotte's study is usefully informed by the psychoanalytic tradition of Lacan; indeed, Freudian interpretations of *noir* have abounded over the years, as have Marxist ones. There is certainly much to be said for both approaches. Part of the argument of this book is to suggest another and thus far neglected line of philosophical interpretation, derived from Pascal.

8   "Nietzsche and the Meaning and Definition of Noir," in *Philosophy and Film Noir*, p. 19. Conard's essay also provides a decent summary of the various attempts at definition of film *noir*.

9   Pascal insists both that God is hidden and the he is in some sense present. How can God be both hidden and present? Hiddenness is opposed, not to presence, since someone or something can hide in our very midst; it is, rather, opposed to manifestness. For Pascal, the signs of God's presence surround us, but they are hidden from us because we know not how to read the signs and because sin occludes our vision. Pascal thus criticizes the modern project of theodicy, just as it was getting started. As Susan Neiman shows in her book *Evil in Modern Thought: An Alternative History of Philosophy* (Princeton: Princeton University Press, 2004), the reduction of God to pure reason at once demands and makes impossible the resolution of the problem of evil. She comments, "Both grace and atheism leave the connection of virtue and happiness up to chance. Reason demands that the connection be systematic. . . . If the link between virtue and reward were accidental, the watch wouldn't work--to use another favorite Deist metaphor. What watchmaker would design a mechanism with the wheels and cogs turned randomly one way then sometimes another, without any warning whatsoever?" Even at the moment the modern, scientific project of theodicy was first getting under way, Pascal insisted on the "hiddenness of God": Whatever evidence there is of God's presence points not to the truth of Deism but to a redeeming God who enters history to take evil upon himself. Like Kierkegaard and Dostoyevsky after him, Pascal agreed in advance with Neiman's concluding note that "the picture of reason as inherently systematic is fatal to any form of philosophy we will want to preserve."

10   Lucien Goldmann, *The Hidden God: A Study of Tragic Vision in the Pensées of Pascal and the Tragedies of Racine* (London: Routledge and Kegan Paul Ltd, 1964). Although, as we shall see, Goldmann's interpretation of Pascal and tragedy is a fertile resource for uncovering the philosophical roots of *noir*, his exegesis of Pascal is not ultimately adequate to the whole of Pascal's thought. First, Goldmann reads Pascal, not on his own terms, but as one moment, an early and immature moment, in the development of modern philosophy. Pascal thus appears as an incomplete modern, who discovered the rudiments of dialectic thought but was unable to achieve the historical synthesis of Hegel or Marx. Second, Goldmann distorts and thus fails to appreciate the proper role of the heart in Pascal's conception of human nature (*The Hidden God*, pp. 195, 200). Goldmann's tragic Pascal is a Pascal stripped of his cogent religious response to the impasse at which the uncertain but searching human being arrives on the basis of a purely rational quest. That tragic impasse

might well capture the quintessential *noir* character. And this is why Goldmann's Pascal is so useful for the interpretation of *noir*. But this is only part of Pascal's integral vision of the human condition. For theologically informed interpretations of Pascal, see Jean-Luc Marion, *Descartes' Metaphysical Prism* (Chicago: University of Chicago Press, 1999) and Hans Urs von Balthasar, "Pascal" in Hans Urs von Balthasar, *The Glory of the Lord, A Theological Aesthetics Volume III: Studies in Theological Styles: Lay Styles*, trans. Andrew Louth, John Saward, Martin Simon, and Rowan Williams, ed. John Riches (San Francisco: Ignatius Press, 1986), p. 184. Also see my "Pascal and the Ethics of Thought," *International Philosophical Quarterly* Summer (2005), pp. 203-220.

11 Pascal, #72.

12 *The Hidden God*, p. 25.

13 *The Hidden God*, p. 36.

14 See Alasdair MacIntyre's essay on Goldmann's book in *Against the Self-Images of the Age* (Notre Dame: University of Notre Dame Press, 1971). Also of interest on Pascal is Sara Melzer, *Discourses of the Fall: A Study of Pascal's Pensees* (Berkeley: University of California Press, 1986); Leslie Armour, *"Infini Rien": Pascal's Wager and the Human Paradox* (Carbondale, Ill: Southern Illinois University Press, 1993); and Jean Mesnard, *Pascal* (Tuscaloosa: University of Alabama Press, 1969). The best general biography is Marvin O'Connell, *Blaise Pascal: Reasons of the Heart* (Grand Rapids, MI: Eerdmans Publishing Company, 1997).

15 *The Hidden God*, p. 44.

16 *The Hidden God*, p. 105.

17 See Ian Jarvie, "Knowledge, Morality and Tragedy in The Killers and Out of the Past," in *The Philosophy of Film Noir*.

18 See the chapter entitled, "A Puzzle of Character," in *Unless the Threat of Death Is Behind Them: Hard-Boiled Fiction and Film Noir* (Baltimore: The Johns Hopkins University Press, 2006), pp. 171-206.

19 Sara Melzer, *Discourses of the Fall: A Study of Pascal's Pensées* (Berkeley: University of California Press, 1986), pp. 100-101.

20 Stanley Rosen, "A Central Ambiguity in Descartes," in *The Ancients and the Moderns: Rethinking Modernity* (New Haven: Yale University Press, 1989), p. 32.

21 Pascal is also famous of course for his work in the theory and application of probability, some variant of which surfaces in his famous wager for the existence of God.

22 Pascal, #132.

23 Pascal, #138.

24 Pascal, #134.

25 Pascal, #73.

26 As quoted in *The Hidden God*, p. 71.

27 Pascal wonders whether this longing is explicable on its own terms or any natural terms.

28 Nicholas Christopher, *Somewhere in the Night: Film Noir and the American City* (New York: Henry Holt and Co., 1997), p. 16. On the modern city and *noir*, see the fine book by Edward Dimendberg, *Film Noir and the Spaces of Modernity* (Cambridge: Harvard University Press, 2004).

29 Pascal, #166.

30 Pascal, #655.

31 For a summary of such attempts at definition, see Mark Conard, "Nietzsche and the Meaning and Definition of Noir," in *The Philosophy of Film Noir*. Important statements can be found in James Naremore, *More Than Night: Film Noir in its Contexts* (Berkeley: University of California Press, 1998); Nicholas Christopher, *Somewhere in the Night: Film Noir and the American City*; Andrew Spicer, *Film Noir* (Essex: Pearson Education Limited, 2002); Foster Hirsch, *The Dark Side of the Screen: Film Noir* (London: De Capo Press, 1981); Foster Hirsch, *Detours and Lost Highways: A Map of Neo-Noir* (New York: Limelight Editions, 1999); R.

Barton Palmer, *Hollywood's Dark Cinema: The American Film Noir* (New York: Twayne, 1994); and Alain Silver, *The Noir Style* (Overlook, 1987). *Film Noir Reader*, edited by Alain Silver and James Ursini (New York: Limelight Editions, 1996) brings together a number of seminal essays on *noir*. For example, it contains a selection from Raymond Borde and Etienne Chaumeton's early *Towards a Definition of Film Noir*, as well as indispensable essays by Durgnat, Schrader, Profirio, and Damico. Also of interest is *Film Noir Reader 3: Interviews with Filmmakers of the Classic Noir Period*, edited by Robert Profirio, Alain Silver, and James Ursini (New York: Limelight Editions, 2002).

32 In his recent book *American Jesus: How the Son of God Became a National Icon*, Stephen Prothero describes our cultural Jesus as an other-directed personality type, eager to please, and readily amenable to the wishes of whatever group will have him. See Stephen Prothero, *American Jesus: How the Son of God Became a National Icon* (New York: Farrar Strauss & Giroux, 2004).

33 Dan Brown, *The Da Vinci Code* (New York: Doubleday, 2003).

34 *Harry Potter and the Sorcerer's Stone* (London: Bloomsbury, 1998); *Harry Potter and the Chamber of Secrets* (1999); *Harry Potter and the Prisoner of Azkaban* (1999); *Harry Potter and the Goblet of Fire* (2000); *Harry Potter and the Order of the Phoenix* (2003); *Harry Potter and the Half-Blood Prince* (2005).

35 One of the most instructive features of *Harry Potter,* as of a television series such as *Buffy the Vampire Slayer*, concerns the depiction of evil as non-being, as a lack or want of some good that ought to be present but is not. Evil is shown to be parasitic, secondary to, and dependent on, the good. In his fine book of cultural criticism, *The Death of Satan: How Americans Lost the Sense of Evil* (New York: Farrar, Strauss and Giroux: 1995), Andrew Delbanco makes much of our inability to overcome a dualistic, Manichean conception of good and evil, a conception that tempts us to identify our enemies as evil others with whom we must contend. By contrast, Delbanco proposes, for its ethical and political advantages, an Augustinian conception of evil as privation, as a pocket of nothingness in a good world.

36 Steven Sanders advances this thesis in his essay, "Film Noir and the Meaning of Life," In *The Philosophy of Film Noir*, pp. 91-105.

37 A complimentary argument is put forth by Read Mercer Schuchardt who traces the roots of *noir* to the 1927 film, *The Jazz Singer*, which depicts "not the fall of man, but the fall of God." Given the contingency of trends in filmmaking, Schuchardt suggests that just as the main character in *The Jazz Singer* paves a path away from the Jewish synagogue, so too *noir* may eventually find its way back. In an odd way, *Pulp Fiction* does precisely that, in Jules' adopting of the position of an Old Testament prophet or wayfaring penitent, obliged to wander the earth. See "*Cherchez la Femme Fatale*: The Mother of Film *Noir*," in *The Philosophy of Film Noir*, pp. 49-68.

38 See Mark Edmundson, *Nightmare on Main Street: Angels, Sadomasochism, and the Culture of Gothic* (Cambridge: Harvard University Press, reprint edition 1999).

39 As Steven Sanders notes, the strong sense of fatalism in *noir* seems to undermine not only the possibility of optimism and progress but also existentialist transcendence through the embrace of self-creative freedom. This is but one of a number of problems facing Porfirio's famous claim that *noir* is existentialist. See "Film Noir and the Meaning of Life," pp. 97-98.

40 Some might argue that the embrace of aristocratic nihilism is merely a matter of the elimination of external restraints (in the form of the demise of the production code) on Hollywood filmmaking. Certainly the elimination of the code was a precondition for the making of many neo-*noir* films. But what I have called the democratic world of classic *noir* is evident not just in the officially restrained world of film but also in much of the *noir* literature of the period. Moreover, while the influence of the production code on classic *noir* films may be said to have curbed the possibility of depicting criminals as getting away with crime, it can hardly be blamed for the *noir* tendency to depict even good or marginally good

characters as deprived of happy endings. This study, at any rate, is not much interested in trying to determine the elusive social causes of *noir*, but in an analysis of the narratives on their own terms.

41 Gnosticism is a complex historical phenomenon, much in the news of late because of attention given to the Gnostic gospels and because of Dan Brown's devotion to its version of Christian history. For a balanced assessment of Gnosticism, see Pheme Perkins, *Gnosticism and the New Testament* (Minneapolis: Augsburg Fortress Publishers, 1993). Also see Hans Jonas, *The Gnostic Religion* (Boston: Beacon Press, reprint edition 2001). Eric Voegelin famously made Gnosticism central to his analysis and critique of modernity. See *Modernity Without Restraint* in *The Collected Works of Eric Voegelin, volume 5*, edited with an introduction by Manfred Henningsen (Columbia: University of Missouri Press, 2000), especially pp, 254-256 and 297-298. Harold Bloom has made Gnosticism the basis for his interpretation of contemporary religion in *American Religion: The Emergence of the Post-Christian Nation* (New York: Simon and Schuster, 1993). His tendentious thesis is that American religion, no matter its apparent denominational creed, embodies at its core a Gnostic creed, which stresses that knowledge of an inner self, free from nature, time, community, and history, is the source of salvation. But classical Gnosticism and the sort we detect in contemporary films need not be tinged with the sort of isolated selfishness Bloom finds in contemporary religion. Indeed, in its origins, Gnosticism was connected to ample metaphysical claims about the structure of reality and the place of the individual within it. For our purposes, contemporary Gnosticism involves an experience of world as an alien land from which the key task is to escape and to return to a proper home, separated from the body and the vagaries of time. The instrument or means of salvation, understood as release from time and the body, is knowledge (*gnosis*), achievable by only a few noble souls. Of course, *noir* itself involves a confrontation with illusion; it also often involves a desire to escape. Yet, where other-worldly solutions are entertained, it is not by an escape from this world but by the intervention of the other world into this one.

42 There is a return here to something of the purity of Sade's own Enlightenment aspirations; for, as we shall see in later chapters, Sade can be read not so much as an anti-Enlightenment figure, but rather as an odd fulfillment of the Enlightenment goals of control over nature and the transparency of human desire and its fulfillment through rational mechanisms. See Roger Shattuck, *Forbidden Knowledge: From Prometheus to Pornography* (New York: St. Martin's Press, 1997).

43 See Jon Young, "Happiness, Hope, and Faith in *Thirteen Conversations About One Thing,*" in *Thinking About Religion* 3 (2004).

44 Of course, *The Passion* abandons all sorts of features of classic *noir*, but as a dark, penitential narrative of religious quest, it is without competition. Moreover, the accent of the entire film is on suffering, death, abandonment and mockery and on the faithfulness, forbearance, and charity with which one endures these. The resurrection is shown very briefly at the end but it comes almost as an afterthought, as indeed it seems to have been in Gibson's own mind. This does not mean that the film is skeptical about that indispensable doctrine in the faith of the church, but it does mean that the accent is on the penitential path to redemption, not its full realization.

45 Both Shyamalan and Gibson, who worked together on *Signs*, can be quite overt in the resolution of their dramas and in their affirmation of a providential orchestration of events, even if Shyamalan is clearer about the fact of providence than he is about who is in control of things. Although Shyamalan's quests are deeply penitential, they sometimes border on facile transcendence in their conclusions. By contrast, Gibson's *Passion* is an extended penitential path, traversed first not by us but by a humiliated God; yet, here as elsewhere in Gibson's corpus he may have profited from Shaymalan's sense of restraint and indirection in the depiction of violence.

46 Pascal, #449.

47 A less overt attempt at recovery of Christian symbolism can be found in the novel, *The Children of Men* (New York: Alfred A. Knopf, 1993), from the British author P.D. James, a book made into a recent film by Alfonos Cuaron. See chapter 10 of this book.

2 The Dangerous Edge of Things

1   Naremore, *More Than Night*, p. 80.

2   A wonderful collection of Greene's reviews, with interviews on the topic of film and selections from film scripts, is available in a volume entitled *The Graham Greene Film Reader: Reviews, Essays, Interviews & Film Stories*, edited by David Parkinson (New York: Applause Books, 1995).

3   *The Graham Greene Film Reader*, p. 414.

4   *The Graham Greene Film Reader*, p. xxxii.

5   *More Than Night*, p. 65.

6   *The Graham Greene Film Reader*, p. 409.

7   *The Graham Greene Film Reader*, pp. 132-134.

8   *The Graham Greene Film Reader*, p. 408. A concern with all too easy or all too cozy moral relationship between films, critics, and audiences pervades Greene's comments about the art and purpose of film criticism. He insists that it is not the critic's business to assist film's social function; instead, the critic should engage in a kind of satire; he should attack the reader and force him to laugh at what he had previously taken for granted.

9   *The Graham Greene Film Reader*, p. 415.

10 See, for example, Paul Buhle and Dave Wagner, *Radical Hollywood: The Untold Story Behind America's Favorite Movies* (New York: The Free Press, 2002).

11 "Les Americains aussi font des films *noirs*," *Revue du cinéma* 2 (1946), p. 67.

12 See, for example, Hirsch, "The Crazy Mirror: Noir Stylistics," in *The Dark Side of the Screen*, pp. 71-111.

13 Dostoevsky, *Demons*. This is of course but one strain, the most radical strain, of Enlightenment thought, but it is one that has proven surprisingly influential.

14 *More than Night*, p. 35.

15 Nancy Gish, *The Waste Land: A Student's Companion to the Poem* (Boston: Twayne Publishers, 1988), p. 37.

16 *Voices in the Dark*, p. 218.

17 *The Heart of the Matter* (New York: Penguin Books, 1948), p. 197.

18 See George Orwell's review of Graham Greene's *The Heart of the Matter*: "The Sanctified Sinner," *The New Yorker*, July 17, 1948, pp. 61-63.

19 *The Power and the Glory*, p. 65.

20 Georg von Lukacs, *Die Selle und die Formen*, pp. 332-333, quoted in *The Tragic Vision*, pp. 35-36.

21 An early, low-budget film *noir*, called *Detour* (1945) contains a majority of the standard motifs, plot devices, and stylistic features of American *noir*. Although not very successful or influential in its time, it has become a useful object in the academic study of *noir*, what Paul Cantor identifies as a "textbook illustration" of the genre. Exploring the links between the intellectual views of the film's German director, Edgar G. Ulmer and those of the Frankfurt School, Cantor argues that the America depicted in film *noir* tells us more about European, anti-American prejudices than about America. Despite a passing admission that much of American film *noir* has roots in American fiction, Cantor concludes, "film *noir* is as American as apple streudel." Cantor nicely points out the points of convergence between Ulmer's film and the Frankfurt School's vision of the Hollywood dream factory or culture industry, that creates artificial needs in citizens, arouses needless desires and

then fails to fulfill the longings it provokes. According to this vision, America is socially a land of lonely drifters, and physically, a vast wasteland. But there are a number of problems with taking *Detour* as normative for film *noir*. It is a mediocre film, cheaply made, illustrating none of the dramatic complexities of the best of film *noir*. So unsophisticated is *Detour*'s reflection on fate that it calls to mind the comic one-liner often repeated in the show *Laugh-In*, about the "fickle finger of fate." Cantor's cultural either/or, American or European, conveniently ignores the fact that nearly all American art exhibits strong European influence. Another problem is that Cantor moves far too quickly from noting the important and indisputable European influences on *noir* to the conclusion that the American roots are negligible. Even if the balance ends up being more European than American, this does not justify treating the American roots, for example in the pulp fiction novels of the 1930s, of *noir* as entirely negligible. Indeed, the use of *Detour* as archetypal is a sort of straw man that skirts the dramatic subtlety of *noir* and renders utterly baffling the initial and enduring popularity of *noir* among American audiences. See Paul Cantor, "Film Noir and the Frankfurt School," in *Film Noir and Philosophy*, pp. 139-161.

22 Chandler, *The Simple Art of Murder*, as quoted in Hirsch, *The Dark Side of the Screen*, p. 33.

23 *Unless the Threat of Death is Behind Them*, p. 67. But even this ends up "hollow and empty," as Chandler's later novels on an older, more cynical, and more weary Philip Marlowe indicate. See Irwin, pp. 59-68.

24 *Leviathan*, Part I, chapter XI.

25 *Leviathan*, Part I, chapter XIV.

26 *Leviathan*, Part I, chapter XIV.

27 On the incompatibility of love and detective work, see Irwin's *Unless the Threat of Death if Behind Them*, pp. 238-239.

28 See John Cawelti, *Adventure, Mystery and Romance: Formula Stories as Art and Propaganda* (Chicago: University of Chicago Press, 1977), p. 143. Cawelti's thesis informs Deborah Knight's interpretation "On Reason and Passion in *The Maltese Falcon*," in *Film Noir and Philosophy*, pp. 207-221.

29 See *Radical Hollywood*, p. 328.

30 Pascal, #73.

31 *Film Noir Reader*, p. 87. For a critique of the existentialist reading of *noir*, see Irwin, *Unless the Threat of Death is Behind Them*, pp. 2-16.

32 *The Myth of Sisyphus and Other Essays* (New York: Vintage Books, 1991), p. 91.

33 *More Than Night*, p. 285.

34 Camus, "An Absurd Reasoning," in *The Myth of Sisyphus*, p. 30.

35 No single film stands as a paradigm for all of *noir*, but for a certain very influential strain in *noir*, *Double Indemnity* comes as close as possible. See, for example, James Damico's "Modest Proposal," *Film Noir Reader*, p. 103, in which the author attempts to add clarity to all the vague talk about whether *noir* is a genre by offering an initial definition, which reads as if it had been lifted directly from the plot of *Double Indemnity*.

36 *Film Noir*, p. 76.

37 In this respect, *Double Indemnity* has much grander narrative ambitions than those associated with the barely conscious narrator in *Detour*.

38 *Unless the Threat of Death is Behind Them*, p. 74.

39 *Leviathan*, Part I, chapter V.

40 *Somewhere in the Night*, p. 88.

41 *Radical Hollywood*, p. 328.

42 *Voices in the Dark*, p. 52.

43 "Les Americains aussi font des films *noirs*," p. 67.

44 Pascal, #79.

45 Pascal, # 78.

46 Pascal, #55.
47 *Film Noir Reader* 3, interview with Lizabeth Scott, p. 198.
48 "Paint it Black," *Film Noir Reader*, p. 38.
49 Donald Spoto, *The Art of Alfred Hitchcock* (New York: Anchor Books, 1992), p. 281.
50 *Detours and Lost Highways*, p. 15.
51 *Discourses of the Fall*, pp. 93-94.
52 *The Graham Green Film Reader*, pp. 52 and 163.
53 Foreward to Quentin Falk's *Travels in Greeneland* (London: Reynolds and Hearn, 2000).
54 Francois Truffaut, *Hitchcock*, p. 317.
55 Spoto, p. 257.
56 Truffaut, p. 203.
57 On the "wrong man" theme in classic *noir*, see Hirsch, *The Dark Side of the Screen*, pp. 176-180.
58 Truffaut, p. 204.
59 Truffaut, p. 206.
60 Spoto, p. 206
61 The story may well be a divine comedy, but if it is, as the literary critic Northrup Frye noted in his study of T. S. Eliot, then it is a very peculiar sort of comedy, one that contains a tragedy as its penultimate act. See Northrup Frye, *T.S. Eliot: An Introduction* (Chicago: University of Chicago Press, 1981).

3 Beyond Good and Evil

1 Cynthia Freeland, "Penetrating Keanu," in *The Matrix and Philosophy* (Chicago: Open Court), p. 214.
2 Nietzsche, *Will to Power*, translated by Walter Kaufmann (New York: Vintage, 1968) "European Nihilism," #2. I have examined Nietzsche and his indirect influence on contemporary popular culture in *Shows About Nothing* (Dallas: Spence Publishing, 1999).
3 *Thus Spoke Zarathustra* in *The Portable Nietzsche*, translated by Walter Kaufmann (New York: Penguin, 1968), p. 129.
4 *Will to Power*, #22.
5 *Will to Power*, #22.
6 *Beyond Good and Evil*, translated by Walter Kaufmann (New York: Vintage, 1966), p. #257.
7 For the best defense of Nietzsche on these matters, see the chapter on Nietzsche in Richard Bernstein's *Radical Evil: A Philosophical Interrogation* (Cambridge, UK: Polity Press, 2002). Bernstein focuses on Nietzsche's concept of unreleased *ressentiment* as a chief source of evil in modernity, underlying phenomenon such as anti-Semitism. Still, it is not clear that Bernstein comes to terms with the consequences of Nietzsche's embrace of nihilism. According to the perceptive analysis of Peter Berkowitz in *Nietzsche: The Ethics of an Immoralist* (Cambridge: Harvard University Press, 1996), the fundamental tension in Nietzsche is this: Although he wished to base right making on right knowing, to ground a proper evaluation of levels of creative power on a rank order of character, his complete repudiation of any sort of natural, civil, or religious standard puts his entire project into question. As Berkowitz puts it, Nietzsche "pursues the antagonism between knowing and making to its breaking point."
8 The primacy of the will stultifies the understanding and ends up paralyzing the will itself, since there is nothing in light of which the will might deliberate and act. Nietzsche's project of incessant self-overcoming would seem to lead to precisely the sort of nihilism that he detests. As Stanley Rosen puts it, "Chaos empties rank-ordering of its significance." *The Question of Being*, p. 249. For Rosen's view of the "central problems" in Nietzsche, see also pp. 132, 151, 158-159, 220.

9 *Birth of Tragedy* (New York, 1967, Kaufmann translation), p. 46.

10 *Birth of Tragedy*, p. 46.

11 *Birth of Tragedy*, p. 97.

12 *Birth of Tragedy*, pp. 96 and 98.

13 *Birth of Tragedy*, p. 111.

14 *Birth of Tragedy*, p. 112.

15 *Birth of Tragedy*, p. 19.

16 For more on these internal contradictions in Nietzsche, see Peter Berkowitz, *Nietzsche: The Ethics of an Immoralist.*

17 For Dostoevsky, art has at least two functions in the face of the threat of nihilism: one is to construct dramatic arguments that display in the lives of characters the consequences of modern social theories (*Notes from Underground* and *Crime and Punishment*), while the other is to cultivate an alternative memory of a way of life increasingly marginalized in modernity (*The Brothers Karamazov*). Dostoevsky's more developed view of these matters includes an account of the human propensity to reduce all things, including the self, to nothingness. The propensity is rooted in a rebellion against submission to any authority other than one's own will, a rebellion whose ultimate source is the proud refusal of transforming, sacrificial love.

4 Neo-Noir

1 The result fuses two forms of decadence, that of Nietzsche's superman and that of the Gnostic hero. Recall the line from Voegelin about Gnosticism taking the form of a "will of nature that transforms itself into the superman" (*Modernity Without Restraint*, p. 255).

2 *Detours and Lost Highways*, p. 10.

3 "Les Americains aussi font des films *noirs*," p. 67.

4 In a certain strain of late twentieth-century films, there is a trajectory toward comic nihilism, the result of the dominance of surface aesthetics, which jaded audiences come increasingly to anticipate and to find entertaining for its own sake. I have traced this trajectory in the horror genre in *Shows About Nothing*. None of this entails an irreversible direction in the style or ethical content of films. Indeed, in the horror genre, the films of M. Night Shamyalan, and in neo-*noir*, the films of Christopher Nolan, would run counter to these tendencies.

5 Jim Thompson, *The Getaway* (New York: Vintage Crime, 1958), p. 180.

6 Spicer, *Film Noir*, p. 139.

7 Pascal, #166.

8 *Oedipus Rex*.

9 *Birth of Tragedy*, p. 60.

10 *The Hidden God*, p. 44.

11 "Chinatown and Generic Transformation in Recent American Films," in *Film Genre Reader*, ed. by Barry Grant (Austin, University of Texas Press, 1986), p. 184.

12 *More Than Night*, p. 209.

13 *More Than Night*, p. 35.

14 Pascal, #121.

15 *Will to Power*, #32.

16 *Beyond Good and Evil*, #259.

17 Machiavelli, *The Prince*, translated by Leo Paul de Alvarez (Irving, TX: University of Dallas Press, 1980), p. 101.

18 *The Last Gentleman* (New York: Farrar, Straus, and Giroux, 1966), p. 280, as quoted in Andrew Delbanco's *The Death of Satan*, p. 202.

19 Kierkegaard, *The Concept of Irony*, translated by Howard Hong and Edna Hong (Princeton

University Press, 1992), pp. 248 and 253 as quoted in Andrew Delbanco's *The Death of Satan*, p. 202.

20 *More Than Night*, p. 35.

5 *Sci-Fi Noir*

1 As we have already observed, the Enlightenment is a complex phenomenon. As will become clear in the body of this essay, I will be concentrating on a certain strain of Enlightenment thought, one of which Dostoevsky ably dissects.

2 "Android and Machine," *Science Fiction at Large*, ed. Peter Nicholls (New York: Harper & Row, 1976), p. 202.

3 *The Rebel* (New York: Vintage, 1991).

4 *The Science Fiction Film*, (Cambridge University Press, 2001), p. 210.

5 "The Imagination of Disaster," in *Against Interpretation and Other Essays* (New York: Dell, 1966), p. 223.

6 *The Myth of the American Superhero*, p. 47.

7 Larry Wachowski interview, quoted in *The Gospel Reloaded: Exploring Spirituality and Faith in The Matrix* by Chris Seay and Greg Garrett (Colorado Springs: Pinon Press, 2003), p. 11.

8 Derrida's *Double Session* in *Dissemination* (Chicago: University of Chicago Press, 1981), p. 288.

9 Pascal, #201.

10 Cynthia Freeland, "Penetrating Keanu," p. 214.

11 *Film Noir Reader I*, p. 87.

12 Dostoevsky, *Notes from the Underground*, translated by Pevear and Volokhonsky (Vintage, 1993).

13 For a discussion of the historical and polemical context of the book, see the excellent discussion in Joseph Frank's *Dostoevsky: The Stir of Liberation*, 1860-1865 (PrincetonL Princeton University Press, 1986), pp. 310-347.

14 *Notes*, p. 13. All references to *Notes from the Underground* are from the superb recent translation by Pevear and Volokhonsky.

15 *Notes*, p. 24.

16 *Notes*, p. 24.

17 *Notes*, p. 37.

18 *Notes*, pp. 129-130.

19 Adrienne MacLean, "Media Effects: Marshall McLuhan, Television Culture, and 'The X-Files'," *Film Quarterly* 51 (Summer 1998), pp. 2-9.

20 *Nightmare on Main Street: Angels, Sadomasochism, and the Culture of the Gothic*, (Harvard University Press, 1997).

21 From *Conversation Between D'Alembert and Diderot*, quoted in *Notes from Underground*, p. 133.

22 "Penetrating Keanu," p 215.

23 Seay and Garrett, *The Gospel Reloaded: Exploring Spirituality and Faith in The Matrix*, p. 42.

24 *The Gospel Reloaded*, p. 44.

25 The most popular Gnostic tale of spiritual quest is undoubtedly Dan Brown's best-selling *The Da Vinci Code*, recently made into a film. What starts as an attempt to distinguish the fragile, bodily life of mortal human beings ends up implicitly denigrating the limits of bodily existence. The murder of the curator in the Louvre sets the plot in motion. The quest to solve the murder brings together Sophie Neveu, a young detective and granddaughter of the curator, with Robert Langdon, identified as a Harvard "symbologist." Their quest

unveils battles between secret societies, in one of which, the Priory of Sion, the curator was the leading member. For a book that propounds a subversion of patriarchy by the eternal feminine, *The Da Vinci Code* embodies a blandly traditional gender relationship between the elder, experienced male (Langdon) and the youthful, naïve female (Sophie). One of Langdon's great paternal moment of pedagogy comes as he listens calmly to Sophie's distraught confession that she had a "rift" with her grandfather after she inadvertently discovered his participation in a strange sexual ritual. Langdon patiently asks Sophie whether the ceremony took place around the time of the equinox, with androgynous masks. When she responds affirmatively, he explains that she witnessed an ancient ceremony called "Hieros Gamo" or sacred marriage, which celebrates the "reproductive power of the female." What appears to be a "sex ritual" has in fact nothing to do with eroticism. "It was a spiritual act," a means of achieving "*gnosis*—knowledge of the divine."

The term gnosis calls to mind, as Brown's book does explicitly in many other ways, the ancient religious cult of Gnosticism, which sought a complete transcendence of the body and an ascension to a realm of pure spirit. The most advanced members of the sect were thought to have already transcended the realm of the body. That's the supposition behind Langdon's assertion that the sexual ritual was void of eroticism.

But this is where Brown's use of Gnosticism itself becomes incoherent. The great emphasis in the book's final chapters is not upon transcending the body to achieve pure spirit, but upon the "power of the blood coursing through the veins of Sophie Neveu," whose parents are both from "Merovingian families—direct descendants of Mary Magdalene and Jesus Christ." The Priory of Sion guards the secret in order to protect the "surviving royal bloodline." It is interesting to note that the Priory of Sion is not ancient, as Brown's book says it is, but is rather a mid-twentieth-century invention intended to advance unseemly political interests in France.

There is double trouble here for Brown's heroes. First, how do we get from the Gnostic repudiation of the body in favor of the spirit to the assertion that what is most significant is pure biology, a bloodline? Second, why should anyone today care about the protection of a royal bloodline? On the one hand, Brown wants to demote Christ, who is no longer to be conceived as divine, but merely as an influential human; on the other hand, Brown wants to elevate Christ's human bloodline, his royal genealogy. But unless we harbor nostalgia for hereditary monarchy, why should we be moved by this or deem it worthy of protection? Is there not something deeply troubling about Brown's enthusiastic embrace of the purity of blood? The conclusion of the book confirms Pascal's ominous aphorism, "He who tries to make himself an angel ends up as a beast."

6 *Feminist Neo-Noir*

1   *BtVS* contains an implicit response to the theses of Andrew Delbanco, according to whom we now lack a "coherent symbology" to feed our "unslaked craving for transcendence." Given our culture's preoccupation with demonic evil, Delbanco worries about the "gulf" that has "opened up in our culture between the visibility of evil and the intellectual resources available for coping with it." His dire thesis is that "if evil...escapes the reach of our imagination, it will have established dominion over us all." See *The Death of Satan*, p. 9-10. The loss of animating narratives of hope, inspiring stories of noble human quests, is particularly dangerous for children. Delbanco writes, "nothing is more alarming than the impoverishment of our children's capacity to imagine the future." Suffering the multiple deprivations of national, religious, and familial culture, children can come to exist in a moral vacuum, filled more often than not by pop culture. And, as the film critic Michael Medved observes, pop culture in contemporary America is Hollywood culture, especially TV culture. See *Hollywood vs. America* (New York: HarperCollins, 1992).

2 *Forbidden Knowledge*, p. 239.
3 *Nature and Culture: Ethical Thought in the French Enlightenment.* (Baltimore: Johns Hopkins University Press, 1963).
4 Andrew Spicer, *Film Noir* (Longman, 2002).
5 *Film Noir,* Spicer is quoting Jim Collins, p. 150.
6 *Detours and Lost Highways*, p. 244.
7 *Civilization and its Discontents*, p. 81.
8 Nietzsche, *On the Genealogy of Morality* (Indianapolis: Hackett Publishing, 1998), p. 36.
9 Marquis de Sade, *Philosophy in the Boudoir.* translated by Richard Seaver and Austryn Wainhorse (New York: Grove Press, 1965), pp. 283-284.
10 *Philosophy in the Boudoir*, p. 211.
11 Foucault, *Madness and Civilization: A History of Insanity in the Age of Reason* (New York: Random House, 1965), p. 210.
12 *Dialectic of Enlightenment*, p. 74. On Sade, see Roger Shattuck's *Forbidden Knowledge: From Prometheus to Pornography.*
13 *Parade Magazine* (30 January 1994).
14 John Paul II, *Veritatis Splendor* (Boston: St. Paul Books, 1993), p. 65.
15 *Sex, Economy, Freedom, and Community* (New York: Pantheon, 1998), pp. 153-136.
16 *Sex, Economy, Freedom, and Community*, p. 122.
17 *Sexual Personae* (New York: Random House, 1991), p. 3.
18 *Sexual Personae*, p. 29.
19 *Pensées*, #408.
20 Sade, *Philosophy in the Boudoir*, p. 254.
21 *The Real American Dream: A Meditation on Hope* (Cambridge: Harvard University Press, 1995), p. 103.
22 J. P. Telotte, *Voices in the Dark*, pp. 17, 86.
23 For a discussion of *noir's* treatment of these themes, see my *Shows About Nothing: Nihilism in Popular Culture from The Exorcist to Seinfeld*, pp. 10-53.
24 Nicholas Christopher, *Somewhere in the Night: Film Noir and the American City*, p. 20.
25 *Voices in the Dark*, pp. 220, 222.
26 *Detours and Lost Highways*, p. 183.
27 In severing any link between freedom and nature and in asserting an absolute autonomy, the most popular contemporary conception of freedom ends up treating the human body as a raw datum, devoid of meaning (*Veritatis Splendor*, p. 65). By contrast, *BtVS* occasionally glimpses another possibility, that in the human body, we might "discover the anticipatory signs of the expression and promise of the gift of self" in love (p. 66).

7 Questions about One Thing

1 Roy Anker, *Catching Light: Looking for God in the Movies* (Grand Rapids, MI: Eerdmans, 2004), p. 347.
2 *Sex, Economy, Freedom, and Community*, p. 143.
3 Pascal, #183.
4 Pascal, #171.
5 Tocqueville, *Democracy in America*, Volume 2, the Henry Reeve text (New York: Random House, 1945), p. 104
6 Wendell Berry, *Sex, Economy, Freedom, and Community*, p. 125.
7 This is the structure of Shakespearean comedy and even of what Stanley Cavell calls the comedies of remarriage from 1940s Hollywood film; see *Pursuits of Happiness: The Hollywood Comedies of Remarriage* (Cambridge: Harvard University Press, 1981).
8 As quoted in *The Hidden God*, p. 71.

9 Interview with *Time Out New York*, quoted in Charles Taylor's review of *Magnolia* for *Salon. com* (12/17/1999).
10 See Charles Taylor's review of *Magnolia* for *Salon.com* (12/17/1999).
11 Pascal, # 148.
12 Pascal, # 68.

8 *Wide Awake*

1 Pascal, #427.
2 Walker Percy, *Lancelot* (New York: Farrar, Straus & Giroux, 1977), pp. 53-54.
3 I have discussed both these films in detail in *Shows About Nothing*.
4 Pascal, #149.
5 Andrew O'Hehir, "A Higher Power," *Salon*, August 2, 2002.

9 *Paint It Red*

1 "Tarantino Point Blank," Richard Roeper, *Chicago Sun-Times*, October 5, 2003.
2 Undated, anonymous review can be found on *Esplatter.com*.
3 Dennis Prager, "*The Passion*: Jews and Christians Watching Different Films," *TOWNHALL*, October 28, 2003
4 *NewsMaxWires* Interview (March 10, 2003).
5 Mel Gibson, *The Passion: Photography from the Movie "The Passion of the Christ"* (Tyndale House Publishers, 2003).
6 Rene Girard, "On Mel Gibson's *The Passion of the Christ*," in *Anthropoetics* 10, no. 1 (Spring/ Summer 2004). See also Girard's *Violence and the Sacred* (Baltimore: Johns Hopkins University Press, 1977).
7 In his influential book, *The Transcendental Style in Film* (Berekeley: University of California Press, 1972), Paul Schrader objects to Hollywood depictions of holiness for using a style of "identification rather than of confrontation." The "viewer is not lifted to Christ's level"; instead, Christ brought "down to the viewer's" level (p. 164). Of course, one of Schrader's targets is a "realism" that focuses on imannence rather than transcendence. As Girard intimates, *The Passion* embodies a kind of realism that forces viewers to confront something wholly other, something so offensive to conventional assumptions that it shatters the comfortable relationship between audience and film.
8 On this and other features of the life of the early Church, see Robert Wilken, *The Spirit of Early Christian Thought: Seeking the Face of God* (New Haven: Yale University Press, 2005).
9 *The Spiritual Exercises of St. Ignatius*, translated by Anthony Mottola (New York: Image Books, 1964), p. 93.
10 In the science fiction horror film, *Mimic*, from Guillermo del Toro, the rosary, which invokes Mary's care over a sinful, alienated humanity, plays a suggestive role.
11 Pascal, #316.
12 "Who Killed Jesus?" *Newsweek* (February 16, 2004).
13 Schrader cites this scene in his discussion of the role of "stasis" in religious film. See *The Transcendental Style in Film*, p. 52.
14 O'Connor, *Collected Works*, p. 806.
15 In an interview concerning the role of redemptive suffering in his superb horror-fairy tale, *Pan's Labyrinth*, Guillermo del Toro acknowledges Blatty's influence on his own work: "One of the most important movies in my life, emotionally is William Peter Blatty's *Twinkle, Twinkle "Killer" Kane* [aka *The Ninth Configuration*]. It's a movie about redemption through sacrifice and the giving of your blood to save others that speaks to the soul of somebody

who believes in a messiah. It deals with the fragility of faith, which is essential to Blatty's work—how faith is almost intangible and yet incredibly strong.... I think that's the same thing that occupies Blatty: faith, the state of grace, immortality, redemption. And these are things that are important for me too. See "Girl Interrupted," del Toro interview with *Sight and Sound* (December, 2006). On the possible points of intersection between horror and Christianity, see the interview with the director of *The Exorcism of Emily Rose*, Scott Derrickson, "Horror: The Perfect Christian Genre," in *Christianity Today* (August 30, 2005).

16 The engagement of scientific and religious conceptions of human nature and destiny is a regular theme in Blatty's work, nowhere more intellectually captivating than in his book and film, *The Ninth Configuration*.

17 This is the thesis of Lucien Goldmann's *The Hidden God: A Study of Tragic Vision in the Pensées of Pascal and the Tragedies of Racine*, the limitations of which as an exegesis of Pascal we hinted at above and now make explicit.

18 Pascal, #149.

19 Pascal, #189-91.

20 Pascal, #192.

21 Pascal, #265, #267.

22 Pascal, #47.

23 Pascal, #449.

24 "Pascal," p. 190.

25 "Pascal," p. 210.

26 "Pascal," p. 206.

27 Marion, *Descartes' Metaphysical Prism*, p. 314.

28 Pascal, #449.

10   The Children of Men

1   *Film as Religion: Myths, Morals, and Rituals* (New York: New York University Press, 2003).

2   *Film as Religion*, p. 123-126.

3   The problem with the identification of film as religion, which is distinct from our thesis that some films embody a religious or quasi-religious quest, is the sheer banality of it all. Lyden himself is reduced to deriving vacuous lessons from the likes of Hannibal Lecter in *Silence of the Lambs*, a character both "horrible and sympathetic...a brutal killer with almost superhuman powers, yet he helps Clarice and seems to like her." *Film as Religion*, pp. 244-245.

4   *We Hold These Truths* (Lanham, MD: Rowman & Littlefield Publishers, Inc., 2005), originally printed, 1960.

5   Another problem with Lyden's thesis about film and religion concerns the formation of viewers. How can films impart the sort of character formation that religions have traditionally provided? Lyden poses the problem as one of enforcing a moral vision. Conceding that film cannot do this, he counters that neither can religion, at least not any longer. The argument at this point looks less like an elevation of film than a demotion of religion. Lyden overlooks here one of the key elements of religion, even in a functional account: ritual practice. The goal of ritual is not principally to enforce a moral code but to form character so that believers come to see and respond to the world in distinctive ways. Traditional religions take such transformation very seriously and see it as a task that involves regular discipline, a habituation of one's passions and actions. Contemporary films offer no such pedagogy; taken as religious, popular films leave us with a very misleading perspective on character transformation, as if the depiction of a virtue or a vice on a particular occasion could be sufficient to change us in some deep way. On this, see Stanley Hauerwas, *Vision*

and Virtue (Notre Dame: University of Notre Dame Press, 1981).

6   Of course, taking pluralism in film and religion seriously would involve expanding the study of the religious quest beyond the parameters of the current book. Pascal gives hints, in his unfinished apology for the Christian faith, that an adequate account of religious interpretations of the human condition would have to include careful attention at least to the major world religions.

7   Brooks, *On Paradise Drive* (New York: Simon and Schuster, 2004), p. 161.

8   *The Whole Equation: A History of Hollywood* (New York: Knopf, 2004), p. 74.

9   *The Whole Equation*, pp. 49 and 98.

10   *The Whole Equation*, p. 74.

11   *The Moviegoer* (New York: Alfred A. Knopf, 1961), p. 18.

12   *The Whole Equation*, p. 296.

13   On the influence of Pascal on Tocqueville, see Peter Augustine Lawler, *The Restless Mind* (Lanham, MD: Rowman and Littlefield, 1993). Also see the discussion of restlessness and the inability to live in the present as marks of the man of success in the hard-boiled tradition in Irwin's *Unless the Threat of Death is Behind Them*, pp. 102-110. As Irwin points out, the virtues and aspirations of the young man become, in old age, the vices and despair of the failed criminal or detective. Hence, Tocqueville's point is made, as is that of Pascal.

14   Pascal, #47.

15   *The Children of Men*, p. 7.

16   *The Children of Men*, p. 11.

17   *The Children of Men*, p. 15.

18   *The Children of Men*, p. 167.

19   *The Children of Men*, p. 79.

20   By contrast, Cuaron selects the easy, comfortable symbol of a child — the mere fact of birth and innocence. Indeed, in a film from which all Christian referents have been systematically erased, the title itself, *The Children of Men* — a direct quotation from *Psalm* 90, a prayer in the burial service for the dead — is stripped of all symbolic resonance.

21   *The Children of Men*, p. 73.

22   "Rapidly Rises the Morning Tide: An Essay on P.D. James's *The Children of Men*," *Theology Today* 51 (1994), pp. 277-288.

23   *The Children of Men*, p. 282.

24   *Discourses of the Fall*, p. 76.

25   *Discourses of the Fall*, p. 142.

26   In *Beyond Good and Evil*, Nietzsche describes the faith of Pascal as a "continual suicide of reason—a tough, long-lived, wormlike reason that cannot be killed all at once and with a single stroke," translated by Walter Kaufmann (New York: Random House, 1966), #46. J. L. Mackie, *The Miracle of Theism: Arguments for and against the Existence of God* (Oxford: Clarendon Press, 1982), pp. 200-204.

27   Pascal, #83.

28   Pascal, #93.

29   *Pascal's Wager: A Study of Practical Reasoning in Philosophical Theology* (Notre Dame: University of Notre Dame Press, 1985).

30   *Leviathan*, I, 11.

31   Pascal, #641.

32   *Leviathan*, I, 13.

33   At one point, he writes, "I will write down my thoughts here as they come and in a perhaps not aimless confusion. This is the true order and it will always show my true order by its very disorder. I should be honoring my subject too much if I treated it in order, since I am trying to show that it is incapable of it" (Pascal, #532).

34   Pascal, #121.

35 Pascal, #47.

36 Pascal, #73.

37 Pascal, #905.

38 Pascal, #110.

39 Pascal, #382.

40 "Pascal" in *The Glory of the Lord, A Theological Aesthetics Volume III: Studies in Theo-logical Styles: Lay Styles*, translated by Andrew Louth, John Saward, Martin Simon, and Rowan Williams, edited by John Riches (San Francisco: Ignatius Press, 1986), p. 184.

41 Pascal, #400.

42 Pascal, #427.

43 Pascal, #427.

44 Pascal, #116.

45 *Discourses of the Fall*, p. 138. Another problem with Melzer's interpretation, a deficiency that repeats the errors of Voltaire and Valery in their critiques of Pascal, involves a failure to treat the *Pensées* as a dialogical work that contains numerous voices ranging from various states of unbelief—indifference, horror, longing—to sympathetic and even exulting faith. The objection on the part of Voltaire and Valery is that Pascal is a sophist who hypocriti-cally pretends that he shares the horror of the unbeliever. For a response, see Jean-Jacques Demorest, "Pascal's Sophistry and the Sin of Poesy" in *Blaise Pascal*, edited with an intro-duction by Harold Bloom (New York: Chelsea House Publishers, 1989), pp. 37-52.

46 This is the thesis of Lucien Goldmann's *The Hidden God*. As we have already noted, Gold-mann's book has certain limitations. First, Goldmann reads Pascal, not on his own terms, but as one moment, an early and immature moment in the development of modern phi-losophy. Pascal thus appears as an incomplete modern—Goldmann calls him the "first modern"—who discovered the rudiments of dialectic thought but was unable to achieve the historical synthesis of Hegel or Marx. Second, Goldmann distorts and thus fails to ap-preciate the proper role of the heart in Pascal's conception of human nature (*The Hidden God*, pp. 195, 200).

47 Pascal, #449.

48 One reason for this is that Pascal, for all his criticisms of Enlightenment science as provid-ing a comprehensive vision of the human condition, does not reject the certitude of the mathematical or physical sciences. On the contrary, he is both proponent and exponent of math and science.

49 "Introduction" to Pascal's *Pensées* (New York: E.P. Dutton, 1958), p. xix.

50 Pascal, #112.

51 "Notes on Film Noir," *Film Noir Reader I*, p. 63. It is instructive that Pascal does not condemn the godless; nor does he feel a generic pity for them; instead, he distinguished between the indifferent and the seekers, that latter of whom embody a tragic nobility.

52 *Voices in the Dark*, p. 218.

53 *Voices in the Dark*, p. 220.

54 Pascal, #114.

55 Pascal, #45.

56 Pascal, #405.

Index

A NOTE ON THE AUTHOR

With his earlier book *Shows About Nothing,* THOMAS S. HIBBS
established his reputation as one of the most interesting critics
writing today. His reviews and essays appear regularly in the
national media. A former professor of philosophy at Boston
College, Dr. Hibbs is now the Dean of the Honors College
and Distinguished Professor of Ethics and Culture at Baylor
University in Waco, Texas.

This book was designed and set into type

by Mitchell S. Muncy,

with cover design by Stephen J. Ott,

and printed and bound

by Bang Printing,

Brainerd, Minnesota.

℃

The text face is Minion Multiple Master,

designed by Robert Slimbach

and issued in digital form by Adobe Systems,

Mountain View, California, in 1991.

℃

The paper is acid-free and is of archival quality.

52